Nature Walks in New Jersey

A Guide to the Best Trails from the Highlands to Cape May

Glenn Scherer

D1112071

APPALACHIAN MOUNTAIN CLUB BOOKS
BOSTON, MASSACHUSETTS

Nature Walks in New Jersey

Glenn Scherer

Cover Photograph: Tom Till
All photographs by the author unless otherwise noted
Cover Design: Elisabeth Leydon Brady
Book Design: Carol Bast Tyler

Distributed by The Globe Pequot Press, Inc.

Library of Congress Cataloging-in-Publication Data
Scherer, Glenn.
Nature walks in New Jersey: more than 45 scenic nature hikes throughout the
Garden State / Glenn Scherer.
p. cm.
Includes bibliographical references (p.) and index.
ISBN 1-878239-68-6 (alk. paper)
1. Hiking—New Jersey—Guidebooks. 2. Nature study—New Jersey—
Guidebooks. 3. New Jersey—Guidebooks. I. Title.
GV144.42.N5S24   1998
917.4904'43—dc21   98-35787
                                                        CIP

The paper used in this publication meets the minimum requirements of the
American National Standard for Information Sciences—Permanence of Paper for
Printed Library Materials, ANSI Z39.48–1984.∞

**Due to changes in conditions,
use of the information in this book
is at the sole risk of the user.**

Printed on recycled paper using soy-based inks.
Printed in the United States of America.

10 9 8 7 6 5 4 3 2   00 01 02 03

Contents

Inner and Outer Coastal Plain Provinces

Atlantic Shore Region

List of Nature Essays

Appendices

*To my parents, who introduced me
to the natural world,
and to Marty Fletcher.
She and I continue to enjoy
New Jersey's wild places together.*

Locator Map

RIDGE &
VALLEY
PROVINCE

HIGHLANDS
PROVINCE

PIEDMONT
PROVINCE

INNER
COASTAL PLAIN
PROVINCE

OUTER
COASTAL PLAIN
PROVINCE

ATLANTIC
SHORE
REGION

N

1. Mount Tammany

2. Raccoon Ridge

3. Millbrook Village and Van Campens Glen

4. Merrill Creek Reservoir

5. Paulinskill Valley Trail

6. Ridge and Valley Trail

7. Sussex Branch Trail

8. White Cedar Swamp

9. Monument Trail

10. Wallkill River N.W.R.

11. Pinwheel's Vista

12. Terrace Pond

13. Bearfort Ridge Firetower

14. Long Pond Ironworks S.P.

15. NJ Botanical Gardens at Skylands

16. Wyanokie High Point

17. Four Birds Trail

18. Beaver Brook Trail

19. Tripod Rock and Bear Rock

20. Black River and Kay Environmental Center

21. Schooley's Mountain

22. Great Falls of the Passaic River

23. The Palisades

24. Hackensack Meadowlands

25. Branch Brook Park, Newark

26. Great Swamp Outdoor Education Center

27. Leonard J. Buck Garden

28. Delaware and Raritan Canal State Park

29. The Delaware River at Prallsville

30. Holmdel Park and Longstreet Farm

31. Poricy Park

32. Shark River

33. Wells Mills

34. Pakim Pond

35. Whitesbog

36. Dot and Brooks Evert Preserve

37. Rancocas Nature Center

38. Apple Pie Hill Firetower

39. Batsto Village and Nature Trail

40. Parvin State Park

41. Sandy Hook

42. Cattus Island

43. Island Beach State Park

44. Holgate

45. Brigantine

46. Cape May Point State Park

Walks and Highlights

Distance (Miles)	River/ Brook	Lake/ Pond	Swamp/ Marsh	Beach	Scenic Vista	Unusual Plants	Special Geology	Birds/ Animals
3.5	✔				✔		✔	
5.8			✔		✔			✔
5.1	✔	✔	✔			✔		
4.1	✔	✔	✔		✔			✔
6.4	✔	✔	✔			✔	✔	✔
4.2		✔				✔	✔	✔
3.7		✔	✔			✔		✔
1.5			✔			✔		
3.5		✔			✔			✔
3.5			✔			✔		✔
2.6					✔	✔	✔	✔
4.0		✔	✔		✔		✔	
3.6					✔		✔	
3.0	✔	✔					✔	
1.0–1.7			✔		✔	✔		✔
3.1	✔				✔		✔	
5.6		✔	✔		✔			✔

Distance (Miles)	River/ Brook	Lake/ Pond	Swamp/ Marsh	Beach	Scenic Vista	Unusual Plants	Special Geology	Birds/ Animals
6.2	✔	✔	✔		✔			✔
3.0	✔		✔		✔	✔	✔	✔
3.6–5.1	✔	✔	✔			✔		✔
2.9	✔	✔			✔	✔		
1.5	✔				✔		✔	
5.5	✔				✔	✔	✔	
1.5			✔		✔	✔		✔
2.0	✔					✔		✔
1.5–3.0		✔	✔			✔		✔
1.5	✔	✔				✔	✔	
4.0	✔					✔		✔
6.5	✔				✔	✔		✔
4.1–5.1	✔	✔	✔			✔	✔	✔
2.5	✔	✔	✔			✔	✔	
2.5	✔		✔			✔		✔

Distance (Miles)	River/ Brook	Lake/ Pond	Swamp/ Marsh	Beach	Scenic Vista	Unusual Plants	Special Geology	Birds/ Animals
6.0		✔	✔			✔		✔
6.8		✔	✔			✔		✔
2.5		✔	✔			✔		✔
1.5	✔		✔			✔		✔
1.5	✔					✔		✔
8.0			✔		✔	✔	✔	✔
2.0								
4.6	✔	✔	✔			✔		✔
1.0–2.1		✔		✔	✔	✔		✔
3.2		✔		✔	✔	✔		✔
4.1		✔		✔	✔	✔		✔
5.5				✔	✔			✔
3.1–8.0		✔	✔		✔	✔		✔
2.0		✔	✔	✔	✔	✔		✔

Acknowledgments

I would first like to thank my friend Jean LeBlanc, who walked with me on most of the hikes in this book, wrote five chapters and several more sidebars, and who proofread the entire text. She is a fine naturalist and a patient teacher. I would also like to thank fellow walkers Wendy and Jim Elwell, Paul DeCoste, Ron Dupont, Emilie Jeanneney, George Lightcap, Rick Patterson, Ed Lenik (Sheffield Archaeological Consultants), Bob Canace (Ridge and Valley Conservancy), Marjorie Barrett (Paulinskill Valley Trail Committee), and Jack Epstein (National Park Service). Many others helped in researching and/or reviewing the hikes: John Garcia and Celeste Tracy (New Jersey Department of Environmental Protection), Anne Lutkenhouse (New York–New Jersey Trail Conference), Bob Rooke (Morris County Parks), Bob Barth (Canal Society of New Jersey), Karen Carlo Ruhren (the Nature Conservancy), Emile DeVito (New Jersey Conservation Foundation), and Dick Anderson (New Jersey Audubon Society). One of the pleasures in creating this book came from talking with volunteer and professional park managers and trail builders who love our state's natural and cultural heritage for its own sake. Though too numerous to list here, their heartfelt interest in this project and informed assistance was invaluable.

Introduction

This book is about discovery: the discovery of New Jersey's vast outdoors. It represents an unfolding adventure for me, and I hope it provides a rewarding experience for you.

As a child I was introduced early to New Jersey's natural world: I climbed Mount Tammany in the Delaware Water Gap, wandered the woods behind my house near Merrill Creek, and hiked the Appalachian Trail. But as I gained greater appreciation for my state's wildness, I was appalled to see it slipping away. By the late 1960s, I joined with cynical friends in lampooning New Jersey as the "Garden Apartment State," a place where condos sprang up like mushrooms. It seemed that pavement surely would overwhelm the last deer and warbler. In his 1964 book *New Jersey Out-of-Doors,* naturalist Leonard Lee Rue III predicted:

> All living things except people will continue to diminish in numbers in our state.... Our birds of prey, the hawks and owls, will be drastically reduced.... Wild turkey propagation will fail.... The bald eagle will join the ranks of the dodo.... The beaver will have no place in New Jersey.... [The black bear's] disappearance is inevitable...

Thankfully, these words of doom were heeded as a warning. All wildness did not disappear before an onslaught of neat lawns and mini-malls. In 1998 Rue declared, "I live in our state because I've got more wildlife in my backyard than anyone anywhere in the country. Thank God I was wrong!"

Today New Jersey is in the midst of a green renaissance. This spontaneous rebirth began at the grassroots level in the 1960s. Zealous community groups, innocent of politics and policies, organized to kill the Tocks Island Dam on the Upper Delaware, prevent construction of a jetport in the Great Swamp, and stop the building of a "city of the future" in the Pine Barrens.

The act of green transformation rolled on into the 1990s, as factory sites and dumps were remade into parks at the Great Falls and Meadowlands; as abandoned railroads and canals became greenways along the Paulinskill, Millstone and Delaware Rivers; as lost towns, ruined iron furnaces, and forgotten farms were preserved at Long Pond, Batsto, Wells Mills and Holmdel. Priceless Atlantic beachfront that might have been covered in condos stayed the territory of migratory shorebirds.

Volunteers saw to it that trails snaked into the new preserves. Now people come to walk and enjoy the first peepers of spring, the fireflies of summer, the eagles of autumn, and the solitude of winter. They come to reconnect with forest, field and wetland. They come to learn. They come for peace.

The struggle to preserve New Jersey nature continues. Population and economic growth, pollution and habitat loss remain relentless problems. Our flora and fauna will be in danger so long as progress and profit rule. But now ordinary people, in alliance with town, county, state and federal officials, have decided that the restoration of a natural balance is not only worthwhile but vital.

In researching this book I saw places I've walked since childhood with new eyes and explored fabulous parks that were new to me. I've tried to create a narrative that reads as well from the armchair as it does out on the trail.

I hope this book will serve as a map to some of New Jersey's many green treasures. Let it take you to places near your home and far afield. Put on sturdy walking shoes and pack a lunch, water, insect repellent and a rain jacket. Take along the flower book, tree book and bird book.

Don't rush. Hike slowly. Take time to see and your sensitivity will grow. With sensitivity comes wonder and a greater appreciation for New Jersey's spectacular natural diversity. With appreciation may come the urge for action, the desire to volunteer with others in the preservation of our green spaces for future generations. Have a good walk!

The Territory

New Jersey is a small state (the fifth smallest in the U.S. at just 7,509 square miles). It is, however, the most densely populated. Its 7.7 million people are spread over the land at an average density of 1,029 persons per square mile. We're packed in more tightly here than in India or Japan. The state evokes stereotypical images of super highways lined with oil refineries and housing developments. But there is another New Jersey. More than two million acres of the state are forested today, with some counties possessing more woodland now than they did a century ago.

This little state encompasses some of the most diverse natural landscape and habitats concentrated within a small area to be found anywhere in America. This book divides the state into five unique regions:

The Ridge and Valley Province covers 625 square miles in New Jersey's northwest corner, about eight percent of the state. The region's mountain ridges are topped by remote crags and blanketed by mixed oak forest. Its fertile limestone valleys are a checkerboard of picturesque farms, sugar maple and mixed hardwood forests and small villages. Geographically, the Ridge and Valley Province is part of the larger Appalachian Geologic Province running from Canada to the southern United States. In our state, it includes the erosion-resistant sedimentary rock of the 43-mile-long Kittatinny Range (reaching an elevation of 1,803 feet) plus the lowlands of the Delaware River Valley and Great Valley of the Appalachians.

The Highlands Province is a rugged mountainous region, part of a larger geologic province called the New England Uplands (which includes New York's Hudson Highlands and Vermont's Green Mountains). It encompasses 900 square miles and 12 percent of the state, and runs in a narrowing wedge from the border with New York southwest to the Delaware River. Its billion-year-old banded gneiss bedrock (achieving heights of 1,500 feet) is separated by very narrow limestone and shale valleys. The magnetite iron in these ridges once supported a thriving nineteenth-century iron industry. Today, the mixed oak forests of these peaks are home to black bear, coyote and white-tailed deer.

The Piedmont Province is a shale-and-sandstone lowland composed of gently rolling hills that display only a 400-foot elevation change between New York Harbor and the Delaware River. A few erosion-resistant igneous ridges, such as the Palisades and Watchung Range (rising to 850 feet), overlook the landscape. The 1,500-square-mile region (about 20 percent of the state) is made up of an urban and suburban corridor connecting New York City and Philadelphia. While this metropolitan landscape holds the largest concentration of the state's population, it also includes a surprising number of natural gems: the Great Swamp, fine urban parks, gardens and greenways.

The Inner and Outer Coastal Plains are the largest of New Jersey's geographic regions. The two provinces combined cover 4,475 square miles and nearly 60 percent of the state, and stretch east from the Delaware Bay to the Atlantic Ocean. This vast sandy lowland gently slopes to the sea. A series of small gravel hills (just 373 feet high) divide the Inner Coastal Plain from the Outer. At the heart of the Outer Coastal Plain are the Pinelands, resembling the Pine Barrens of Long Island and Cape Cod, but covering many more remote acres. While the flat topography seems less than exciting, the flora is fascinating, with many ancient plant species now recognized as living fossils.

The Atlantic Coastal Region, a narrow band of tidal wetlands, stream mouths, back bays, barrier islands, sand dunes and ocean beaches, is not truly a geographical province. But its unique ecosystems demanded a separate section in this book. This habitat, shaped by the sea, supports some of the most unusual flora and best birding on the East Coast. Highlights include Cape May, a focal point in the ancient annual songbird, raptor and butterfly migration; plus the Edwin Forsythe National Wildlife Refuge, where bald eagles, osprey and snow geese roost within a few miles of Atlantic City gaming tables.

The Trails

Natural New Jersey is accessible by a vast network of public and private trails. There are more than a thousand miles of federal, state, county, and township trails already in existence, with many more miles being built each year.

Private organizations including the Appalachian Mountain Club, New York–New Jersey Trail Conference, the Nature Conservancy, New Jersey Conservation Foundation, New Jersey Audubon Society, Canal Society of New Jersey, New Jersey Rails-to-Trails Conservancy, and Sierra Clubs are all active in building new trailways and in maintaining and upgrading existing ones. Obviously, with so many hike possibilities, it was hard to narrow down the walks for this book.

The walks selected were chosen to profile the many faces of natural New Jersey. They are equally distributed over the state's five distinct geographic areas. Each hike focuses on one or more aspects of New Jersey's unique natural history, such as the Great Eastern Forest, Atlantic white cedar swamps, beaver colonies, or barrier island ecology. In some cases, a historical resource—such as a nineteenth-century canal, iron mine or farming community—is explored, along with its intimate connection to the land. A few hikes highlight annual natural events: cherry blossom time in Branch Brook Park, the raptor migration over Kittatinny Ridge and songbird migration at Cape May.

The book's hikes vary in length from one to eight miles, with the average length being about four miles. Eight miles may seem like a great distance, but the longest hikes are (with a few exceptions) the easiest, passing over level terrain, such as an old railroad bed, a canal or a beach. The walks traverse federal, state, county, municipal and private (conservation group) lands.

Each hike has been selected to provide the most enjoyable experience to the hiker. In nearly all cases, only clearly marked trails with easily found trailheads are featured. A very few hikes use unblazed trails, but these offer such exceptional natural value that I couldn't bear to delete them.

Most walks are easy or moderate (crossing level or hilly terrain), while some are challenging, especially climbs to the state's major summits, such as Mount Tammany in the Delaware Water Gap or Pinwheel's Vista on the Wawayanda escarpment. Steep ascents have been minimized wherever possible to allow children, seniors, and even the disabled to enjoy the walks. But, of course, this is the woods, and hikers should come prepared for a workout on all kinds of terrain and in all kinds of weather.

Accurate directions are given to each trailhead from interstate, state and county roads. Parking and park facilities are listed with phone numbers, as are adjoining nature and environmental centers or related museums.

I'm sure that such a large work, encompassing so many diverse habitats and trails, left out people's favorite walks, missed fascinating local facts, or made errors. I welcome readers' comments, views and corrections concerning this book. You may e-mail me at gscherer@warwick.net or write me at P.O. Box 512, Highland Lakes, NJ 07422.

Getting Started

It is beyond the scope of this book to teach you how to hike, but I have included some tips to get started.

What to Bring: Walkers must be prepared for the unexpected when venturing into the natural world. To quote an old Russian proverb: "There is no bad weather, only bad clothing." Sturdy waterproof footgear is a must, as is rain gear. Dress in layers so you can add or remove clothing depending on temperature. Carry a small pack containing a lunch, snacks, and at least two quarts of water. Carry insect repellent, sunscreen, hat, watch, toilet paper, flashlight, extra clothing (such as a sweater, gloves and dry socks), compass, whistle, small first-aid kit and trash bag. Remember that whether hiking in the mountains or on the beach you will be exposed to sun, wind and precipitation.

On the Trail: Carefully read the hike description in this book before setting out. Check weather reports shortly before your trip. Always try to take a walking companion with you. On arriving at a trailhead, check bulletin boards and visitor centers for present trail conditions, and changes in trail routes and blazing. Align the maps in this book with those shown at the trailhead.

Leave No Trace: New Jersey's trails receive heavy use. Every walker has a responsibility to protect our parks. Never litter. Carry out what you carry in. While it's OK to bring home small souvenirs (seashells, acorns, and hickory nuts), it's not all right to pick flowers or remove wildlife. Stay on trails and avoid trampling plants. Respect animals and other hikers by traveling quietly. Take only photographs. Leave the lightest of footprints.

Trail Safety

Hiking is an exhilarating and enjoyable pastime. With a little extra effort, it can also be a very safe activity. The following list of common hiking hazards is not meant to scare you, only to make you aware of outdoor safety.

Getting Lost: If you lose your way, don't panic. Stay in one spot and carefully look for trail blazes. Study the map. Discuss your position with fellow walkers. Do not leave the trail. Do not push on without ascertaining your location. If you can't figure out where you are, retrace your steps to determine where you went wrong. Never divide up your group or hurry when lost. Three blasts on a whistle is a distress signal in the woods.

Insect Pests: Mosquitoes and ticks are everywhere in the outdoors. Tiny deer ticks (smaller than a sesame seed), sometimes infected with Lyme disease, are common in New Jersey. Lyme disease is usually (but not always) indicated by a red bull's-eye rash at the tick bite site, followed in days or weeks by aching joints and muscles, fever, flu-like symptoms and headaches. If untreated, chronic arthritis and neurological problems can result. Use insect repellent (preferably containing DEET) and wear a long-sleeved shirt and long pants tucked into socks. Light-colored clothing makes tick spotting easier. Check your body after a hike and take a shower on returning home. If a tick has embedded itself under the skin or if you experience unexplained symptoms, see a doctor.

Poisonous Plants: Poison ivy and sumac are common in our area. Learn to identify poisonous plants. The old adage "leaves of three, let it be" is a good maxim. Wash skin immediately when it is exposed to a poisonous plant. If a poisonous plant rash becomes serious see a doctor.

Drinking Water: Stop regularly to sip water. The hotter the day, the more water you need. Drink only the water you bring with you. No matter how pure streams and ponds look, they may contain invisible bacteria that can cause serious intestinal illness.

Hypothermia: One of the greatest hazards in the outdoors is hypothermia, in which the body is drained of heat. It can occur well above freezing temperatures. Wet clothing, wind, sudden temperature drops, and precipitation can all bring on the condition. Shivering, lethargy, mental slowing and confusion are symptoms. If you suspect hypothermia, remove wet garments, replace with warm clothes, and seek shelter immediately.

Heat Emergencies: Sunburn, heat weakness, heat cramps, heat exhaustion, and heatstroke can all result from overexertion in high temperatures and high humidity, and from sun exposure. Drink plenty of water on the trail. If someone shows the first symptoms of being overheated (heavy sweating, high pulse rate, fatigue and general weakness, headache, and mental and physical inefficiencies), rest in a cool, shaded place and apply cold, wet compresses. Use sunscreen to protect against sunburn.

Staying safe in the outdoors is ultimately a matter of being prepared, of staying calm in an emergency, and of using common sense. Take proper precautions and stay aware so that every hike can be a safe hike.

Ridge and Valley Province

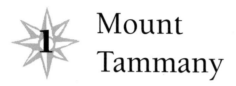

1 Mount Tammany

Delaware Water Gap National Recreation Area

- 3.5 miles
- 3 to 4 hours
- Elevation gain 1,200 feet
- Challenging; a 1.5-mile climb

Breathtaking views of the Delaware River and Mount Minsi

The Kittatinny Ridge (meaning "Endless Mountain" in the Lenape Native American language) comes to an abrupt, spectacular end at Mount Tammany. The 1,527-foot ridge plunges 1,200 feet into the Delaware Water Gap. This river gorge, one of New Jersey's most acclaimed natural treasures, has attracted painters, hikers, canoeists and fresh-air lovers since the 1800s.

While the Dutch settled the Upper Delaware River Valley as early as 1700, it was tourism that made the Gap famous. After the Civil War, railroads brought vacationing urbanites to the natural beauty of the Gap. Guests lounged at luxury hotels built in the grand style of the best Adirondack resorts. Refined Victorians sat on hotel verandahs, took the "water cure" at the Christian Home Sanitarium, and sought out "the sublime in nature." Filmmaker D. W. Griffith even chose the spot as backdrop for a scene in *Birth of a Nation*.

Today the great resorts are burned or gone bust, but the Gap remains, protected within the Delaware Water Gap National Recreation Area. The gorge serves as gateway to the Upper Delaware River Valley, a tapestry of folded mountains, tumbling waterfalls and forested bottom land supporting black bear, migrating golden eagles and spawning shad.

Mount Tammany

Mount Tammany is one of the most popular hiking destinations in New Jersey. To beat the crowds, set off early on a weekend, on a weekday, or in winter. The climb is strenuous and demands sturdy hiking boots (as do most of the walks in this book). Give yourself plenty of time to enjoy the views.

This 3.5-mile loop hike utilizes the Red Dot Trail, Blue Dot Trail and Appalachian Trail. It boasts fine vistas from Mount Tammany and ends with a stroll through a shaded ravine along a cascading brook.

Begin at the I-80 rest area parking lot. Follow the Red Dot Trail's red-on-white painted blazes uphill. The trail immediately elevates your heart rate with a brief steep climb, a promise of things to come. The path levels out, and though you're still within earshot of traffic, you're now surrounded by calming forest.

The Red Dot Trail parallels Dunnfield Creek (below to your left), on what geologists call a kame terrace (sorted sand and gravel left behind by outwash from the Wisconsin Glacier, which filled the Gap just 15,000 years ago). In a short distance the path veers sharply right and begins to climb. Tulip trees quickly give way to sweet birch, red oak and chestnut oak.

After a 0.5-mile ascent, the hard work pays off with a first look into the gorge. Mount Minsi (named for a Lenape clan) rises on the Pennsylvania side of the Gap. The flank of Mount Tammany (your destination) also looms. The Delaware River snakes gracefully between the peaks. Arrow Island, at midriver, points south to the Great Valley of the Appalachians. This wide valley is part of a much larger geological feature, a lowland stretching from Alabama to New York (see chapter 6).

The trail rises along a spine of Mount Tammany, passing over shale and sandstone sheets called *redbeds* (named for their color, caused by high iron content). The forest on this exposed slope is an open canopy of chestnut oak, with an understory of lowbush blueberry. Autumn hikers are rewarded when turning blueberry leaves transform the forest floor into a vibrant scarlet blanket.

The most difficult part of the climb comes thirty to forty minutes into the hike with a steep rock scramble up a talus slope (boulders broken loose from above by frost action). This ascent is tricky when wet or icy.

Notice that the redbeds are being replaced by a dark gray rock called Shawangunk conglomerate. This stone explains the existence of the Kittatinny Ridge. It forms an erosion-resistant backbone, averaging 1,600 feet in elevation, extending from the Water Gap north along the New Jersey border for forty-three miles, and continuing into New York as the Shawangunk Ridge. The range also flows southward, rising on the far side of the Gap as Mount Minsi and reaching far into Pennsylvania.

At 1.3 miles into your walk the Red Dot Trail arrives at Mount Tammany's summit, bursting into the open at a boulder-strewn vista. Lichen clings to the rocks, scrub oak grows in low twisted thickets, and a few pitch pines battle for survival. Dry conditions and brutal winter storms prevent the growth of larger trees. Below to the right is the visage of Lenape chief Tammany, a stony profile imagined by nineteenth-century visitors.

Look west to see the folded strata of Mount Minsi and its jumbled talus slopes; tree clumps tenaciously cling to the mountainside. The Delaware River flows south into the Great Valley. To the northwest is the Pocono Plateau. Autumn visitors may see migrating hawks soaring southward. Humans also take advantage of the ridge's updrafts: this is a popular glider flight path.

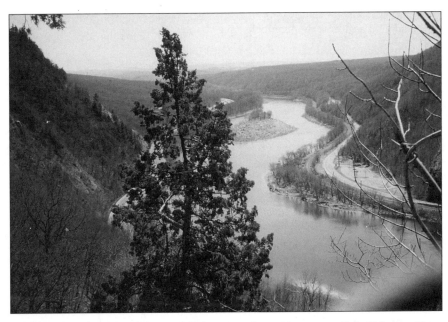

The first view from the Red Dot Trail looks out on the snaking curves of the Delaware River and Arrow Island. Photo credit: George Lightcap

Climb back to the top of the rock slope and look to the right for the Blue Dot Trail, leading north along Mount Tammany's narrow crest. Follow the trail for 0.3 mile along the ridge.

Step off-trail and study the bases of the trees; you'll see that they're fire damaged. Heavy use of the Water Gap by inexperienced campers has resulted in wildfires. These fires harm the environment, but have benefits. Fire-resistant pitch pines, for example, thrive in burnt-over areas. Fire also converts leaf litter into fertilizer, causing a fast release of minerals to plants.

At 1.6 miles the Blue Dot Trail turns left, steeply descending from the ridge, at first on a narrow trail, then on a fire road. The flora quickly changes from a hardy ridge-top chestnut oak forest to a sheltered woods dominated by maples and a mountain laurel understory.

At 3.1 miles, the Blue Dot Trail descends into Dunnfield Hollow, crosses Dunnfield Creek on a bridge, then turns left and intersects with the Appalachian Trail (AT). The last 0.4 mile of the walk is along the white-blazed, 2,100-mile, Maine-to-Georgia Appalachian Trail. The AT follows a gently descending woods road beside the stream, which cascades over falls and tumbles through chutes into pools. It is shaded by hemlock, yellow birch, and rhododendron. The hemlocks are dying, their branches stripped of needles. They've fallen victim to hemlock woolly adelgid, an insect accidentally imported to the U.S. from Asia on ornamental trees. In 1998, New Jersey introduced a tiny ladybug which, it is hoped, will control the adelgid and save the hemlocks (see chapter 23 sidebar).

Dunnfield Creek is popular with trout fishermen, and you're likely to share this peaceful grotto with them. At 3.5 miles, cross a small bridge, reaching the Dunnfield Natural Area parking lot. The rest area parking lot is a few hundred yards to your left and reached via a small unmarked trail.

🪨 WATER GAP GEOLOGY

The view from Mount Tammany inspires visitors to wonder how this great gorge was formed. Many imagine the mountains came first, with the Delaware River backing up behind the ridge in a vast lake before eventually cutting a gap through from north to south.

Geologists doubt this story. They think the erosion-resistant sandstone strata of Kittatinny Ridge began as muddy sediment layers at the bottom of an ancient shallow sea. These layers were compressed into rock, then were uplifted and folded into the ancestral Appalachian Range, mountains which 230 million years ago rivaled the present-day Rockies. Through time, these old peaks eroded away. Then, in another episode of mountain building, Kittatinny Ridge was raised about 80 million years ago.

The Delaware River probably started as a fast-moving mountain stream on the south (Atlantic Ocean–facing) slope of Kittatinny Ridge. It found weaknesses and fissures in the Shawangunk conglomerate and redbeds, cutting downward at a point that would eventually become the Water Gap (this cutting action is what geologists call *stream headward migration*). Once the gap was formed, the stream linked up with others on the north side of the ridge, forming the Upper and Lower Delaware River Valley as we know it.

Today, the twin sentinels of Mount Tammany and Mount Minsi tower above the landscape, while the river grinds its course deeper into the bedrock.

Hours, Fees and Facilities

Trails are open daily, year-round. Call the Delaware Water Gap National Recreation Area for Kittatinny Point Visitor Center seasonal hours.

Getting There

Traveling west through the Delaware Water Gap on I-80, follow signs for the Rest Area exit. Park in the rest area lot on the right. Traveling east on I-80, cross the river and take the first exit in New Jersey. Pass the Kittatinny Point Visitor Center, then turn left, passing under I-80. Turn right at the end of the underpass, then left into the rest area parking lot.

For More Information

Delaware Water Gap National Recreation Area Headquarters, Bushkill, PA 18324; 717-588-2451. Kittatinny Point Visitor Center: 908-496-4458.

2 Raccoon Ridge and Appalachian Trail

AMC Mohican Outdoor Center

- 5.8 miles
- 4 hours
- Elevation gain 500 feet
- Challenging; a rocky 1.4-mile climb

Hawks migrate south by the thousands

Every autumn, New Jersey plays host to the raptor migration, one of nature's most mysterious and magnificent events. Starting in late August, peaking in September and October, and fading into November, birds of prey sweep down from northern skies, riding thermals and updrafts on outstretched wings. For some, like the osprey, this is a journey of 6,000 miles, beginning in Canada and concluding in Argentina.

Autumn hawk watching is akin to meteor-shower watching. Annual observers gather on Appalachian Mountain crags in crisp winds or during the last sultry days of Indian summer to stare attentively up at empty skies. Then the birds come, often in clusters, like sudden shooting stars, growing from specks into shining, silvery silhouettes. They surge briefly past the lookouts, swiftly dipping and climbing on air currents, then disappear southward.

More than fifteen raptor species regularly glide through the region: soaring buteos (red-tailed, red-shouldered, broad-winged and rough-legged hawks); bullet-shaped falcons (kestrels, merlins and peregrines); swiftly maneuvering accipiters (goshawks and sharp-shinned and Cooper's hawks); northern harriers (also called marsh hawks); majestic ospreys, golden and bald eagles; and the unjustly maligned carrion eaters (turkey vultures and black vultures). All these raptors also fly our skies in the spring, during northern migration, but weather conditions cause them to be more dispersed then.

One of the best places to view the great autumn migration is atop Raccoon Ridge, a peak in the Kittatinny Mountain Range. In fact, raptor counts here are only 10 to 15 percent below those at Hawk Mountain, Pennsylvania, a world-renowned raptor-watching spot. But, while Raccoon Ridge boasts many hawks (more than 15,000 in a typical migration), human crowds are smaller. You'll rarely run into the binocular-wielding mobs encountered in Pennsylvania.

This 5.8-mile out-and-back hike along the Appalachian Trail (AT) to Raccoon Ridge is not just a climb to a birder's paradise. It rewards walkers year-round with a sweeping 360-degree view of the Delaware River Valley and the broad, fertile farmlands of the Great Valley of the Appalachians.

Start at the AMC's Mohican Outdoor Center lodge. Face the lodge and turn left, walking 0.2 mile down Mohican Road. This edge environment supports light-loving plants, including sassafras with its mitten-shaped leaves. Note the red maple swamp to your right. This is a good place to watch for deer at twilight.

Leave the road, turning right onto the white-blazed Appalachian Trail. (This 2,100-mile footpath runs from Maine to Georgia. There are 73 miles of AT in New Jersey).

Immediately cross Yards Creek on a footbridge. A single red maple stands on the opposite stream bank. This tree's leaves are smaller than those of the sugar maple; reaching four inches across, they are differentiated by coarse, irregular teeth on leaf margins. Red maples are common to wet bottomlands.

In 0.1 mile, the AT intersects the Coppermines Trail. Its wooden sign is affixed to a sweet birch (also called black birch), one of the most numerous trees of New Jersey uplands. Its twigs and leaves give off a distinct and refreshing odor of wintergreen. Old-fashioned birch beer was brewed by fermenting this tree's sap.

Stay on the AT, following the white blazes. As the path begins its rocky climb to the steep, well-drained ridge top, the water-loving red maples vanish, replaced by chestnut oaks. These hardy trees, with their deeply furrowed bark, are the masters of northern New Jersey's harsh, bone-dry mountaintops. Beneath the chestnut oaks spreads a carpet of lowbush blueberries. They offer a delicious diversion in late summer and a scarlet leaf show in the fall. Pitch pine and mountain laurel, both of which thrive in thin, acidic hillside soils, now join the forest mix.

At 1.4 miles into the walk, the AT achieves the top of Kittatinny Ridge and reveals a series of stunning views east over the Great Valley of the Appalachians. This wide valley stretches from Alabama to the Hudson River. The New Jersey portion is underlain by the state's second most important freshwater aquifer (the state's largest aquifer is in the Pine Barrens).

Also visible below are the reservoirs of the Yards Creek pumped-storage facility. This public-utility project, when originally planned in the early 1960s, would have destroyed Sunfish Pond, New Jersey's most famous glacial lake. Vocal public protest resulted in the rescue of this National Natural Landmark and in a revamped Yards Creek electrical power facility.

The hike continues along the Kittatinny Ridge through an oak forest where elusive kinglets, red-eyed vireos, white-throated sparrows, and chickadees reveal themselves through their song. These little songbirds provide frequent snacks for hungry raptors.

A stand of mockernut, pignut and shagbark hickories now closes in around the hiker. Here we saw one of nature's most fearsome looking insects. The hickory horned devil is the largest native North American caterpillar, a five-inch long, spine-covered creature with protruding horns at either end. The horned devil, like

Birders are alert to the swift flight of "sharpies" (sharp-shinned hawks).

many other insects, associates with a particular plant species. It relies largely on hickories for food and camouflage.

The AT weaves over to the west side of the ridge and gives a partial view of the Delaware River Valley and the Pocono Plateau beyond. At 2.7 miles, the trail leaves the Delaware Water Gap National Recreation Area and passes a sign welcoming walkers to Worthington State Forest.

At 2.9 miles, the trail comes out onto a grass- and sedge-covered vista. Wind-swept Raccoon Ridge is little more than 100 feet wide here. The 1,500-foot peak, topped by a rock cairn, gives 360-degree views south toward the Water Gap, north to Rattlesnake Mountain, northwest to the snaky bends of the Delaware River, and east to the Great Valley of the Appalachians.

Autumn hawk watching is at its best from this vantage point. We climbed here one unseasonably warm, windless October day. Hawks usually sit out such after-noons, preferring to ride strong winds occurring just after the passage of cold fronts. Surprisingly, we were treated to a spurt of migrating raptors. Most numer-ous were sharp-shinned hawks (birders call them "sharpies"). With rounded wings and narrow tails they can deftly pursue small birds through thick woods. Several peregrine falcons, with pointed wings and long streamlined tails, zipped by our lookout. These birds hunt in open country and are among the world's fastest birds. A single northern harrier also swept by. The mature male harrier is called the "gray ghost" by birders, perhaps for its deathly silent, low-level hunting flights conducted just a few feet above marshy grasslands.

Under the best conditions, Raccoon Ridge birders spot hundreds of raptors every hour. A single species, the red-tailed hawk, for example, accounted for nearly a thousand sightings on one remarkable day in 1987. But numbers matter little. Whether you see one raptor or a thousand, these great, graceful birds are a thrill to behold. After enjoying the summit, return the way you came to the Mohican Outdoor Center.

🪶 *RAPTURE OVER RAPTORS*

Built to hunt, raptors amaze naturalists with their endurance, acute senses, speed and agility. Look at just one species: the red-tailed hawk. This common bird's four-foot wingspan makes it an accomplished and powerful glider, a quality vital to the conservation of energy required during long, grueling migrations.

The red-tail's telescopic eyesight allows it to spy a scampering mouse from 100 feet in the air. Its vision is specially adapted for rapid change of focus, allowing it to track tiny prey while conducting aerial dives at 120 mph. A red-tailed hawk, like most hunter-predators, is an opportunist. It often sits atop trees or utility poles and waits. Then it swoops on almost anything that moves. These birds eat insects, rodents, fish, toads, snakes, small birds, skunks, and rabbits.

But even these immense carnivores fall prey to predators. A friend had the once-in-a-lifetime privilege of seeing a golden eagle attack a red-tailed hawk. The immense eagle, with its six-foot wingspan, dove on the bird, seized it in midair, and killed it instantly with its razor-sharp talons.

Hours, Fees and Facilities

The Appalachian Trail is open year-round. AMC's Mohican Outdoor Center is also open all year, renting bunks to club members and nonmembers. AMC's Camp Mohican, a 1920s-vintage Boy Scout camp, invites outdoor enthusiasts to enjoy ice climbing, canoeing, hiking, wildflower identification, and other workshops. The AMC is also locally active in volunteer trail building.

Getting There

From I-80 east or west, take NJ 94 north for 8 miles to Jacksonburg. Turn left on Mohican Road and follow it for 3.5 mi. (bearing right at forks along the way). Turn left on Gaisler Road, go 0.5 mi., and turn right onto Camp Road. Follow for 1.0 mile. Park either at the Mohican Outdoor Center gate or the main lodge.

For More Information

AMC Mohican Outdoor Center, 50 Camp Road, Blairstown, NJ 07825; 908-362-5670.

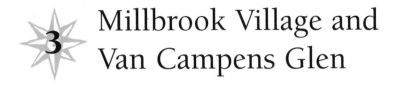

Millbrook Village and Van Campens Glen

Delaware Water Gap National Recreation Area

- 5.1 miles
- 4.5 hours (not counting village tour)
- Elevation gain 300 feet
- Moderate; one stream crossing with some climbing at waterfalls

Hike through history on the Old Mine Road

The fertile bottomlands of the Upper Delaware River Valley have been shaped by farm life for untold generations. Native Americans cultivated pumpkins, squash, beans, and maize in the soft soils of riverside plots. Dutch farmers settled here in the early 1700s, and the English followed later, planting wheat, rye, flax, and potatoes and raising cows, hogs, and sheep.

These isolated valley farms, cupped between the sheltering hands of the Kittatinny Ridge to the east and the Pocono Plateau to the west, measured change more by the seasons than by American history. While tiny communities sent sons to fight in the Revolution, Civil War, and two world wars, dairy cows continued to be milked every day and corn harvested every autumn.

The rhythms of pastoral life were not disrupted until a catastrophic 1955 flood on the Lower Delaware River brought the Army Corps of Engineers to the Upper Delaware in 1962. Their flood-control plan was to build the Tocks Island Dam, which would convert the upper valley into a thirty-seven-mile-long lake, drowning forest and field. A battle erupted, one of the most significant environmental fights of the 1970s. Locals both won and lost. The dam was never built, but residents were forced from their homes and most of the valley became federal property.

This hike within the Delaware Water Gap National Recreation Area is a walk through history. It begins and ends at Millbrook Village, a recreated nineteenth-century farming community. It explores the Old Mine Road, Van Campens Glen (named for the earliest Dutch settlers), and meanders over a manicured twentieth-

Millbrook Village and Van Campens Glen

century estate. If the Corps of Engineers had won the day, all these treasures would be submerged under a hundred feet of water.

Arrive at Millbrook Village early and save the town tour until hike's end. From the north end of the parking lot, cross the paved road and enter the woods on the Orchard Trail. This orange-blazed path leads 0.5 mile uphill through abandoned farmlands which are slowly returning to forest, a classic example of field succession.

Fruit trees and open pasture are gone, replaced by light-loving red cedar, sassafras and gray birch. But reminders of farm days linger: ornamental lilac bushes, Japanese barberry and buckthorn (planted as hedges) grow along old stone walls and near the ruins of a springhouse. They compete with native hay-scented fern, milkweed and winterberry. Shade tolerant trees—beech, dogwood and sugar maple —are also taking hold. They'll eventually push out most of the light-loving vegetation. In autumn and winter, views east to the Kittatinny Ridge are exceptional.

At the hill's crest, the Orchard Trail intersects with Hamilton Ridge Road, an abandoned section of the original Old Mine Road. Turn left here.

The Old Mine Road was once touted as the first commercial highway in America. Myth had it that the 104-mile byway was built around 1650 by Dutch miners hauling Delaware Valley copper to the Hudson River. But ore found south of Millbrook is of such low grade that historians doubt if any sane prospector would ever have gone to the trouble. The Old Mine Road was probably constructed by farmers in the 1700s. It was once dotted by blockhouses as protection from Indian raids. Washington moved his Continental army along the road to shield his troops from prying British eyes.

Follow Hamilton Ridge Road gently downhill for about two miles. This walk over crumbling, moss-covered pavement is easy. It passes through former pastures, now a crazy quilt of native and introduced plant species. Oaks, white ash, mockernut and pignut hickories coexist with privet (a garden escapee with tubular white flowers), Japanese barberry (with showy red berries in autumn), and buckthorn. White-tailed deer don't seem to mind the mix. They freely browse along overgrown stone fences and near a farmhouse foundation.

When Hamilton Ridge Road ends at 2.5 miles into the walk, turn left on another road. At 2.7 miles turn left again on a paved section of Old Mine Road. In a few hundred feet, turn right into the Van Campens Glen parking lot. At the end of the lot, follow the yellow-blazed Van Campens Glen Trail into the woods.

The glen, the almost exclusive domain of native species, is a shaded grotto. Eastern hemlocks predominate. These trees create their own micro-climate, with temperatures several degrees cooler than in the surrounding forest. They also cast dense "blue" shade because, like other conifers, they filter out light across the complete spectrum. Tulip trees and beeches grow in the gorge, too, and reach high to gather sunlight. Rhododendron and spicebush (identified by its acrid scent) fill out the understory, while wood, polypody and Christmas ferns add lacy decoration to steep rock slopes. Hepatica also grows in deep shade, a delicate lavender flower blooming in early spring. In days past, plant shape often indicated medicinal use to herbalists (a doctrine called "signatures"). Hepatica's three-lobed, rounded leaves once suggested it as a liver cure, a bogus assumption.

The trail climbs steeply on stone and log steps along the left side of the brook, rising above the lower Van Campens Falls and passing through clefts in the redbeds (Bloomsburg Formation sandstones stained by iron deposits). The path then descends steeply through sweet birch, reaching a small level plain beside the stream. This area is covered in a mature stand of sycamores, tulip tree, and yellow birch. Resist the temptation to leave the trail. Where people have trampled, nothing grows; where they have not, native ferns abound.

As you head upstream (about 0.5 mile into the gorge and 3.3 miles into the hike), watch for a place where the yellow blazes indicate a sharp turn to the right as the path crosses the brook on steppingstones (this crossing can be difficult in high water).

Just ahead is the highlight of the walk, upper Van Campens Falls, plunging over violet-hued sandstone. Fly-fishermen stand waist deep and cast the wide pool at the falls' base for native trout (no bait fishing is allowed).

A quick rock scramble to the top of the falls is the most challenging part of the hike. Watch closely for the yellow blazes following along the top right edge of the glen. The stream pinballs below through the narrow slotted gorge, bouncing off eroded walls and plunging in white sheets of foam into pools.

A man-made stone wall on the brook's left bank, probably the remains of a dam, marks the head of the glen. Follow the yellow blazes north, as the ravine widens into a little valley and passes through a forest of sugar and red maple, beech, and oak. The path parallels the stream, crosses two roads, then dips down into the brook's shrubby floodplain, where it passes beneath power lines.

At 4.2 miles into the hike, the yellow-blazed trail ends as it crosses Van Campens Brook on a wooden bridge. Continue straight ahead, curving to the right along the gravel roads of Watergate, the 1950s estate of George Busch (there is no political affiliation!).

All that remains of Busch's retreat are a stone dam capped by a Victorian turret, and the grave of his beloved dog Bozo (look for the marker under a tall Norway spruce). Canada-goose droppings and rabbit pellets dot the mowed grass, now a National Recreation Area picnic ground.

Follow the gravel road closest to Van Campens Brook, passing a number of small ponds where there's evidence of former beaver activity. Gnawed river birch and speckled-alder logs (favorite beaver food), a ruined lodge, and beaver mudslides prove the recent presence of the animals, as did a beaver skeleton we uncovered in the brush.

The road continues straight ahead, reaching the outskirts of Millbrook Village at about five miles. Just past the one-room schoolhouse, make a short detour left to the town cemetery. The tilted nineteenth-century stones of Permella Sutton, Uriah Hill, Abram Garis and others stand beneath mature oaks and a seventy-foot-tall paper birch.

The road leads on into Millbrook Village and to the parking lot. This rural community once was home to seventy-five people. Today, summertime volunteers demonstrate weaving, blacksmithing, woodworking and milling to visitors. The sugar shack (for boiling down maple syrup), cider mill, smokehouse, gristmill, general store and Methodist church supported the physical and spiritual needs of surrounding nineteenth-century farms. Today, the sleepy village is home only to wild animals. We've watched wintering juncos here and, in spring, have seen a mother groundhog carry her young by mouth to a stream-side burrow just opposite the gristmill.

Hours, Fees and Facilities

Delaware Water Gap National Recreation Area trails and Millbrook Village grounds are open dawn to dusk year-round. Millbrook Village buildings are open from late April until the end of October, Wednesday through Sunday. Craft demonstrations are on weekends only. No admission fee.

Getting There

From I-80 west, take the last exit in New Jersey. Turn right and travel north for about 12 miles to Millbrook Village.

For More Information

Delaware Water Gap National Recreation Area Park Headquarters, Bushkill, PA 18324; 717-588-2451. Millbrook Village: 908-841-9531.

Merrill Creek Reservoir

- 4.1 miles
- 2.5 hours
- Easy; streamside areas are wet

*A changing ridge-top habitat supports bird
and wildflower diversity*

A contemporary visitor to Merrill Creek views the placid, sun-dappled surface of a 16-billion-gallon lake encircled by forest and field atop Scotts Mountain. But this is my home ground, where I wandered as a child and where I witnessed the swift remaking of the natural landscape by human beings.

In the 1960s, I played explorer here with boyhood friends, puzzling out humankind's past influences. After a spring rain, black chert arrowheads shone against the red clay of plowed farm fields, revealing a 12,000-year Native American legacy. Amid dense second- and third-growth forest, we found incongruous walls and sunken roads, evidence of abandoned eighteenth- and nineteenth-century farms. We explored old homesteads—overgrown, stone-lined cellar holes—with the same romantic zeal as Schliemann uncovering Troy.

In the mid-1970s, seven public utilities announced plans to flood the mountaintop with a gargantuan reservoir. My father, a retired public-utility employee, couldn't bear to see this wooded ridge, where he had hunted deer, rabbit and pheasant, drowned. He was quickly converted from an advocate of progress into an ally of environmentalists.

My dad doggedly fought the project. The utility companies won. Giant earth movers came; stripped away forest and field; tore a 225-foot deep, 650-acre hole in the ridge; and erected an ugly half-mile-long earthen dam. A 3.5-mile-long tunnel, blasted through bedrock, connected the top of Scotts Mountain to the Delaware River. Water was pumped from the river into the reservoir and stored for use by downstream power plants during drought times.

The human change carved into Scotts Mountain both impoverishes and enriches the environment, harming some species while favoring others. Where white-tailed deer once ran, largemouth bass now swim. Where deep-forest warblers once thrived, edge and meadow birds like goldfinches now flourish.

This 4.1-mile loop hike within the 290-acre Merrill Creek Environmental Preserve explores the north shore of the reservoir, passing through a remnant of the

Merrill Creek Reservoir

deciduous, conifer, streamside, wetland and field habitats that once covered all of Scotts Mountain.

To begin the walk, face the main entrance of the visitor center and turn right, walking around to the side of the building. Follow the red gravel path toward the reservoir. Straight ahead a sign points to hiking trails. Pass through an open meadow where yellow winter cress blooms in spring and wild bergamot, goldenrod, and bull thistle flower in fall.

Enter the woods, following the blue-blazed Shoreline Trail to the left. Tulip tree, chestnut oak, and sweet birch rise high overhead, while the understory is filled out by sassafras, red maple, flowering dogwood, witch hazel, and spicebush. Wildflowers dot the leaf litter. Sunny colonies of rue anemone bloom white in late April along with a scattering of blue violets and less common yellow violets. In autumn, wood asters abound in deep shade.

The blue-blazed trail parallels the reservoir and follows a sunken road, its edges stacked high with cobbles by nineteenth-century farmers. Here we found a shrew run, small tunnels ending abruptly on either side of the road and connected by a muddle of tiny footprints. Shrews tunnel through soft forest humus, gaining safe passage from predators. The road, too hard packed for tunneling, must be traversed above ground, exposing the animals to attack.

Another tiny forest creature, the ant, colonizes the roadside. Ants and humans are both considered social animals, though their evolutionary lines diverged about 600 million years ago. Ant species have proven wildly successful, with an estimated million billion ants populating the world today.

Between 0.6 mile and 0.8 mile you'll find evidence of another social species along the blue trail: the ruins of the Cathers farmhouse, a springhouse, the Cathers/Shafer farm, and a lime kiln. Near these field-stone farm foundations stand old apple trees, planted for fruit, and gnarled sugar and silver maples, planted to provide maple syrup. Their low, spreading branches attest to the open sun in this area when it was farmed. The forest found here today is composed of pillar-like trees which reach high before branching to gather sunlight. Non-native barberry, multiflora rose and white violets (with purple centers) are also plentiful at the farms. Next to a boardwalk in a small wetland below the springhouse native blue marsh violets bloom in spring, while great lobelia flowers bright blue in late summer.

A few yards past the lime kiln, detour left and stroll down a short trail to the wildlife observation blind on the reservoir shore. Merrill Creek supports many waterfowl. On an April visit we watched buffleheads, chubby diving ducks aptly called "butterballs." Males are easily identified by a large, roundish white head patch. Without the reservoir there would probably be few buffleheads found on Scotts Mountain. Flooded dead trees bordering the shore provide ideal nesting cavities for the birds.

Return to the blue trail. Follow it to the woods edge, where it turns sharply right (1.1 miles). The trail becomes a mowed path climbing a grassy knoll from which you can look west over the reservoir to the Great Valley of the Appalachians and beyond to Kittatinny Ridge. In this meadow, benevolent human efforts attempt to offset naturally destructive human mistakes. Bluebird boxes placed here attract eastern bluebirds, a species made scarce by aggressive European starlings intentionally introduced to America. To the left of the path, Spanish chestnut trees have been planted. They are an exotic replacement for native American chestnut trees destroyed by a fungal blight accidently introduced to the U.S. in 1904

The blue trail quickly descends to the reservoir edge, reenters the woods, and gets rocky. This reservoir cove, with its drowned trees, offers good birding. In spring, insect-gathering tree swallows swoop above the water, while double-crested cormorants sit on stumps drying their wings. Hysterical laughter, the call of the northern flicker, is heard from birds resting on dead limbs. Pileated woodpeckers, in search of carpenter ants, have blasted huge cavities in rotting trunks.

The blue-blazed Shoreline Trail ends at 1.7 miles. Turn left on the orange-blazed Creek Trail. At 2.0 miles, make a detour a hundred feet left onto a footbridge over Merrill Creek. These woods of sweet birch; beech; and red, white and chestnut oak resemble the forest that once covered the 650 acres submerged by Merrill Creek Reservoir.

The orange trail moves away from the creek briefly, passes a junction with the green Orchard Trail (2.1 miles), and then returns to the creek for the most secluded part of the walk. Sleek tulip trees and peeling yellow birches rise above gracefully spreading spruce limbs. In late April a blaze of golden marsh marigolds, trout

The ruins of a nineteenth-century farmstead.

lilies with yellow drooping blossoms, white dwarf ginseng, and false rue anemone bloom amid greening skunk cabbage and false hellebore.

The orange Creek Trail forks at a wooden bench (2.4 miles). Take the left fork straight ahead as it follows the creek, then turns right and away from the stream. The trail climbs through a stand of pine, the remains of a sprawling pine plantation where I once played hide-and-seek with boyhood friends.

At 2.8 miles, the orange trail passes through a stone wall, turns sharply right on a woods road, and loops back to the bench by the stream (3.0 miles). Turn left, retracing your steps along the brook back to the junction with the green-blazed Orchard Trail (3.3 miles). Follow the green trail as it climbs through oak and sweet birch. Look for an amazing sight: six one-foot diameter tulip trees all rising from a common trunk. Such multiple-trunked trees often sprout from cut stumps.

At 3.6 miles, the green trail reaches the gravel, wheelchair-accessible Eagle Trail. Detour briefly right and stroll through a black cherry grove to the wildlife observation blind at a field edge. Walk silently and you may see a fox as we did. The fox, hearing our approach, quickly disappeared, using an old woodchuck burrow to make good its escape.

Retrace your steps back to the green trail and follow it along the gravel path through the ruins of the Beers Farm, where sweet-scented ornamental white lilacs blossom in springtime. Follow the green blazes straight ahead across a paved road into an old orchard. Take both right forks on the green trail, which returns you to the visitor center at 4.1 miles.

Hours, Fees and Facilities

The visitor center is open seven days a week, 8:30 A.M. to 4:30 P.M., but is closed Thanksgiving, Christmas Eve, Christmas Day, New Years Day and Easter.

Getting There

From I-80 take Exit 12, Hope/Blairstown. Follow County 521 south 1.0 mile to Hope town center. Continue straight on County 519 south for 16 miles. Bear left on 519 south at a Y intersection with County 646. In 1.3 miles, look for a small Merrill Creek sign and turn left on Fox Farm Road. In 4.5 miles turn right at a stop sign onto Richline Road. In 0.6 mile make a right onto Merrill Creek Road. Follow signs right to visitor center.

For More Information

Merrill Creek Reservoir, 34 Merrill Creek Road, Washington, NJ 07882; 908-454-1213.

5 Paulinskill Valley Trail

Blairstown to Marksboro

- 6.4 miles
- 4 hours
- Easy; flat

A streamside stroll along a historic railway

In 1881 the New York, Susquehanna and Western Railroad (NYS&W) brought progress and the promise of prosperity to the rural Paulinskill River valley in western New Jersey. Today, the trains are gone. What remains is a lush, twenty-six-mile-long greenway and trail where nearly a quarter of New Jersey's plant species, plus numerous bird and animal species, thrive.

At its height in 1916, the railway's iron tracks were polished silver by forty passing trains per day. They brought coal from Pennsylvania to New York City, fueling America's Industrial Revolution. They also carried milk, ice, wood, and farm produce to the urban East, while bringing manufactured goods, petroleum products, fertilizer, and city-weary vacationers west. Alfred Ringling even shipped his circus elephants via the NYS&W. But by 1962, truck lines had replaced train lines and the rails turned to rust. Track was torn up, and the abandoned railway became a dumping ground.

A 1985 state plan to turn the railroad into a linear greenway met fierce opposition from adjoining property owners and politicians. That's when local citizens formed the Paulinskill Valley Trail Committee. They garnered overwhelming public support for the new trail corridor. Established as Kittatinny Valley State Park in 1992, the Paulinskill Valley Trail is testimony to the power and promise of grass-roots efforts. Today the trail is a boon to hikers, bikers, horseback riders and fisher folk.

The Paulinskill Valley Trail begins at Columbia on the Delaware River, runs roughly northeast, and ends at Sparta Junction in Sussex County. The section hiked here, between Blairstown and Marksboro, is an easy, perfectly level woods walk paralleling the Paulinskill River. It boasts fine wildflowers, ferns and birds. The walk can be done as a 6.4-mile-out-and-back trip, or a 3.2-mile one-way hike with cars spotted at both ends.

Paulinskill Valley Trail

Begin hiking at the Blairstown parking lot. Pass through the gate north onto the Paulinskill Valley Trail and notice the two tall catalpa trees flanking you. With their floppy, foot-long, heart-shaped leaves, these showy specimens are hard to miss. Most catalpas are tropical species. Those found in New Jersey are usually planted as shade trees. These two may once have landscaped the Blairstown train station. You won't see another catalpa for the rest of the hike.

The trail quickly passes under Route 94, shooting straight ahead under a dense canopy of Norway maple, sugar maple, elm and ailanthus. Whenever you spot ailanthus trees (with eleven to forty-one leaflets along a single stem), you know you're walking in a disturbed forest where humans have left their mark. These exotics were introduced from China. Once planted as speedily growing shelter belts along roadsides and railroads, they now spread out of control, forcing out native trees (a far more valuable source of food for wildlife). The ailanthus, easily confused with sumac, is distinguished by its rank, disagreeable odor.

The Paulinskill River flows as a lazy little stream to your left and is lined by water-loving silver maples, sycamores, basswood and box elders. Spectacular wildflower displays proliferate in these damp woodlands and thickets, peaking in spring but progressing through autumn. Canada mayflower, sweet cicely, Mayapple, bloodroot, early saxifrage, wild columbine, Solomon's seal, and asters all blossom at trailside. Bloodroot, a fragile, solitary white flower with a golden orange center, was especially useful to Native Americans. Its underground stem provided a deep red dye for baskets, clothing and face paint. It also served as insect repellent.

Soon the trail passes a rock outcrop cut by the railroad. While most of the treadway lies on soft river-valley soils or on grittier glacial tills, such rock cuts reveal the Kittatinny limestone underlying this portion of the Great Valley of the Appalachians. This 3,000-foot-thick blue-gray limestone layer consists of compressed organic materials deposited in warm, shallow seas more than 480 million years ago. Today these shady, calcite-rich outcrops support unusual plants. Look for the walking fern. This rare evergreen grows only in limestone. Wherever its long, gracefully pointed leaf tips touch the ground, another plant sprouts. Thus the walking fern strides, step by step, across its stony domain (see sidebar).

The trail briefly escapes the cover of sugar maple, white ash and hickory at 0.7 mile into the hike. It enters the open, crosses the Paulinskill River on a bridge, intersects sleepy East Crisman Road, and arrives at Paulina Dam. The picturesque little milldam on your right creates a quarter-mile-long lake where painted turtles, wood ducks, common mergansers, and swans congregate among lily pads. The trail hugs the lake shore under willows and amid wildflowers. Fragrant white plumes of lizard's tail and erect yellow spikes of common mullein intermingle here from June to September

At this spot we saw a rare sight: a bat flying in broad daylight. It settled its body awkwardly on a shore-side reed, becoming the perfect imitation of a dried leaf. Little brown bats (only about 3.5 inches wide) are nocturnal and most often seen at twilight, darting above water bodies and feeding on clouds of insects. A bat spotted during the day may be rabid or hurt and is best avoided. You should not touch wildlife you discover on your walks.

The trail passes a small wetland blanketed in pickerelweed and cattails at 1.3 miles. Flocks of goldfinches often perform their bouncing acrobatic flight just above the marsh. This "wild canary" is a New Jersey native and our state bird. An edge-habitat bird, it feeds on the seeds of thistles, dandelions, and wild sunflowers, which thrive at field boundaries and in shrubby wetlands. Goldfinches are among the most visible of the Paulinskill Valley Trail's numerous songbirds.

Crossing a second bridge puts the river back on your left-hand side. The stream now rushes through a series of rapids that challenge canoeists during spring high water and attract trout fishermen year-round. The trail then passes

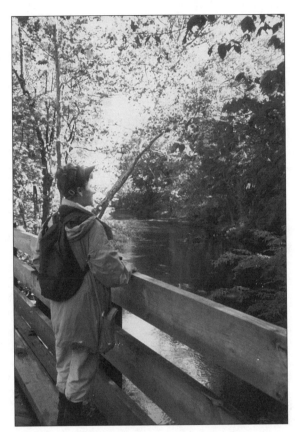

View from a scenic footbridge over the Paulinskill River.

Mile Marker 81, an artifact of the age of steam. These cement posts gave railroaders the track mileage west from Jersey City.

At 2.0 miles, the path crosses the river on a third trestle. The river's edge is lined with black walnut trees and big-tooth aspens. Aspens attest to how recently this area returned to woods; they are pioneer trees which fill in forest clearings.

A concrete pillar etched with the letter W tells walkers they've reached Marksboro. Such markers once warned train engineers of approaching road crossings and cued them to blast their whistles. At 3.2 miles, the trail arrives at the Marksboro Paulinskill Trail parking lot. An old stone mill, now a residence, stands on the far side of the stream. Hikers should either return the way they came or use a second car parked here earlier to retrieve their car in Blairstown.

The Paulinskill Valley Trail is an outstanding but tenuous triumph for environmentalists. Just sixty-six feet wide, this elegant green thread will need the continued support of local residents and hikers to prevent adjoining farmlands from disappearing under suburban development.

🌿 *FABULOUS FERNS*

The moist, limestone-rich lowlands of the Great Valley of the Appalachians supports luxurious fern growth. Hikers along the Paulinskill find Christmas fern (an evergreen whose leaflets are shaped like tiny Christmas stockings), maidenhair fern (growing on a graceful circling axis), polypody (found only on rock outcrops), fragile fern, hay-scented fern, walking fern, and the greatest concentration of glade fern in the state.

Ferns are among the most ancient of plants. During Carboniferous times, more than 230 million years ago, they grew to tree size in jungle swamps. These great ferns were compressed to form the coal once transported by the NYS&W Railroad. Today, there are 10,000 known fern species in the world, most of diminutive size. Ferns remain extremely successful, with their microscopic spores carried by the jet stream for possibly thousands of miles. There are about 100 commonly occurring fern species in our region.

"All you need to learn about them is a hand lens and a fern guide," says Marge Barrett, one of the founders of the Paulinskill Valley Trail. "While they may seem bafflingly similar at first, you can identify them by their shape and by the fruit dot patterns appearing on their undersides during late summer and fall."

Hours, Fees and Facilities

The Paulinskill Valley Trail is open from dawn to dusk daily.

Getting There

From I-80 take NJ 94 to Blairstown. At the north edge of town, turn right onto Footbridge Lane at a sign for Footbridge Park. If you reach a right turn for County 616, you've gone too far. Park by signs for the Paulinskill Valley Trail. Follow the trail north, back toward the parking lot entrance. For shuttle hikers, place a second car 3 miles north of Blairstown. Follow NJ 94 north just past the Marksboro Country Store, and turn left on County 659 west toward Stillwater. In 0.3 mile, cross the Paulinskill River and turn left into a parking lot.

For More Information

Kittatinny Valley State Park, P.O. Box 621, Andover, NJ 07821; 973-786-6445.
    To volunteer with the Paulinskill Valley Trail Committee, call 908-852-0597.

6 Ridge and Valley Trail

White Lake Natural Area, Warren County Park

- 4.2 miles
- 3 hours
- Easy; with small ascents and descents

A walk through a lowland limestone forest

First time visitors to the rolling hills of Warren and Sussex County farm country sometimes comment on how much the area reminds them of Virginia's Shenandoah Valley. The resemblance is not coincidental: the valleys are one and the same.

The Great Valley of the Appalachians shadows Appalachian ridge tops from Alabama to the Hudson River. This broad lowland, characterized by whphy, is dotted with hunchbacked limestone outcrops, a latticework of limestone caves, bottomless sinkhole lakes, cold springs that gush from pristine aquifers, and small streams that surge out of solid stone and disappear as quickly back into it.

White Lake Natural Area, Warren County's first county park, is also one of the first examples of karst topography in New Jersey to be protected. "For years, people have been actively saving the high ridges, which is a good thing," says Bob Canace, President of the Ridge and Valley Conservancy. "Meanwhile the lowlands were being lost to roads, homes and malls. Here, we've set aside over 1000 acres of significant limestone forest, a great legacy."

The conservancy is also pressing forward with the Ridge and Valley Trail, an ambitious greenway project which will eventually cut for twelve miles across the Great Valley, connecting with the Appalachian Trail atop Kittatinny Ridge.

This circuit hike uses 2.7 miles of the Ridge and Valley Trail, beginning at Marksboro, penetrates the new preserve, then returns via the White Lake Loop Trail, for a round-trip total of 4.2 miles. The walk is highlighted by a crystal clear sinkhole lake, rare carnivorous plants, hemlock and sugar maple forest, and the ruins of a limestone marl works and limestone kiln.

Note: the White Lake Natural Area is so new that its trails were still under construction at the time of this book's publication. The precise trail

Ridge and Valley Trail

corridor may vary from the description found here due to the results of an ecological survey. Call the Ridge and Valley Conservancy at 908-362-7989 to determine current trail status. Stay on trails and woods roads to avoid trampling sensitive flora.

From the Marksboro Paulinskill Valley Trail parking lot, turn left and walk west, along County 659, being careful of traffic. Head uphill, following the small gray slate shingle blazes, painted with a white "Ridge and Valley" slash. The trail passes through a road cut revealing layers of Martinsburg shale (these shales share this portion of the Great Valley with the limestones).

A hundred yards past the intersection with Paulinskill Road (on the left) and Primrose Road (on the right), the trail turns right, leaving the macadam and striking out along an abandoned railroad spur of the New York, Susquehanna and Western Railroad. This rail line once transported ice harvested at White Lake to a local creamery. The path passes under white ash, sycamore, sugar maple and red cedar, and overlooks several sprawling country farms.

The old spur quickly passes a wetland on the right bordered with limestone outcrops and goes by a limestone sinkhole to the left. The limestones and dolomites in the Great Valley form calcite-rich rock layers 3,000 feet thick and are composed of the accumulated and compressed secretions of ancient algae mats that lived on tidal flats as much as 2 billion years ago. The stone itself was formed between 650 million and 440 million years ago. Today, rainwater (containing a weak natural acid) seeps into the porous rock, combines chemically with it, and dissolves it away, pitting, scouring, and hollowing it out. Limestone-loving trees— red cedars, sugar maples and chinkapin oaks (also called yellow oaks)—are plentiful in these soils.

A short side trail cuts left to the limestone marl works, an impressive, two-story stone ruin dating from the 1890s, with gracefully arched doorways and windows. Marl, a soft, calcium-rich limestone clay dredged from White Lake, was processed to make cement and fertilizer. The industry failed in 1900.

The side trail continues to the edge of White Lake. With its ivory-colored marl shoreline and crystal-clear water, this beautiful spot seems to resemble a Caribbean beach. The marl supports rare grasses and sedges and is dotted with numerous pitcher plants. This carnivorous plant holds a small pocket of water within its upstretched lips. Unfortunate insects trapped inside are dissolved and digested by the plant to provide it with nutrients it can't obtain from the soil.

The lake itself is a sinkhole (a so-called karst depression) with no inlet. It is supplied by pure groundwater springs. The lake is alive with snails and mussels that feed on calcium-rich plants and detritus and utilize that food to make their shells. The water also holds black bass and is visited by ospreys and migratory ducks. Look for raccoon tracks and scooped-out depressions where this mammal digs out mollusks. Because this environmentally sensitive area supports so many fragile plants, please stay on the blazed trail.

Return to the main trail and follow it along an old logging road through a mixed deciduous forest and past the ruins of a 1950s Girl Scout camp. We found black bear droppings near here, and others have reported seeing a red fox trotting across the path. Trees grow well in these soils. Look for a huge white oak and a black cherry tree that require two people's arms to stretch around them.

The Ridge and Valley Trail enters a dark hemlock grove, where the healthy trees seem unaffected by the hemlock woolly adelgid (an exotic insect that is wiping out Eastern hemlocks). Beeches, sweet birches and tulip trees mix with the conifers. Christmas ferns adorn exposed benches of moss-covered limestone. Look closely at the outcrops and you'll see lenses and nodules of dark black stone. This glasslike chert was prized by Native Americans because it could easily be chipped into stone scrapers, arrowheads, and other tools.

The trail descends steeply for a hundred feet into a linear karst valley eroded out of a broken fold in the limestone. To visualize how this little valley was made, imagine a layer of limestone under immense pressure. The rock layer bent upward until the crest of the fold snapped in two (like a bent green stick breaking). Rainwater then eroded away a small, straight valley along the joint planes at the top of the shattered limestone fold.

The trail climbs out of the karst valley, arriving at one of the best-preserved lime kilns in Warren County. These graceful, keyhole-arched stone kilns, representing eighteenth-century Moravian technology, were loaded from the top with alternating layers of wood and limestone, then set ablaze. The resulting calcium-rich powder was hydrated, loaded on wagons, and spread on farm fields. Up to eighteen cords of wood were needed to supply a single season's kilning.

Just beyond the kiln, the White Lake Loop Trail enters from the left. Continue straight ahead on the Ridge and Valley Trail as it winds through more limestone outcrops, entering and exiting small groves of oak and hemlock, hickory, sweet birch, and black walnut.

Look under the small limestone outcrops for signs of life. Fox and other mammals use these spaces as natural dens, leaving behind hair or small bones (the remains of meals). Also look for misplaced boulders that don't seem to match the ashen gray dolomite or blue-gray limestone. These tough sandstones and quartzites were dragged from as far away as the Kittatinny Mountains and Catskills. They are glacial erratics, dropped like giant marbles by the retreating Wisconsin Glacier more than 15,000 years ago.

At 2.7 miles into the hike, the Ridge and Valley Trail continues straight ahead, running for another 1.8 miles to a parking area at Sunset Lake Road. Turn left, following the cedar shingle (with blue-painted ripple) blazes of the White Lake Loop Trail.

This path winds for about a half-mile through old pasturelands grown up with red cedar, black walnut, white pine and sugar maple. The trail turns left at a gravel driveway, then forks onto a woods road, returning back to the junction with the Ridge and Valley Trail near the lime kiln. Follow the Ridge and Valley Trail right, back the way you came, to your car.

Hours, Fees and Facilities

White Lake Preserve is open dawn to dusk year-round.

Getting There

From I-80 drive north on NJ 94 to Blairstown. Staying on NJ 94, travel a little more than 3 miles farther north, just past the Marksboro Country Store, and make a left on County 659 west, toward Stillwater. In 0.3 mile, cross the Paulinskill River and turn left into the trail parking lot.

For More Information

Ridge and Valley Conservancy, P.O. Box 146, Blairstown, NJ 07825; 908-362-7989.

7 Sussex Branch Trail

Kittatinny Valley State Park

- 3.7 miles
- 3 hours
- Easy; flat

A haven for deer and wild turkey

For thousands of years the fertile lowlands of the Great Valley of the Appalachians have supported wildlife and attracted human beings. This gently sculpted valley stretches from Alabama to New York and runs in a forty-five-mile-long, twelve-mile-wide, diagonal swath across northwest New Jersey.

At the end of the last Ice Age 12,000 years ago, Paleolithic hunters moved up and down this trough, chasing caribou herds across a frigid New Jersey landscape that was covered in open tundra and spruce forest. A global warming trend melted the ice and caused the rise of a great deciduous forest, stretching to the Mississippi River. The vast woodlands became home to wolf and cougar and their prey, elk and deer.

White settlers quickly claimed the prime real estate of the Great Valley. They deforested it, building farms and estates, roads and railroads. Wildlife was hunted to oblivion. Elk and cougar disappeared from New Jersey by 1840, wolves by 1855, and white-tailed deer by 1900. Only in the twentieth century have people felt secure enough in their hold on the Great Valley to allow nature's limited resurgence.

This 3.7-mile loop hike, starting on the Sussex Branch Trail and circling through Kittatinny Valley State Park, offers a chance to see plentiful deer, wild turkeys and songbirds. The flat terrain invites families with children, and cross-country skiers.

The trailhead parking lot on US 206 is bordered by native chinkapin oak, elm, and aspen along with introduced catalpa, apple, and ailanthus. In springtime, walk a few yards left to a limestone outcrop. The drooping red, fool's-cap-shaped blossoms of wild columbine thrive upon the calcite-rich rock. These flowers, narrow tubes with pollen hidden deep inside, allow access to just a few pollinators. Hovering ruby-throated hummingbirds, with needle-like bills and an attraction to red,

Sussex Branch Trail

private residence
(old estate
house) ■

gravel road →

Twin Lakes
(private)

gate

field

Lake
Aeroflex

path to
cement
dock

Goodale Road

White Pond
(private)

Sussex Branch Trail (old railroad grade)

hangars
runway
airplane tie
downs

park
office

KITTATINNY
VALLEY
STATE PARK

Gardners Pond

206

START

P.

Limecrest Road

have evolved a specialized pollinating/nectar-gathering partnership with columbine. Be careful when leaving the path—poison ivy lurks at trailside.

Leave the parking lot, following the Sussex Branch Trail through a gate into the woods. This twenty-one-mile-long trail began life in 1849 as the mule-powered

Sussex Railroad, hauling ore from the Andover Iron Mine to the Morris Canal at Waterloo Village. The line later became a branch of the Erie-Lackawanna Railroad and was abandoned in the mid-1900s.

Today, the rail bed welcomes hikers, bikers and horse riders. The path is lined by tulip tree, ash, maple, and white oak. In autumn, the forest floor explodes with color. Yellow spikes of common mullein and goldenrod rise above the white parasols of Queen Anne's lace and the ornate blue trumpets of great lobelia. Chicory, wood aster, and the scarlet cones of staghorn sumac fill out the color scheme. The earthy scent of wild bergamot permeates the air.

Songbirds add another accent to these woods. The familiar cardinal resides in this edge habitat year-round. It loves the dense honeysuckle thickets, feeding on wild grapes, dogwood berries, and sumac seeds. You might think that the male cardinal's scarlet feathers would betray it to predators. Not so. Deciduous thickets with their green leaves spread green light, while absorbing red and blue portions of the spectrum. The cardinal disappears from sight in its shady habitat. In winter, dense thickets provide protection from hawks.

Within 0.4 mile the raised railroad bed shoots down the middle of a wetland. Quiet, shallow pools support white waterlilies, cattails, pickerelweed, and a beautiful display of water marigolds topped by golden-rayed blossoms. Swans and mallards swim amid surfacing turtles. Notice the silvery gray trunks of dead red maples. This area was a swamp (a tree-filled, seasonal wetland) which has gradually become wetter and changed into a marsh (a treeless, year-round wetland).

The path leaves the marsh and enters deep, cool woods. It passes a small limestone outcrop on the left and an isolated pocket of water that in late summer is dusted with a pea green layer of duckweed, the smallest of flowers.

At 1.0 mile the trail exits the woods, then crosses and parallels Goodale Road. The open meadows and forest of Kittatinny Valley State Park to your right and the cornfields to your left make this the ideal spot for wildlife watching. At dusk, deer congregate at treeline, waiting for darkness before making their cautious way into the corn for a late-night snack. Bold turkeys, in groups of twenty or more, commute from forest to corn in full morning sunlight. Both white-tailed deer and turkey were wiped out by early settlers and had to be reintroduced into New Jersey wilds. The immense deer herds of today are descended from the few animals kept in pens on the Worthington and Rutherford estates. Wild turkeys returned on their own in 1958, when eleven birds flew across the Delaware River from Pennsylvania and began taking back their old haunts.

As the meadow ends to your right (about 1.3 miles into the walk), leave the Sussex Branch Trail, turn right and cross Goodale Road, and enter Kittatinny Valley State Park through a gate. Follow a gravel road along an impressive stone wall lined by stately white ash.

The ash tree's hard wood was once shaped into canoe paddles by Native Americans, and later into furniture and Louisville Slugger baseball bats. This stand, with its tall, straight trunks, may explain why the ancient Norse imagined white ash as a tree that could support the weight of the world. In the woods to your left, look

The 1823 stone farmhouse, expanded to become an estate house in 1906, landscaped with pin oak, white oak, silver maple, and black walnut trees.

for devil's walking-stick, also known as prickly ash. This spiny shrub was planted on Victorian estates as a grotesque ornamental.

Reaching the far corner of the meadow, avoid forks to the left and to the right. Walk straight ahead on the gravel road. At 1.8 miles, the road glides into the open, passing a landscaped private residence. This stone farmhouse, built in 1823, was expanded in 1906 as an estate house. It is landscaped with pin oak, white oak, silver maple, and black walnut trees. Follow the gravel road as it swings right, sweeping alongside hemlock-lined Aeroflex Lake.

At 2.3 miles a clear path leads left to the lake and a cement dock, a fine lunch spot. Sunfish rise to snap up crumbs on this, the deepest glacial lake in New Jersey.

Continue to the end of Aeroflex Lake and pass left along the end of a small airport runway. Stop by the park office, built in 1872, to pick up info or use rest rooms, then walk the road between the airplane tie-downs and Gardner's Pond. Dragonflies buzz above the purple loosestrife, and butterflies flit among black-eyed Susans (see sidebar).

At the pond's end (3.2 miles) veer right, following the road into the woods. The road passes a small red maple swamp, then reaches what was once an estate gate. The road passes between planted juniper, spruce and box trees. The box is a

European native and a once popular ornamental. Its branches were trimmed into fantastic topiaries, while its hard wood was formerly used in carving. The road passes a remarkable seven-trunked silver maple before returning to US 206. A right turn leads quickly to your car.

🌰 FLIGHTS OF WONDER

A dragonfly zigzags across the sun-drenched marsh; a seagull sweeps over the lake; a single-engine plane arcs toward the runway. Kittatinny Valley State Park is a study in flight, a place to let your imagination soar.

A flight-friendly wing is the secret to flying. An effective wing is convex above and flattened below, rounded in front and with a rear edge tapered to a point. This elegant design moves air faster across the upper wing surface than below. This reduces air pressure above the wing, resulting in lift.

Unlike airplanes, birds have flexible airfoils to control air speed and direction. Bird flight is actually a combination of wing movement alternating with swooping glides. Flight is a high-energy enterprise for birds; wing feathers wear out quickly and must be replaced.

A pilot must guard against losing too much air speed and stalling a plane. Birds land by gliding to a stall precisely over the spot on ground, water or limb where they wish to "fall." Such efficient avian gliders as turkey vultures and sea gulls actually lose altitude at the same rate warm air rises. Thus, these feathered gliders fall without falling.

The cellophane-like, intricately veined wings of an adult dragonfly allow this hunter to fly at 25 mph and catch mosquitoes in flight. The scale-covered, leaf-like wings of a monarch butterfly carry this insect at top speeds of only 6 mph, but the seemingly fragile butterfly can flap itself hundreds of miles to Mexico during autumn migration.

—sidebar by Jean LeBlanc

Hours, Fees and Facilities

Trails are open from dawn to dusk year-round. The park office is open daily.

Getting There

The Sussex Branch Trail parking area is located on NJ 206, 0.2 mile north of Andover on the right and 3.2 miles south of Newton on the left.

For More Information

Kittatinny Valley State Park, P.O. Box 621, Andover, NJ 07821; 973-786-6445.

To volunteer with New Jersey RailTrails, write P.O. Box 23, Pluckemin, NJ 07978.

White Cedar Swamp Trail

Dryden Kuser Natural Area, High Point State Park

- 1.5 miles
- 2 hours
- Easy; with gentle climbing

The wonders of an Atlantic white-cedar swamp

Not so long ago swamps evoked primal fear and disgust. Their slime-covered pools, muck, mosquitoes, and dismal forests thwarted America's drive toward wilderness conquest. For the past century, people could find no better use for these trackless wastelands than to drain, bulldoze and plop subdivisions down where they had been, attaching prettified names like "Willowbrook" or "Pleasant Valley" to the once swampy locales. And good riddance too...

Luckily, hydrologists, botanists and biologists have set us straight. Today, we recognize wetlands as vital to our own survival and to planetary biodiversity. These self-cleaning organic sponges are recognized as natural waste treatment plants. They capture polluted runoff and purify it, while recharging groundwater drinking supplies. Hikers have also recognized these once forbidding places as magical – they are the habitat for large mammals like the black bear, and haven to strange flora like insectivorous sundews or magnificent Atlantic white cedars. The National Wildlife Federation estimates that 43% of threatened and endangered species rely on wetlands at some stage in their life cycles.

The 850-acre Dryden Kuser Natural Area in High Point State Park played a role in raising New Jersey's wetland consciousness starting in the 1960s. The preserve's highly accessible 1.5 mile Cedar Swamp Trail draws hikers into the mysterious world of an Atlantic white-cedar swamp. (You can pick up a numbered Nature Guide at the High Point State Park office).

The walk begins at a gate from which a road leads downhill through a deciduous forest of chestnut oak, white oak, pignut hickory and sweet birch. Notice the 25-foot-tall American chestnut immediately to the left of the gate. It is identified by its long, narrow, oblong leaves with sharp curved teeth. This tree dominated upland forests just a century ago, growing to over a hundred feet.

White Cedar Swamp Trail

The spiny fruit and leaf of the American chestnut.
These once giant trees were laid low by a fungal
blight introduced from Asia.

Its fruit was food to animals, Native Americans and pioneers. A fungal blight accidentally introduced to New York City on imported Chinese chestnut trees wiped out these American giants. But hope springs eternal for the chestnut: young sprouts rise from the roots of long dead trees, grow into spindly saplings, then are blighted. We've seen female chestnuts on this hike in early fall, with ripe spiny fruit. Perhaps an offspring will one day develop blight immunity.

The gradually descending road is lined with large sassafras trees. These can be tricky to identify at first, since mature specimens have very few of the mitten-shaped leaves characteristic of younger trees. Sassafras can be positively identified by its spicy, aromatic scent. Bracken fern and hay-scented fern also grow on this drier ground.

Two stone pillars mark the entrance to the Dryden Kuser Natural Area 0.25 mile into the walk. The preserve is named for a state senator, New Jersey Audubon Society president, and the son of parents who donated their High Point retreat to New Jersey as a park. The wet ground at this spot supports water-tolerant red maples.

At the natural-area plaque (0.4 mile), fork left on the Cedar Swamp Trail. The trail encircles the swamp, following the natural boundary between upland and wetland and providing a unique opportunity to see how moisture and soil type dictate plant habitat. In the upland to the left, oaks, sweet birch, and witch hazel dominate. To the right is the swamp, where rhododendron, Atlantic white cedar, and Eastern hemlock rise on sphagnum moss (peat moss) hummocks amid pools of rust brown water. These evergreens are tolerant of the sodden, acidic, nutrient-poor soils, as is skunk cabbage. Graceful, vaselike displays of cinnamon fern also grow in the wetland.

The swamp, cradled between two Kittatinny Range ridges, is a relic of the last Ice Age. The retreating Wisconsin Glacier dammed this little depression 15,000 years ago, creating a thirty-acre lake. The water body was gradually filled in by a sphagnum moss bog (a permanently flooded, open peatland whose highly acidic waters won't let organic material decay). Conifers then gradually filled in the bog at its margins until no open water remained, turning the area into a swamp (strictly defined as a tree-covered wetland). This northernmost New Jersey Atlantic white cedar swamp is a crossroads for biodiversity. New England plants mingle with southern species.

The trail rises above the swamp (0.6 mile), giving good views over the wetland. Look for a large sour-gum tree, also called black tupelo, at the nature guide's number 11 station along the trail. This swamp-forest tree is uncommon in northern Jersey, though numerous on the Inner Coastal Plain. It can be identified by its deeply furrowed bark and sharply pointed, shiny leaves, turning scarlet in autumn. The bluish black fall berries are favored by birds.

The trail descends back toward the swamp and cuts through it on a boardwalk (1.0 mile). Notice that shade-tolerant hemlocks dominate the wetland canopy, but wherever an opening has appeared (caused by either a tree-fall or the trail itself), light-loving Atlantic white cedars have seized the opportunity to grow. The white cedar is normally a coastal tree, spreading southward from Maine. Its wood has been variously used in war- and music-making: it produced charcoal for Revolutionary War gunpowder and served as pipes in the first American church organs. The hemlock has flat, flexible needles, while the cedar has more bristly, scalelike needles.

Great rhododendron forms a thick, impenetrable understory along the boardwalk. This shrub blooms with showy flowers in mid-July, and its long, waxy leaves curl cigarlike at winter's onset. The colder the weather, the tighter the curl. Wild calla, more common to southern Canada than New Jersey, is plentiful at this spot. Its heart-shaped glossy leaves are topped in summer by a pudgy spike of yellow flowers partly enclosed by a white hood. A tight cluster of crimson berries make this a showy member of the arum family in autumn.

While on the boardwalk, stoop and notice the thick, spongy sphagnum moss blanket covering the shallow water pools on both sides. This unassuming aquatic evergreen actually initiated the bog ecosystem at High Point 15,000 years ago (see sidebar). Acids and tannins released from dying sphagnum moss inhibit decay-causing bacteria that normally enrich wetland soils. Thus, only hardy plants able to survive under nutrient-starved conditions—plants like the Atlantic white cedar, rhododendron and calla—can join sphagnum moss in this acid-rich ecosystem.

Just beyond the boardwalk, the trail reaches a major intersection (1.1 miles). The left branch leads to a bridge crossing of a stream on the Monument Trail (see chapter 9). The right branch leads back to your starting place at the parking lot in 0.4 mile, where tree-shaded tables provide a fine spot for a picnic.

🌲 *SECRETS OF SPHAGNUM MOSS*

This lowly evergreen has one thing in common with North America's beavers: its ability to utterly transform an aquatic environment. Growing in thick green mats, sphagnum moss (commonly called peat moss) is perpetually growing at the water's surface but dying just below the waterline. The dead part of the plant releases acids and tannins which sterilize the water, preventing decay from occurring. Dead layers of vegetation sink to the bottom, creating thick deposits of organic matter sometimes hundreds of feet thick (in the Dryden Kuser Natural Area swamp, sphagnum moss has nearly filled in a glacial lake that was twelve feet deep). Specialized shrubs and trees anchor their roots in the dead material and rise above the floating raft of living moss.

Humans have found many uses for sphagnum moss. Because it is sterile and absorbs up to twenty times its own weight in water, it was used as a wound dressing during World War I. Britons have long cut and burned peat as fuel. Its most frequent use today is by gardeners and farmers as moisture-holding mulch.

According to John Eastman, in *The Book of Swamp and Bog,* one of the least-understood features of sphagnum moss bogs is their ability to moderate climate. Bogs stay cool in spring and summer, possibly reducing temperature extremes in the air around them. With almost half of all U.S. boglands now gone, and with other nations fast depleting this resource, we may unknowingly be destabilizing our weather systems and possibly inviting environmental unbalance.

Hours, Fees and Facilities

The Cedar Swamp Trail is open from dawn to dusk year-round.

Getting There

Take I-80 west to NJ 23 north through the town of Sussex. Eight miles north of Sussex, climb Kittatinny Ridge and turn right into High Point State Park (the park headquarters building is on the left side of NJ 23). Within 1.0 mile reach Lake Marcia, and follow signs to the Cedar Swamp Picnic Area. Follow the road to a dead end at the picnic area parking lot.

For More Information

High Point State Park, 1480 State Route 23, Sussex, NJ 07461; 973-875-4800. Stop at the office for the Cedar Swamp Guided Nature Walk booklet.

9 Monument Trail

High Point State Park

- 3.5 miles
- 3 hours
- Elevation gain 300 feet
- Moderate; some rocky footing and climbing

A ridge-top walk among forest mammals

People sometimes fail to recognize how the accidents of geology shape our daily lives. New York City skyscrapers, for example, can exist only because bedrock underlies shallow soils at the central and southern parts of Manhattan Island. Likewise, the rugged, erosion-resistant ridges of the Kittatinny Range at High Point have made New Jersey's northwest corner into a haven for forest mammals, rather than a home to humans.

The tough Shawangunk conglomerate that forms the backbone of the Kittatinny Ridge was born in the deposition of sand and gravel by streams 440 million years ago. These formations compressed, folded, faulted, tilted and uplifted into mountains once as high as the Rockies. Worn down over millions of years, a new mountain-building period left a several-mile-wide range cresting at 1,803 feet above sea level at High Point.

These ridges are domain to large forest mammals and have attracted hunters for thousands of years. Native Americans tracked mastodon and caribou through boreal spruce forest just 12,000 years ago. More recently, white-tailed deer were stalked and beavers trapped by Native Americans and white settlers. By the early 1900s, the Kuser family established a ridge-top estate and game park. Fences enclosed elk and reindeer herds, from which individual animals were loaned to department store Santas at Christmastime. When the Kusers donated their mountain retreat to the state in 1923, local papers whined that the new park would serve only as "a stamping ground for wild and destructive animals."

Today, High Point State Park's Monument Trail, a loop of 3.5 miles, explores the home territory of coyote, bobcat, bear, fox, deer, raccoon, porcupine, skunk, rabbit, and other mammals. Most of these animals are elusive, so you're unlikely to see them; if you know what to look for, however, signs of their presence are everywhere.

Begin hiking at the High Point Monument parking lot (to avoid crowds, go early in the day or off-season). Walk behind the rest rooms and look for the circular, red-on-top, green-on-bottom metal markers of the Monument Trail. Follow them uphill a few hundred yards to the right of the monument. This 220-foot-tall, trim stone pinnacle resembles the Washington Monument and was built in 1930 to honor New Jersey veterans. The tower is presently closed for repairs (July 1998) but 360-degree views at the base are great year-round. Look east to the Great Valley of the Appalachians (locally called the Wallkill River valley) and to the ramparts of the New Jersey Highlands on Wawayanda Mountain. Look north to the town of Port Jervis, New York and the Catskills, west to Pennsylvania's Poconos, and south along the Kittatinny Ridge toward the Delaware Water Gap.

Blooming next to the monument at summer's end is bristly, bright blue viper's bugloss, or blueweed. At home in limestone (found only in the valleys below), this invading wildflower may have caught a ride to New Jersey's highest summit in the limestone-rich pea gravel that covers the path. More common to these dry, acid soils are scrub oak, pitch pine, chestnut oak, knapweed and white snakeroot which huddle around the monument. Notice how these plants do not grow very tall, in order to withstand exposure to brutal winter winds.

The path descends past the monument (0.1 mile), where black cherry and big-tooth aspen trees grow in more-protected areas and reach higher to the sky. The path falls farther past a pump house, crosses a road, goes through a rocky area under tall red oaks and red maples, then crosses a second road, reaching Lake Marcia (0.3 mile). This glacial pond was scraped out by the Wisconsin Glacier more than 15,000 years ago.

The trail circles right, around the lake, where a black tupelo (sour-gum) tree has been gnawed by beavers. Once populating every New Jersey stream, beaver was the first fur-bearing animal to be exterminated in the state. By 1820 they were gone from the wild. Preserved on estates, however, escapees reestablished themselves around 1900. The beaver lodge on Lake Marcia was recently abandoned, though not before the animals killed so many shade trees that water temperatures rose, causing troublesome algae blooms.

At the end of the lake, the trail ascends on a road to the park's nature center and turns right at a Monument Trail sign (0.5 mile). It enters a classic ridge-top forest where assorted oaks and pignut hickories rise above lowbush blueberry bushes and large boulders, erratics left by the Ice Age.

A steep descent on stone steps leads into a ravine where a bridge crosses a small stream (0.7 mile). This stonework, like the rest of this trail, was built by the Civilian Conservation Corps. In the 1930s, when Hitler's answer to global depression was to arm unemployed young men with rifles, Franklin Roosevelt's solution was to equip them with shovels. The CCC built roads, lakes, buildings and trails throughout America's park system.

In this ravine, we once tracked two coyotes on winter snow. The graceful animals left a streamlined "post hole" trail, with the track of one hind food falling directly on top of a front one. In fact, the pair perfectly followed each other, matching footsteps for a long distance, revealing the presence of a partner only when they decided to part company. Domestic dogs, with somewhat similarly shaped prints, leave a sloppy trail of overlapping tracks. Coyotes, smart animals that have outwitted relentless hunting and poisoning, leave other sign. Look for piles of hair at kill sites, or one-inch diameter scat composed of hair and large bone fragments. (Never touch scat with bare hands; it may contain harmful bacteria.)

The trail climbs back to an oak and pitch pine–dominated ridge (0.9 mile), offering northwest views to the graceful bends of the Delaware River at Port Jervis. Along this stretch some pitch pines have succumbed to driving winter winds. The dead trees are riddled with ants, beetles and insect larvae, which provide fine dining for woodpeckers. Flickers and downy and hairy woodpeckers drill small, shallow, roundish holes in bark, while large, prehistoric-looking, pileated woodpeckers blast elongated, cavernous trenches. The pileated is often seeking hidden, vertical galleries of black carpenter ants.

The Monument Trail passes a less sweeping view west, topped by a white pine, then descends to the right, off the ridge top at 1.5 miles, into a small valley that cradles the Dryden Kuser Natural Area. This sheltered upland hosts every northern oak: red, white, chestnut, scrub, scarlet and black oak form a popular animal

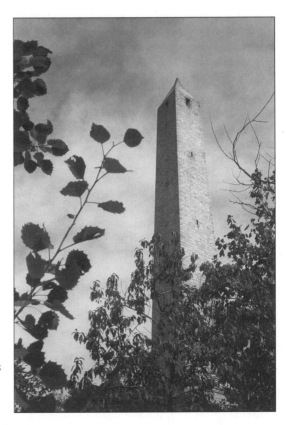

High Point Monument marks the highest ridge top in New Jersey at 1,803 feet.

habitat. Look for frequent dead-falls torn open by skunks, bears and other mammals rooting for grubs.

At the valley's lowest point, the trail crosses a little bridge (2.0 miles). A gravel road to the right leads to the Cedar Swamp Trail (see chapter 8), a fine 1.5-mile addition to this hike if you have an extra hour or two for exploring.

The Monument Trail continues straight ahead and swiftly climbs to a ridge. At the top the trail turns right, heading south. The oak forest has now been replaced by one almost entirely of hickory. There are several great views east from steep ledges into the Great Valley of the Appalachians, and a single view west into the Cedar Swamp. The path becomes less rocky, then exits the woods at the Monument parking lot.

🌰 THE RIDGE TOP GREENGROCER

The dry, winter-ravaged forests topping Kittatinny Ridge may seem like a less than ideal habitat, but these woods provide a cornucopia for feeding mammals.

Pitch-pine cones sate red squirrels and chipmunks. Look for middens, heaps of cones stripped of scales right down to the core with seeds removed. Naturalist Paul Rezendes, in his book *Tracking and the Art of Seeing,* reports seeing squirrels strip cones at the remarkable rate of one every nine seconds.

Acorns, hickory nuts and beechnuts offer a feast to bear, deer, squirrel, shrews, mice and others. Chewed-open nuts with meat removed are easy to find lying on the ground or in hollow trees. Bears love beechnuts so much they'll climb trees for them. Older beeches sometimes display healed-over scars gouged by the animal's five razor-sharp claws.

If you're lucky, you may spot a porcupine hanging motionless high atop a tree, disguising itself as a burl. They debark hardwoods or gobble down spring maple buds.

White-tailed deer leave plentiful sign. Their beds and heart-shaped tracks are easy to find in winter. They nip and tear at twigs, leaving ragged browse marks on favorite foods like birch, maple, hemlock and viburnum.

Hours, Fees and Facilities

The Monument Trail is open from dawn to dusk year-round.

Getting There

Take I-80 west to Route 23 north to the town of Sussex. Eight miles north of Sussex, climb Kittatinny Ridge and turn right into High Point State Park (the park headquarters is on the left side of Route 23). Follow signs to High Point Monument, reached within 1.5 miles. Park by the rest rooms.

For More Information

High Point State Park, 1480 State Route 23, Sussex, NJ 07461; 973-875-4800.

Wallkill River National
10 Wildlife Refuge and
Pochuck Swamp

- 3.5 miles
- 3 hours
- Easy; not recommended for midday or midsummer

Explore the "drowned lands" along the Appalachian Trail

The Wallkill River meanders thirty-seven miles northward to the Hudson, dropping only seven and a half feet in elevation. Twelve thousand years of floods and vegetative growth along this level flood plain have resulted in deposits of rich black dirt. This walk across the "drowned lands," as early settlers called this flood-prone region, focuses on vital wetland habitats that support flora and fauna of almost overwhelming diversity.

This walk takes you from the edge of the Wallkill River, at the boundary between Sussex County, New Jersey, and Orange County, New York, to the base of Pochuck Mountain, where the Kittatinny limestone floor of the Wallkill Valley meets erosion-resistant Precambrian highland gneiss. Two distinctive ecosystems—open, marshy flood plain and deeply shaded red maple swamp—impart a split personality to this walk. The juxtaposition offers tantalizing glimpses into the nature of different types of wetlands.

Human intervention is hastening the refuge's transformation from farm to wetland, so change is one of the few constants here. The nature of land in the refuge varies greatly from year to year, as well as season to season. No hunting will be allowed in this section of the refuge, so an autumn walk will be just as pleasant as a spring walk. In both seasons, you'll marvel at the profusion of wildflowers.

Standing in the refuge parking lot, face Oil City Road and turn left, following the unblazed Liberty Loop Trail along the dike west toward the Wallkill River. In 0.2 mile turn left onto the white-blazed Appalachian Trail. Don't trample the vegetation; poison ivy lurks everywhere. The trail continues straight ahead for the next mile.

This area was an active sod farm until the early 1990s; a network of ditches drained water from the sponge-like black dirt. Now lined with such aquatic vegetation as cattails, these water-filled ditches teem with insects and insect larvae, frogs, salamanders, painted turtles, water snakes, small fish and muskrats. Great

Wallkill River National Wildlife Refuge

Oil City Road (State Line Rd.)

N

Wallkill River

wooded
floodplain

Appalachian Trail (white-blazed)

WALLKILL RIVER
NATIONAL
WILDLIFE
REFUGE

meadows/
wetland

Liberty Loop Trail

P   START

old railroad grade

Pochuck
Swamp

Liberty Corners Road

blue herons and snowy egrets pursue tasty morsels. Smaller birds flit amongst the vegetation, feeding on insects. On higher ground, short-tailed shrews crisscross the meadow in shallow runways, feasting on worms, insects and nestling mice.

All this activity attracts two dozen species of raptors to the area. Rare visitors include golden eagles, bald eagles and peregrine falcons. Red-tailed hawks and American kestrels hunt from on high. A marsh hawk soars just above the vegetation, following the dips and swells like a feathered ship on a sea of flowers and grasses. At dusk, several species of owls patrol the refuge.

Prolonged rain or snow melt floods large areas, summoning flocks of waterfowl. Canada geese, snow geese, black ducks, mallards, wood ducks, mergansers and green-winged teals are just several of the twenty-one species of waterfowl that use the refuge as nesting habitat or migratory way station.

In late summer, bright yellow blooms of evening primrose contrast with purple loosestrife, tall blue lettuce, goldenrod, and chicory. Along the drainage ditches, jewelweed attracts ruby-throated hummingbirds; this flower is a significant autumn food for hummingbirds migrating south.

Purple loosestrife looks gorgeous, but this introduced plant decimates North American wetlands. In Europe insects keep it in check, but here purple loosestrife knows no limits. The seeds—hundreds per flower spike—are indigestible to birds; plus, the plant spreads by underground runners. Butterflies obtain nourishment from the nectar, but flowering plants displaced by purple loosestrife would sustain birds, insects and butterflies. Experimental release of a European beetle that feeds on purple loosestrife is being tested in an attempt to control this noxious exotic plant.

Sycamores with patchwork bark grace the riverbank. Bigtooth aspen leaves whisper in the slightest breeze; red maples and silver maples join in when the breeze intensifies. Indigo buntings dart from limb to limb; watch for vivid blue males and woodsy brown, well-camouflaged females.

At 1.0 mile into the hike the white-blazed AT makes a 90-degree left turn. At least one of the Refuge's 125 species of songbirds is sure to provide musical accompaniment to your walk. On this stretch, a walker can be overcome by unrelenting sunlight. This may be a wetland, but remember: we're not wetland creatures. Without bottled water, you might well quote Coleridge's ancient mariner: "Water, water everywhere, nor any drop to drink."

Common ragweed and great ragweed flourish here. Both have long green flower heads; each individual flower is small and inconspicuous. These flowers are wind pollinated, so they need not be attractive to animal pollinators. Ragweed's airborne pollen torments hay fever sufferers. While goldenrod is often blamed for inducing allergy attacks, its golden flowers are insect pollinated.

Where the trail parallels a drainage ditch, painted turtles sun themselves. Startled frogs squeal a high-pitched "Eep!" before plunging into the water. White blossoms of arrowhead glisten. Holes in the muddy bank mark the entrances to muskrat burrows (see sidebar).

At 1.7 miles, the trail again turns left onto an old railroad grade. On your right is the densely wooded Pochuck Swamp, while more meadow blooms on your left. Bright yellow goldfinches (the females are more olive in hue) frequent stands of thistles; for this bird, thistle seeds are a favorite late summer delicacy. Virginia creeper festoons trees at the edge of the swamp and creeps out along the ground to trail's edge.

At 2.0 miles, a double white turn blaze painted on a post indicates a right turn off of refuge land. Bright sun surrenders to deep shade; take a few moments for

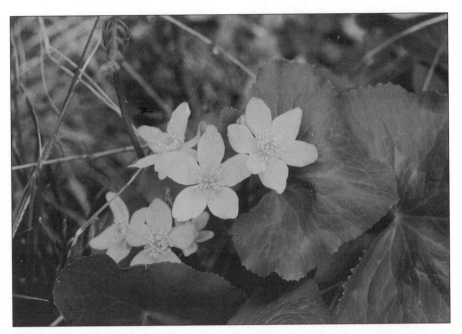

Marsh marigolds bloom with golden flowers as harbingers of spring. Photo credit: Jean LeBlanc

your eyes to adjust before you continue along the boardwalk through Pochuck Swamp.

Red maples block the sky in summer and carpet the swamp with scarlet leaves in autumn. The water level varies, depending upon beaver who sometimes dam the outflow. Step carefully, because even in low water the swamp floor is soft. Watch where you put your hands as well: poison ivy's hairy-looking air roots embrace many tree trunks.

In summer, jewelweed dots the swamp orange and yellow. It is interesting to note that this plant grows in this shade, as well as in the sun-drenched drainage ditches of the refuge. Tracks of white-tailed deer and raccoons reveal where these animals trudged through the mud.

In the swamp, sunlight caresses the ground only before the trees leaf out. Spring, therefore, is the swamp's glory. Jack-in-the-pulpits preach to congregations of purple violets, trout lilies and bloodroot. Royal fern, with its leaf-like fronds, thrives in the waterlogged soil. Sweet viburnum offers fragrant white flower clusters. In April, near the center of the swamp, clusters of low-growing marsh marigolds look like a thousand little suns come down to earth.

At 2.5 miles, the Appalachian Trail rises a few feet out of the swamp to meet Lake Wallkill Road. Be careful not to tread on nodding trilliums, delicate wildflowers with flower parts in groups of three. Rose-breasted grosbeaks, cardinals and scarlet tanagers make it seem as if red flowers have taken wing. A lush stand of Mayapples, their nodding flowers hidden below umbrella-like leaves, thrives on this moist but well-drained gentle slope.

Make your way back through the swamp the way you came. When you emerge onto open refuge land again turn right, away from the Appalachian Trail onto the unblazed Liberty Loop Trail and old railroad bed. In 0.5 mile, turn 90 degrees left onto the dike that parallels Oil City Road and leads back to the parking lot.

🐾 THE SECRET LIVES OF MUSKRATS

The musquash (as Native Americans called this animal) can chew through vegetation underwater without drowning, thanks to incisors which protrude even when its mouth is closed. An important member of the wetland ecosystem, this glossy rodent eats cattails, sedges, waterlilies and rushes, clearing water for use by migrating waterfowl. When swimming, a muskrat uses its tail as a rudder, and can even swim backward. It can stay submerged for more than fifteen minutes.

Muskrats have poor eyesight but good senses of smell and hearing. If you see one cavorting in the water, approach slowly from downwind. Though they may build small lodges out of cattails, Wallkill Refuge muskrats prefer to burrow into the black dirt (sometimes undermining a levee, to the consternation of refuge staff). Entrance holes to these extensive burrows pock the drainage ditches; it is not unusual for an entrance to be underwater. Freshly cut reeds and branches may protrude from an entrance. Muskrats also eat freshwater mussels, frogs, crayfish and fish; their predators include raccoons and mink, which prey on the young.

Hours, Fees and Facilities

The Liberty Loop Trail is open from dawn to dusk year-round (no pets allowed). The AT is is open twenty-four hours a day. Call the Wallkill River National Refuge Area for information on other trails.

Getting There

Take I-287 to NJ 23 north to the town of Sussex. Turn right on County 284 north to Unionville. In Unionville, turn right on State Line Road. (Oil City Road.) Follow it for 1.4 miles over the Wallkill River bridge. In another 0.6 mile look for Wallkill River National Wildlife Refuge Liberty Loop Trail parking lot on right.

For More Information

Wallkill River National Wildlife Refuge, P.O. Box 383, Sussex, NJ 07461-0383; 973-702-7266.

—chapter and sidebar by Jean LeBlanc

Highlands Province

Pinwheel's Vista
11
and Appalachian Trail

Wawayanda State Park

- 2.6 miles round-trip
- 3 hours
- Elevation gain 750 feet
- Challenging; 1.3-mile climb up 400 rock steps

Contemplate the diversity of life and the
mysteries of geological time

The land we know as the New Jersey Highlands was, a billion years ago, an equatorial Himalaya-like chain of mountains towering over a lifeless landscape. Collisions between our ancestral continent and other continental plates formed these megahighlands. Ten to twelve miles within these mountains, incredible pressure and heat melted and metamorphosed old sediments into gneiss. Magma found its way up through fissures and cooled into granite. Magnetite—iron-bearing ore—also crystallized out of these molten solutions. The only life on earth consisted of microorganisms in warm tropical seas; these organisms gave off oxygen as a waste product, setting the stage for all aerobic life to come.

A few hundred million years of erosion exposed the roots of these ancient mountains. Then, about 400 million years ago, another continental collision gave birth to the Appalachians, further contorting the Highlands gneiss. Subsequent continental collisions and continual erosion continued to sculpt the landscape.

Recent touches to this topographic sculpture were added during the Ice Age. When the most recent glacier melted, about 15,000 years ago, it exposed a New Jersey Highlands scraped of topsoil. Scoured bedrock—the ancient gneiss and granite—glistened beneath a prehistoric sun. Sand, gravel and other glacial deposits eventually supported tundra plants. Mastodons and giant sloths roamed

Pinwheel's Vista

over Wawayanda Mountain. Present-day Wallkill Valley filled with meltwater. A lobe of this lake reached into Vernon, New Jersey.

This walk begins at the erstwhile shoreline of this glacial lake, then winds to the top of the gneiss cliffs visible from Route 94 below. The climb of about 600 feet unveils a succession of mountainside plant communities and the animals that today call Wawayanda home.

With Route 94 behind you, leave the parking lot on the white-blazed Appalachian Trail. Backhoes and dump trucks just beyond the trail corridor denote a gravel quarry. This mountainside strip of sand and gravel is a kame terrace, deposited by outwash from the Wisconsin Glacier as it melted.

In spring, male red-winged blackbirds squawk out territories. A killdeer darts through shorter grass, protecting her nest. Summer produces a show of goldenrod, chicory, asters and bergamot.

After 0.2 mile the trail enters the woods. To your left, atop a tumbled stone wall, small shrubby trees form a thicket. The American bladdernut sports drooping clusters of white bell-shaped flowers in spring and puffy, bladderlike fruit in autumn. The leaves, in groups of three leaflets, might be mistaken for poison ivy.

Wawayanda Mountain casts a deep shadow here. Black cherry, red maple and sweet birch prevail, with a few hickories and oaks mixed in. Witch hazel and sassafras comprise the midstory, while maple-leaf viburnum dominates the understory. Spring wildflowers bloom early to take advantage of light streaming through leafless trees. Look for rue anemones, wild geranium and white baneberry (better known by its "doll's eyes" autumn fruit). From late summer until the first frost, resilient wood asters thrive in the cool and shady but rich soil.

At 0.3 mile, the trail winds through a crop of massive boulders. These are chunks of mountain loosened by thousands of years of frost and root action—normal mountain wear and tear. The roots of a white ash tree snake around and into one of the large boulders on your left. Grapevines form exotic-looking garlands. Moisture-loving jack-in-the-pulpits spring up underfoot, and sugar maple and hop hornbeam line the right side of the trail.

The trail begins to climb in earnest now; note the increased amount of light penetrating the forest as you near midslope. Pink-flowered herb Robert decorates the edge of the trail with lacy foliage. After two switchbacks, a small clearing on your right offers a chance to catch your breath. A red oak, its gnarled, twisted, hollow trunk pocked with old pileated woodpecker holes, grows to the left of this bluff. White pines, intolerant of shade, now appear on the side of the mountain, as do beech and basswood. Striped maple, a small understory tree with green-and-white bark and large leaves, loves protected but cool conditions. This species will accompany you to the top of the mountain (but not out onto the open vista).

More switchbacks bear you to the upper-slope vegetative zone most noticeably characterized by mountain laurel and chestnut oak. Thanks to the trail-building technique known as sidehilling, you're actually traversing cliffs. Vertical slabs of gneiss rise on your right, covered with leafy-looking lichens. A lichen is two organisms in one: a fungus that has captured a photosynthetic alga, from which it gleans nourishment even on nutrient-free rock faces. At one turn in the trail, a walker with a good eye for spring flowers might spot pink lady's slippers.

At 1.2 miles, just when you think you can't climb another rock step, the trail levels out. Watch for a low stone wall on your left; a 0.1-mile blue-blazed side trail leads left to the vista.

The immense rock to the right of this blue-blazed trail is not "native" to this mountain. This chunk of dolomitic limestone, light gray and crisscrossed with cracks, is a glacial erratic, dragged from who knows where by the mile-thick sheet of ice. A festive sprig of lime-loving wild columbine sprouts from this boulder in spring.

Suddenly the trail emerges onto the top of the cliff at Pinwheel's Vista. On a clear day, you can see New York State's Shawangunk Mountains to your right and the Catskills behind them. Just visible on the horizon directly in front of you, High Point Monument marks New Jersey's highest elevation.

Sweet birch, red oak and bear oak cling to these cliffs, stunted from near-constant wind and a dearth of soil and moisture. Polypody, a rock-loving fern, carpets a few spots where the feet of awe-struck walkers seldom trample.

A rustling in the leaves on the sheltered side of the cliff may be a rufous-sided towhee scratching for tidbits. Or it might be a chipmunk. Or a black bear. Sun-drenched cliffs also evoke the possibility of a rattlesnake, though these creatures are rare here. Stay calm but alert, and enjoy your visit to this wild world.

As warm air rises from the valley, turkey vultures soar through the air (see sidebar). Hawks and eagles also ride the updrafts, as do monarch butterflies on their autumn migration to Mexico.

Wawayanda Mountain was bald up until the middle of this century. Trees were harvested in the 1800s to provide charcoal for iron furnaces; logging continued until the creation of Wawayanda State Park in 1963. Now, more than three dozen species of trees flourish on this mountain. As you look out from the vista, try to picture the valley glistening with glacial meltwater, or a mountain rising behind you that could compete with Everest for height. As you make your way back along the blue-blazed trail, imagine meeting a mastodon. Turn right onto the white-blazed trail and step carefully down the gneiss steps, knowing you have participated, if only for a few hours, in the billion-year history of Wawayanda Mountain.

🐾 *RIDING THE THERMALS WITH TURKEY VULTURES*

These robust birds are well adapted for their role as nature's sanitary engineers. Sharp beaks and rasp-like tongues are efficient feeding tools. Caustic digestive enzymes destroy bacteria that would lay us low with botulism, anthrax and other nasty diseases. And of course, those featherless heads are easily cleaned after rooting around inside a carcass.

From the Wawayanda vista you can observe this bird's impressive gliding skills. Broad flight feathers on the tips and back edge of each wing spread like fingers, reducing air turbulence and allowing slow, majestic glides with barely a wing beat necessary once the vulture is aloft. On a warm day, watch for a kettle, numerous birds circling on an updraft. On cool but sunny days, you may be lucky enough to look down from the vista at a vulture sunning itself in a tree.

You probably won't find a vulture's nest, but don't feel deprived. Regurgitation of already rotten food keeps the nest smelling uninviting, to say the least, which repels predators. Just find a warm sunny spot on the vista from which to appreciate the vulture's aerial skills. Beauty, after all, isn't in the eye of the beholder, but in the perfection of these birds in their ecological niche.

Getting There

Take I-287 to NJ 23 north to County 515 north. At the Vernon, New Jersey, stoplight, go straight on NJ 94 north for 2.2 mi. to the Appalachian Trail parking area on the right.

For More Information

Wawayanda State Park, P.O. Box 198, Highland Lakes, NJ 07422; 973-853-4462. To volunteer for work on the AT, call the New York–New Jersey Trail Conference, 212-685-9699.

—chapter and sidebar by Jean LeBlanc

Terrace Pond

Wawayanda State Park

- 4 miles
- 4 hours
- Elevation gain 400 feet
- Challenging; rocky, with some hand-over-hand climbing

A Highlands hike to a glacial pond

About a million years ago, the New Jersey Highlands suffered a catastrophe from which they are still recovering. A worldwide climatic cooling trend caused a devastating ice wall to flow irresistibly south from Canada. The advancing glacier bulldozed everything in its path, crushing forests, scraping away topsoil, gouging bedrock, and driving animal life before it.

Wave after wave of ice ravaged northern New Jersey. The most recent glacial epoch, called the Wisconsin Glacier, swept south 100,000 years ago, and reached its maximum expansion just 20,000 years ago. An ice mountain embedded with boulders, gravel and grit dwarfed the state's Highlands, burying and grinding its peaks beneath a mile-thick ice sheet.

Fifteen thousand years ago, a global warming trend caused the glacier to retreat, leaving a lifeless, stony wasteland in its wake. Glacial erratics dotted ice-polished ledges. Shallow glacial depressions became bogs, while deeper gouges flooded and became lakes. On Bearfort Mountain, one such gouge became Terrace Pond. With the glacial retreat, the frigid, lifeless land awoke.

Twelve thousand years ago, a tundra environment of lichen, moss, dwarf birch and Arctic willow existed around the pond. Browsing mastodon and caribou may have drunk from its waters, while saber-toothed tigers, dire wolves and Paleo Native Americans may have hunted herbivores from the crags above. The climatic warming trend eventually brought the return of boreal spruce and fir forest, then deciduous forest resembling today's woodlands.

This rugged, 4.0-mile loop takes walkers to Terrace Pond, one of the most pristine of New Jersey's glacial lakes, and provides ample evidence of the Highlands's glacial past. Cross the road from the parking lot and follow the yellow-blazed Terrace Pond South Trail into the woods. Ignore the blue-blazed Terrace Pond North Trail as it turns left (this will be your return route).

Terrace Pond

The yellow-blazed path climbs steadily with rocky footing through a peaceful mixed oak forest. Red and white oak, chestnut oak, pignut and mockernut hickory and Eastern hemlock reach highest to form a leafy canopy. Beneath them, witch hazel, shadbush, sassafras and sweet birch fill in the middle story. The shrub layer alternates between impressive stands of mountain laurel and sweet pepperbush, while cinnamon fern, bracken fern, wintergreen and mosses rise from leaf litter.

All of this flora testifies to glacial influences. Mountain laurel and Eastern hemlock, for example, grow best in acidic, sandy and rocky soils, an Ice Age legacy. The Wisconsin Glacier scraped nutrient-rich topsoil from Highlands slopes and left behind glacial till, unsorted rock, gravel, sand, silt and clay. Over the thousands of years, plants have struggled to enrich the soils, but the process is slow.

At 0.2 mile the trail crosses a small wetland on planks and passes amid yellow birch and hemlocks. Look for the large shagbark hickory at swamp's edge. Highlands wetlands, like this one, are often glacial in origin, composed of shallow, gouged depressions sometimes without inlets or outlets.

Mountain laurel dominates this hike. This evergreen, with its wildly twisted branches, shiny leaves and rounded crown, contributes to forest beauty year-round. But the best time to see the laurel-lined Terrace Pond trail is in June. That's when the plant is covered in white and pink chalice-shaped flowers. Gently finger a single blossom and watch what happens. The stamens are spring loaded and can catapult pollen onto landing bees. Honeybees and bumblebees thrive on mountain laurel nectar and the honey they make from it, but the plant's foliage is poisonous to humans, as is the honey derived from it.

The trail passes through a rhododendron tunnel, with red maple and witch hazel rising above (0.5 mile). In autumn, witch hazel's elliptical, curly-edged leaves burst into yellow flames of color. Like the mountain laurel, this tree relies on an artillery-like mechanism for propagation. When its seed pods contract, they fire seeds up to twenty feet away. Look for small, witch-hat shaped projections on the leaves. These are galls, tumorous growths, made by parasitic witch hazel leaf-gall aphids. Each hollow, cone-shaped gall holds several immature aphids. When the young insects leave the galls, they feed and live on birches for the next six generations, before a seventh generation grows wings and returns to a witch hazel to lay eggs.

The trail becomes less rocky as it passes easily along a woods road edged by a farmer's stone wall. Nineteenth-century Highlands farms were belated victims of the glacial epoch. Farmers often harvested more cobble-sized stones from their nutrient-poor fields than they did potatoes. The rocks, dropped by retreating ice, had to be hand-hauled and stacked into walls that crisscross the landscape today. When the railroads allowed access to midwestern produce, most Highlands farms failed. These particular fields have been reclaimed by black cherry, white pine and tamarack trees. I once tracked a pair of coyotes along this stretch in winter. Terrace Pond's relative remoteness makes it an ideal place to see bear, fox and coyote sign.

At roughly 1.5 miles and 1.7 miles, two unmarked trails cut to the right as the Terrace Pond South Trail swings sharply left and to the north. Follow the yellow blazes closely as the trail levels out and continues through a diverse forest of oak, hickory, sweet birch, beech and red maple. Also look for Solomon's seal and the rare Indian cucumber-root blooming here in spring.

After passing over a stream on a concrete drainpipe, follow the Terrace Pond South Trail left where the Yellow Dot Trail enters from the right. At about 2.2 miles the path gets more rugged as it climbs to a rocky crag. The scrub oak– and blueberry–embossed vista overlooks a small pocket valley cradled between two ridges, and is an ideal place to enjoy the Highlands's windy silences.

At 2.3 miles the yellow Terrace Pond South Trail crosses the Terrace Pond Red Trail. Go left on the red trail. This is the most strenuous part of the hike, as the trail humps along a series of cliffs. Great gullies, rock faces, glacial erratics and shattered boulders attest to the power of the Ice Age. This strikingly beautiful rock is called puddingstone, a coarse, violet-hued sandstone conglomerate speckled with a kaleidoscopic array of white quartz and other pebbles. These redbeds were laid down more than 350 million years ago by fast-flowing streams depositing mud, sand and abrasion-rounded gravel into an ancient inland sea. Puddingstone is named for a thick concoction made by colonial cooks. The rocky terrain's range of color is broadened by pitch pine, white pine and blueberry bushes (turning scarlet in autumn). Mosses and rock tripe add still other subtle green hues.

A little hand-over-hand climbing and descending brings a first glimpse of Terrace Pond. A further rocky descent takes you to the shore at 2.6 miles, where the red trail ends. Turn left on a white-blazed trail that follows the shoreline.

The roughly rectangular pond is boxed in by high, elephant-skin-textured cliffs that show evidence of glacial gouging and polishing. Remember that it was glacial ice that excavated this pretty, reflective gem. The water itself is covered in lily pads for most of the summer and fall. Sweet pepperbush lines the shore, as does mountain laurel, sassafras, scrub oak, pitch pine and white pine. There are plenty of places to stop for lunch. Enjoy the views, but don't swim: patrolling rangers will ticket you.

At the pond's far end, turn left on the blue-blazed Terrace Pond North Trail, leaving the white trail. This rugged path repeatedly rises over stony ledges then descends and crosses small wet areas on bog bridging. At 3.2 miles, a puddingstone cliff shoots up into the sky like the prow of a sinking ship. From this vantage point, the most far-reaching vista of the day, High Point Monument and the Catskill and Shawangunk Mountains are visible to the west and north.

The blue trail crosses a second and third rocky outcrop, providing another workout, this time without good views. It descends through more puddingstone slots and chutes, then reaches and briefly follows a gas pipeline very steeply downhill. Look for the clearly marked blue trail as it leads left from the pipeline back into the woods. An easy descent through sugar maple, witch hazel, white pine and hemlock leads back to Clinton Road and the parking lot.

Hours, Fees and Facilities

The trails to Terrace Pond are open dawn to dusk year-round.

Getting There

Take I-80 west or I-287 north to NJ 23 north at Wayne. Follow it north of Butler, making a right at the Clinton Road exit. Trailhead parking is 7.5 miles north on Clinton Road on the left.

For More Information

Wawayanda State Park, P.O. Box 198, Highland Lakes, NJ 07422; 973-853-4462.

13 Bearfort Ridge Firetower

Newark Watershed

- 3.6 miles
- 4 hours
- Elevation gain 400 feet
- Moderate; 1.0 mile ascent

A bird's-eye view of Highlands geology

Billion-year-old stone forms the backbone of most of the New Jersey Highlands. Forged deep within the earth, this rock extends in a series of parallel, erosion-resistant ridges, 800 to 1,400 feet high and running roughly southwest to north-east from the Delaware River to the Hudson River.

Highlands geology displays complex, violent change. The story begins in Precambrian times when coastal sediments were plunged ten to twenty miles underground and transformed through intense heat and pressure into metamorphic gneisses and igneous granites. Four hundred million years of melting and cooling caused the mingling of these streaked and layered stones.

This durable Precambrian rock eventually resurfaced as it pinballed off land masses in catastrophic continental collisions. The billion-year-old stone was folded, twisted, broken and forced up into jagged peaks that may have rivaled the Rockies. Further continental collision, rifts, uplifts and erosion left only the bare roots of the once great mountains. Finally, a million years of on-again, off-again glaciation gave the Highlands a superficial facelift, gouging, scraping and smoothing them into the low ridges we see today.

These tough ridges also resist human habitation. Only a few mountain passes gave Native Americans and pioneers access to narrow valleys. Today, geographical lines have been drawn: people, homes and roads (such as NJ 23 and Union Valley Road) occupy the valleys, while deer, bear, raptors, and songbirds occupy upland forests.

This rugged, 3.6-mile-out-and-back hike follows a short section of the Highlands Trail to a state firetower with sweeping views. The Highlands Trail is a joint project of the New Jersey Conservation Foundation, New York–New Jersey Trail Conference, and state and federal partners. When complete, the 150-mile path will traverse the Highlands. The trail section described here is on Newark Water-

Bearfort Ridge Firetower

shed land and requires an inexpensive use permit (call 973-697-2850 for information).

Begin at a small pull-off on the north side of Gould Road. Without crossing the road, walk north into a woods of black cherry and Eastern hemlock, following the turquoise diamond-shaped blazes of the Highlands Trail.

The first 0.8 mile is an easy valley hike, crossing glacial till (unsorted gravel and sand left behind by melting ice) underlain by softer, erosion-prone Paleozoic sandstone, shale and limestone. Sugar maple and white pine grow tall in almost pure stands. These are interspersed with beech, red maple and white oak trees. The pines, all of uniform size, were planted by the Civilian Conservation Corps in the 1930s as part of Franklin Roosevelt's New Deal.

White pine is easily recognized. It's the only eastern pine with five long, soft needles in each bundle. The tree is a mini-ecosystem, supporting eighty species of insect. Its strong, straight limbs are favorite nest sites for sharp-shinned hawks, or "sharpies," able to swoop and snatch up finches and other in-flight prey amid the thick forest canopy. Pine grosbeaks and many warblers (common victims of sharpies) also nest in the trees and feed on seeds at the heart of pine cones. Mice, chipmunks and red squirrels share the pine seed feast. Raccoons often climb white pines for daytime naps (look for territory-marking scat at tree bases).

Not much grows on the forest floor amid the acidic pine needle litter, though sugar maple and sassafras saplings have taken hold, as have partridgeberry and ground pine. Ground pine, a club moss, is a primitive plant originating 300 million years ago. Ancient club mosses grew into trees, formed jungles, and, along with giant ferns, were compressed into coal deposits. In the 1800s tiny club moss spores were dried, placed in pans and ignited to make the first flash photography.

As the white pines thin out, they're replaced by maturing sugar maples. Watch blazes closely: at 0.6 mile, the Highlands Trail falls into a small dip, cuts sharply right, then climbs out of the dip. The trail also crosses beneath a power line where light-loving black cherry, quaking aspen and arrowwood grow.

At 0.8 mile the path crosses Union Valley Road. There's parking for five or six cars here, but a watershed permit is needed (call 973-697-2850 for information).

Beyond the road, the trail begins to rise. Note how flora changes as slope increases, while soil thickness and soil moisture decreases. Sugar maple and white pine quickly give way to scarlet and white oak. The white oak, with its easily recognized round-lobed leaves, is another forest smorgasbord. Its acorns are a preferred food of squirrels, bears, chipmunks and mice. Once sprouted, white oak acorns become hard to digest, so squirrels eat them as they fall, as fast food, rather than storing them up. All manner of birds feed on acorns, including grouse, woodpecker and turkey.

The trail heads straight in from the road, jogs right at about 1.0 mile, then climbs sharply. Chestnut oak, red oak, and sweet birch, dominant trees of Highlands ridges, replace white oaks as the trail rises. Look for oak-apple galls on red oaks. These inch-around, golf-ball-like growths are made by insects that inject twigs with an irritant, causing the brown, tumorlike gall to grow. The insects lay their eggs inside the galls. Oaks support eight hundred species of gall-making insects, most of them small wasps.

The path gets considerably rockier and steeper, passing over stony outcrops. Mockernut and pignut hickories join the forest mix. These deep-rooted trees do well on windy ridges. Their nuts are favorites of wood ducks, fox and squirrel. Look for large rocks near the bases of hickories, their tops speckled with broken shell husks. The rocks serve as raised dining tables, giving gray squirrels safe, elevated observation platforms from which to savor nutmeats.

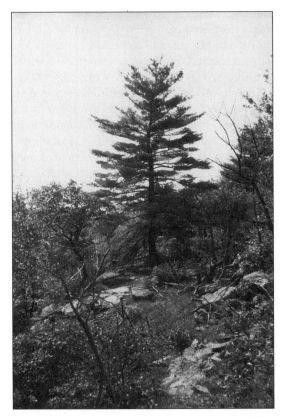

An eastern white pine thrives atop a puddingstone ledge.

The Highlands Trail ascends a series of ledges, zigzagging south and north for brief distances along grassy terraces and sometimes descending into shallow, mountain laurel–filled ravines. Each terrace supports scrub oak and blueberry bushes, rock tripe and the intertwined "antlers" of reindeer lichen. Low-growing scrub oak is also called bear oak, since only black bears find the bitter acorns palatable.

Each ledge offers better views east across Union Valley to Kanouse Mountain. Watch blazes closely; the turquoise diamonds blend in well with forest shadows. Ignore intersections with a white-blazed and blue square–blazed trail. Keep climbing.

Each rock terrace is partially composed of a Highlands oddity called puddingstone. This violet-hued sandstone conglomerate (the color is created by the rock's high iron content) is much younger than most of the Precambrian Highlands. Puddingstone, shot through with creamy white quartz, is all that remains of a long, narrow inland sea or sound into which pebbles and sand were deposited by fast-moving rivers more than 350 million years ago.

The trail flows north, cutting diagonally across a final rock shelf, as the Bearfort Ridge Firetower comes into view between the trees. A rock scramble over puddingstone puts you on the ridge's grassy open summit (1.8 miles).

A climb up the tower gives stunning views over the heart of the Highlands and displays the many humps of southwest-to-northeast-running ridges. The tops of New York City skyscrapers gleam above the Ramapo Mountains to the southeast. Cedar Pond lays just to the west, Clinton Reservoir to the south. Also to the south is deeply etched Berkshire Valley. High Point on Kittatinny Ridge is visible to the northwest, and New York's Catskill Mountains rise to the northwest. New York's Bear Mountain–Harriman State Park lies to the east.

As shadows lengthen at day's end, the true ruggedness of this country is revealed. In winter too, a loss of foliage exposes extreme topography. Only to the southeast do the mountains relent and fade into the flatness of New Jersey's Piedmont. Scanning the lay of the land, it's easy to see how George Washington's Continental army could move freely among the Highlands, safe from attack by the British encamped in the lowlands. Without the natural fortress of the Highlands, the American cause may have been lost.

Picnic tables atop Bearfort Ridge make a perfect lunch spot. When you're through enjoying the view, return the way you came.

Hours, Fees and Facilities

An inexpensive permit is needed from the Newark Watershed Conservation and Development Corporation (NWCDC) to hike the Highlands Trail on Bearfort Mountain. Those without a permit will have illegally parked cars ticketed.

Getting There

Take I-80 west or I-287 north to NJ 23 north. Follow it through Butler. Turn right at the Union Valley Road exit. In 3.3 miles, turn right on Gould Road. The pull-off is 0.3 mile on the left (north) side.

For More Information

NWCDC, P.O. Box 319, Newfoundland, NJ 07435; 973-697-2850.

To volunteer for Highlands Trail construction, call the New York–New Jersey Trail Conference: 212-685-9699.

Long Pond
Ironworks State Park

- 3.0 miles
- 3 hours
- Elevation gain 200 feet
- Moderate; mostly on woods roads

Hike back through history to the time of the fiery furnace

Iron transformed Colonial America. It provided axes and plows with which pioneers subdued the wilderness. It also provided muskets and shot with which they subjugated the native population and overthrew the British Crown. Iron also transfigured the New Jersey Highlands. It made ironmasters wealthy while impoverishing the landscape.

Native Americans long noted black-streaked Highlands stone, but attributed no significance to it. They freely led whites to exposed black rock. Prospectors, hoping to find gold, had to be satisfied with magnetite. By the 1740s the first New Jersey iron mines and furnace were established at Ringwood. The industry quickly spread across the rugged hills as more speculators joined the game.

By 1776 the Highlands were everywhere blasted and tunneled for ore and stripped of forest to fuel hungry furnaces. Smelting fires burned day and night, spewing plumes of acrid smoke. Wagons hauled ore and charcoal out of the hills and moved pig iron to market. Towns sprang up.

Today, casual visitors to the Long Pond Ironworks find an idyllic setting, where nineteenth-century homes and furnace ruins are framed by sycamores and sugar maples. In truth, this was the town of Hewitt, an industrial site that, in its day, was a Little Pittsburgh, a gritty industrial complex that converted Highlands ore into a livelihood for hundreds of people.

This 3.0-mile-out-and-back hike takes walkers to the heart of the Long Pond Ironworks Historic District, along a mine road and to a mine. It offers a chance to visualize the once mighty, and now nearly forgotten, industry that helped turn the U.S. into a world power.

Begin at the Long Pond Ironworks Historical District parking lot. The nineteenth-century general store at the edge of the parking lot is like all the historic buildings you'll see on your walk. It has been stabilized to preserve it but is not yet open for public tours. When state funding is found, the area will be restored as a living history museum.

Face the store and walk around to the left side of the building. Walk parallel to Greenwood Lake Turnpike and away from the store, following a wide grassy path. Pass around a gate and follow a gravel road past the Ward-Ryerson Patterson House (c. 1780), Harty House, and Whritenour House (c. 1800s). Only the Harty House was originally part of the village of Hewitt. The other homes were relocated here in 1986 to save them from the rising waters of the Monksville Reservoir.

The buildings are surrounded by a mix of native and ornamental plants, typical of old town sites. Sugar maples, elms, forsythia and Asiatic bittersweet thrive. In autumn, the viny tendrils of bittersweet put on a colorful show as capsules burst open to reveal flaming orange berrylike fruit. These fleshy seeds survive into winter, a food for birds who spread the plant.

The road enters the woods. To the left stands the nineteenth-century Double Stone House. A huge sycamore and tamarack grow in the yard. Legend says that sycamores love iron-rich soils. While there's no scientific proof to support the claim, archaeologists often find sycamores topping iron-furnace ruins.

To the right are views of the drowned trees of Monksville Reservoir. In the 1980s, before this valley was flooded, archaeologist Ed Lenik discovered eighteen prehistoric Native American campsites dating from 4000 B.C. to A.D. 1680. He unearthed projectile points, knives, scrapers and pottery fragments. Today, mallard ducks and belted kingfishers scout the reservoir for food.

Five minutes into the walk, the road crosses Longhouse Creek on a bridge, then intersects a nexus of roads, once the center of the nineteenth-century village of Hewitt. The blue-dot-on-white-blazed Sterling Ridge Trail enters from the left and exits right. This trail is co-aligned with the Highlands Trail (marked by turquoise diamonds). The Highlands Trail will one day stretch 150 miles from the

This graceful stone arch is all that remains of the 1862 furnace at Long Pond Ironworks. The iron processed here contributed to the Union victory in the Civil War.

Hudson to the Delaware rivers. Follow the Sterling Ridge and Highlands Trail to the right.

The trail quickly passes another arm of the reservoir, then crosses the Wanaque River on a bridge. Before crossing the bridge, walk straight ahead a few hundred feet to see the ruins of the Long Pond furnace complex.

The first of three furnaces, a stone jumble surrounded by troughs of water, is the oldest. Built by Peter Hasenclever in 1766, it produced twenty-five tons of iron per week, some made into equipment for the Continental army. The ruins remained hidden until 1963, when archaeologist Roland Robbins dug beneath a sycamore tree and through a rubble pile to uncover it. Today, yellow-flowered jewelweed, purple-berried pokeweed and the brown nutlets of bur reed lend late-summer color to massive stone blocks.

A second furnace stands just beyond the first. It also profited from warfare. Built in 1862 by Peter Cooper and Abram S. Hewitt, it was a response to the Union army's need for iron during the Civil War. A third, tumbledown furnace stands beyond this one.

The Long Pond furnaces once burned continuously. Wagonloads of ore, charcoal fuel, and limestone flux (to help molten iron flow) were dumped into the egg-shaped stone chambers from above. Immense bellows, powered by water wheels, superheated the fiery mixture. Heat in excess of 2,800° melted the ore, allowing heavier iron to settle to the bottom, where it flowed into sand troughs.

The blast furnaces deafened; they were as loud as a rocket at liftoff. This roar was punctuated by the relentless bang of great hammers at a nearby forge. Columns of fire and smoke rose from the site and could be seen for miles. A film of soot settled on the town and its people. Fatal burns were a hazard, as was lung disease. Long Pond, like most ironworks, was hell on earth.

Walk a few feet farther ahead to a makeshift shed, where two twenty-five-foot diameter water wheels are protected. While both wheels were burned by vandals in 1954, painstaking measurements taken by historians Ron Dupont and George Sellmar (members of Friends of Long Pond Ironworks) allowed one of these marvelous red- and white-pine structures to be restored.

Retrace your steps back to where you left the Highlands Trail and follow it over the Wanaque River on a footbridge. You are now walking a road once used to haul charcoal and ore to the furnaces. It passes through a shaded forest of hickory and maple. The ground, covered in a tangle of bittersweet and grapevines, appears unnaturally lumpy. Beneath leaf litter, humus and slag lie the buried remains of the eighteenth-century village of Long Pond.

The sunken road rises steadily through a grove of Eastern hemlocks. As you climb, look for a small rocky ledge to your left, a sunny lunch spot overlooking the Wanaque River far below.

About a mile into the hike, the hemlocks give way to hardwoods. Beech, sweet birch, hickories and oaks overlook a forest floor dotted with Christmas fern. Try to spot a hard-to-see, flat, grassy thirty-foot circle to your right. This is the site of a charcoal mound. Charcoal was vital to the iron industry, and its production deforested the nineteenth-century Highlands. A typical furnace burned the charcoal equivalent of an acre of trees each day. Soot-covered, reclusive charcoal makers were often shunned as crazies by polite society. They spent months tending smoldering charcoal mounds in the mountains. Each mound was built of wood lengths stacked in a cone and covered with earth. You'll know you've found the mound site if you see tiny pieces of charcoal still hidden in the grass.

At 1.3 miles, the Sterling Ridge and Highlands Trails turn sharply left, leaving the woods road on a narrow path. Continue straight ahead on the unblazed woods road 0.2 mile farther and look for rust-colored ore piles to your right. These fist-sized stones mark the Patterson Mine, dug around 1870 and abandoned in 1903. Explore to your right for two vertical, water-flooded mine pits. Be careful; stay away from the edge of these unstable shafts. Mines were dug with pickax and explosives, and were often several hundred feet deep. Life underground was dangerous. Falling rock, dust-choked air, slippery footing and premature blasts were daily hazards.

When you've finished exploring, return the way you came. As you go, consider this lost way of life. With the 1890s discovery of the ore fields of Minnesota's Mesabi Range, Highlands mining died. In the last hundred years, the forest has slowly reclaimed the scarred landscape left by the excesses of New Jersey's iron miners.

Hours, Fees and Facilities

The Sterling Ridge and Highlands Trails are open dawn to dusk year-round. Please leave ore and other artifacts where you found them.

Getting There

Take I-287 north or south to Exit 57. Follow signs to Skyline Drive. Take Skyline Drive to its end at a ⊤ on the east shore of Wanaque Reservoir. At the ⊤ turn right on County 511 north (Greenwood Lake Turnpike), following it for 5.2 miles to a large white Long Pond Ironworks Historical District sign and parking lot on the right.

For More Information

Ringwood State Park, P.O. Box 1304, Ringwood, NJ 07456; 973-962-7031. Friends of Long Pond Ironworks, P.O. Box 809, Hewitt, NJ 07421; 973-839-0128.

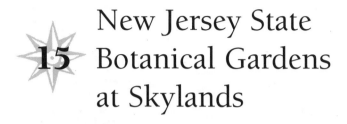

New Jersey State Botanical Gardens at Skylands

15

- 1.0 mile (plus optional additional 0.7-mile side trail)
- 2 to 3 hours
- Easy; flat walk around gardens
- Optional side trail with moderate climb

A feast for the eyes; a boost for the spirit

Nestled amid the oak-hickory-forested Ramapo Mountains, stately Skylands Manor was no ordinary summer escape for investment banker Clarence McKenzie Lewis (1877–1959). Beginning with his purchase of the land in 1922, Lewis began to bring a dream to life. As a trustee of the New York Botanical Garden, Lewis's dream was of a garden and arboretum of his own—one that would serve not only as a showplace but also as a living laboratory to research plants from all over the world.

In 1966, more than a decade after Lewis's death—and the subsequent neglect of the gardens—the state of New Jersey purchased the land and set about restoring Skylands. In 1984 Skylands was designated as the New Jersey State Botanical Gardens. Extensive restoration continued, and intensive activity continues to this day to maintain the gardens and grounds. Also maintained is the multifaceted philosophy of a botanical garden's various roles: aesthetics, public education and recreation, botanical research, conservation, and community pride.

Begin in the Winter Garden, across the road from the gatehouse and visitor center, on the front left lawn of the manor house. This collection of trees, mostly evergreens, was created with an eye toward form, texture and color. Many of the trees around the manor house—as well as the house itself—date from Lewis's time. Massive limbs of a European weeping beech sweep majestically over the lawn. Except for this tree, which is fenced off due to human beings' unfortunate inclination to scarify smooth beech bark, you can use your sense of touch to further enhance your arboreal admiration. The needles of the Japanese umbrella pine look prickly but feel smooth as silk.

Every imaginable shade of green, and even some subtle blues and golds, can be discovered in the foliage of the Winter Garden. You'll feel you're touring the world as you encounter a Japanese cedar, a blue Atlas cedar from the Atlas Mountains of northern

NJ State Botanical Gardens at Skylands

Africa, a Dawyck beech from Scotland, lace-bark pine and ponderosa dragon spruce from China, and Lawson false cypress and Jeffrey pine from Oregon and California.

After wandering amid the trees of the world, cross Maple Avenue to the right of the visitor center and enter the Annual Garden, where a colorful assortment of unusual and familiar plants bloom from June until the first Highlands frost.

Large white ash trees mark the passage from Annual Garden to Perennial Garden. As if the variety of floral form and color weren't enough, these flowers also attract ruby-throated hummingbirds, honeybees and bumblebees (see sidebar), and a rainbow of butterflies. The fruity-lilac-scented butterfly bushes are visited by monarchs, black and tiger swallowtails, and great-spangled fritillaries, to name just a few. A graceful European white birch marks the end of the Perennial Garden. Rows of holes in this and other trees confirm the seasonal presence of yellow-bellied sapsuckers.

Cross Maple Avenue toward the right of the manor house. Interrupted fern, cinnamon fern, royal fern, sensitive fern, maidenhair fern, ostrich fern—these and other shade-loving plants thrive beneath more magnificent trees. Stepping out of this shady area onto the West Terrace provides a sweeping view of the crystalline lakes and verdant hills of the New Jersey Highlands.

From the manor, follow the center walkway through the Magnolia Walk and Azalea Garden. A fountain pool reflects the sky amid cream- , ruby- and sapphire-hued waterlilies. The breathtaking beauty of this area attests to not only the art of landscape gardening, but also to the dedication of volunteers who strive to restore and maintain the grounds of Skylands Manor.

Walk back toward Maple Avenue, away from the manor house and toward the tree-lined lane. Take a close look at the tall, narrow trees that create this living Impressionist landscape. They are not poplars or cedars as one might expect, but a columnar form of sugar maple called sentry maple.

Cross the lawn toward the statues known as the Four Continents, which are located at the far end of the Crab Apple Vista. Pass through the wooded area behind the statues; here horse chestnut, black walnut, white pine, tulip tree and sweet gum intermingle. You can't help but notice that the landscape is becoming less formal. With the Four Continents behind you, head left toward Swan Pond. After admiring impressive flowers and trees, it is a challenge to see well-camou-flaged turtles sunning themselves on rocks.

From the pond, follow the path out toward Swan Pond Road. Rhododendrons, beech, hickory and sensitive fern grow here, as do sugar maples, white ash and slippery elm saplings—all the diversity a northeastern mixed forest has to offer. Remember, you are no longer in a well-tended garden; watch out for poison ivy and mountain bikes.

If you feel like venturing into even wilder territory, turn right onto the green-blazed Halifax Trail about 0.25 mile along Swan Pond Road. This switchbacking trail climbs steeply through a deciduous forest of oak, ash, maple, American chestnut saplings, sweet birch and sassafras. As you ascend, large red oaks and tulip trees shade the way. Farther up the ridge, chestnut oak becomes more abundant. Violets line this walk in spring. In late summer, a patch of woodland sunflowers brightens the trail with yellow blooms. After about 0.25 mile, watch for an unmarked left-hand turn; follow this path for about 100 feet to a rocky vista (if your walk on the green-blazed trail brings you to an intersection with a red-blazed trail, you've gone too far). From this vista, you can see the sentry maples on the manor grounds below. Cupsaw Lake gleams like a diamond amid the rolling Ramapos. As you rest under the chest-nut oaks, you may catch a glimpse of a pileated woodpecker. Make your way back down to Swan Pond Road, bearing right.

About 0.3 mile from Swan Pond, the path to the Bog Garden turns left off the road. Bear left as the path splits. Wildflowers of all shapes and sizes abound, from sky blue forget-me-nots to mauve joe-pye weed, which may reach a height of eight feet. Follow any of the paths to the left to the shady Wildflower Garden. After the formal gardens, cardinal flowers and blue lobelia will seem exotic, though these wildflowers are native to New Jersey.

Make your way back to the visitor center, stopping to explore the meadow, heather garden or rhododendron garden along the way. Every turn of the path promises a new delight.

🐝 THE BUZZ ON BEES

The bees you see gathering nectar are all females. Adult worker honeybees live approximately nine weeks, working in the hive first as nursemaids to the larvae, then as hive-keepers (secreting wax for the honeycomb) and guards, and finally, for the last five or six weeks of their adult lives, as foragers. Worker bees who locate a rich source of nectar return to the hive and tell the other workers, through a sort of interpretive dance, the location of the nectar source. A worker scouting .locations for a new hive performs a similar dance.

Don't be afraid to observe bees. A honeybee bites only as a last resort when she is under attack (just imagine what flailing arms look like from a bee's point of view). A bee can sting only once; when she does, her stinger is pulled from her abdomen, killing her in the process. Stay calm, even if a bee should land on you. She'll soon realize your perfume or shampoo scent is not associated with a food source. As social as these insects are, it is not our society that interests them.

The vast numbers of bees you might see among the flowers at Skylands make it obvious that bees are the most important of pollinating animals. Many species of flowers and bees have coevolved, each dependent upon the other for finding a successful ecological niche. Without bees, the world would be a lot less colorful.

Hours, Fees and Facilities

Open 8:00 A.M. to 8:00 P.M. year-round. Free on weekdays; $4 per vehicle weekends from Memorial Day through Labor Day.

Getting There

Take I-287 north or south to Exit 57. Follow signs to Skyline Drive. Take Skyline Drive to its end at a T on the east shore of Wanaque Reservoir. Turn right on County 511 north (Greenwood Lake Turnpike). In 1.6 miles make the second right onto Sloatsburg Road. In 2.1 miles turn right on Morris Road and follow signs for 1.5 miles to Skylands.

For More Information

Skylands Association, P.O. Box 302, Ringwood, NJ 07456; 973 -962-7527. Garden volunteers meet Wednesday mornings; new volunteers welcome.

—chapter and sidebar by Jean LeBlanc

16 Wyanokie High Point

Norvin Green State Forest

- 3.1 miles
- 3 hours
- Elevation gain 500 feet
- Moderate

A heritage of trail building and a New York City panorama

For those who love hiking, it's easy to imagine that the Garden's State's many trails are ancient. Perhaps, we dream, they were old Indian paths or the trails over which the first settlers moved. In fact, their origins are often far more recent.

By 1910 the New Jersey Highlands attracted a New York City populace grown weary of electric lights, the stench of horse dung, and the roar of the first automobiles. Those far hills beckoned with the romantic illusion of an earlier, simpler, slower time. And so it was that a small rucksack army began fleeing the city on weekends, taking to the mountains in search of adventure.

At first trampers moved west by ferry and train, later by car. But always they struck out on foot into a rural territory only recently returned to woodland. By the early 1900s railroads had bypassed New Jersey's less productive mountain farms and industries. Trampers bushwhacked over newly forested farm fields and hiked to abandoned iron mines and furnaces, to waterfalls and craggy vistas. These wild rambles refreshed tired urban spirits.

Tramping clubs organized and blazed formal trails to favorite spots. In 1912, the New York chapter of the Appalachian Mountain Club laid claim to the Wyanokie Highlands, a jumble of small peaks twenty-five miles northwest of Manhattan. Today, the Wyanokies boast one of the most concentrated trail systems in the state, protected within Norvin Green State Forest.

This 3.1-mile circuit hike samples three Wyanokie Highlands trails and features a waterfall, two iron mines, and a sweeping view of the Manhattan skyline. As you walk, consider that all these paths (like most in this book) were not built with government labor. They were constructed and are maintained by volunteers.

Standing in the Weis Ecology Center hiker parking area, face Snake Den Road and turn left. Take the road 150 yards, then turn right into the woods, following the yellow blazes of the Mine Trail and red blazes of the Wyanokie Circular Trail. The path skirts several residential backyards, then enters a small spruce and hemlock forest. Low stone walls reveal this area to have been a farmer's field. In the nineteenth century, the New Jersey Highlands resembled Scotland, denuded of forest, covered with field and pasture, and broken by stone walls. Only in the past hundred years have forests reclaimed the land.

The trail emerges into a deciduous forest of sugar maple, red oak and eastern hophornbeam. The hophornbeam, with its skinny, vertical strips of scaly bark is named for fruit clusters resembling hops, a beer ingredient. Also called ironwood, the tree's nearly indestructible wood was once shaped into sled runners and wagon parts. Metal has since replaced hophornbeam.

At 0.2 mile turn sharply right, following the yellow Mine Trail as it diverges from the red trail. The path swiftly ascends, descends, and crosses Mine Brook. The trail loops back on itself and recrosses the brook at Wyanokie Falls (0.5 mile). This falls sometimes goes dry, but in springtime it tumbles in a sparkling cascade over jumbled boulders. It is overhung by an American basswood. This tree's June flowers attract bees who make a minty, gourmet-quality honey from the nectar.

The yellow Mine Trail descends and crosses the red Wyanokie Circular Trail, then steeply climbs Ball Mountain (named for round glacial erratics left behind by the retreating Wisconsin ice sheet). Ascending through sweet birch and chestnut oak, the trail arrives at a vista (0.8 mile) that looks west to Wyanokie High Point. Rock slabs are framed in lowbush blueberry and striped wintergreen. Watch blazes closely: just beyond a second vista the trail turns right and descends, while an unmarked woods road goes straight ahead.

The yellow trail descends steeply to the Roomy Mine (1.1 miles). This abandoned iron mine is dug in solid rock, is stable, and is entered by many hikers (though a hard hat and flashlight are recommended). If you choose to go in, avoid the upper entrance. Crawl in through the lower tunnel. Inside, a twenty-five-foot chamber opens to the sky and to a fifty-foot-long shaft. Look for drill marks where black powder charges were set. Dug in 1840, the Roomy Mine produced iron until 1857. Today, the cool tunnel is home to bats. Place a compass on the tailings pile outside; they're so iron-rich that they skew the needle (a prospecting technique once used to locate ore deposits).

In a short distance, the yellow Mine Trail turns left as it rejoins the red Wyanokie Circular Trail on a gently descending woods road. At 1.5 miles, the blazed trails both turn sharply right, crossing Mine Brook on a bridge. Before crossing the water, detour a hundred yards straight ahead on the old road to the Blue Mine. This flooded mine dives nearly five hundred feet underground and required large water wheels and pumps to keep it dry. Now, it's an ideal home for mosses and mosquitoes.

Retrace your steps and cross the trail bridge, arriving in a short way at the ruins of a stone shelter built by the New York chapter of the Green Mountain Club (GMC), which became active in the Wyanokies in 1916 (see sidebar). Eccentric Will Monroe, a burly bearded Montclair professor and friend to Walt Whitman,

Wyanokie High Point

organized this club. He blazed some of the Wyanokies' best trails as a rehearsal for his work on Vermont's Long Trail. Monroe was famous for skyline trails that climb and wind through tight, rocky passageways to the best vistas.

Just beyond the lean-to, the yellow Mine Trail turns right. Stay on the red-blazed Wyanokie Circular Trail as it climbs very steeply through pillarlike black and white oak, beech and tulip trees, reaching one of Will Monroe's finest New Jersey lookouts (2.1 miles). Slabs of tilted rock, edged by scrub oak, chestnut oak and pitch pine, look east from the nearly bald top of Wyanokie High Point out over Wanaque Reservoir to the Manhattan skyline. Near evening, the World Trade Center and Empire State Building glow scarlet with reflected sunlight. This is also a perfect spot for lunch.

Just beyond the highest vista, the red Wyanokie Circular Trail continues straight ahead and the blue-blazed Hewitt-Butler Trail enters from the right. Follow the blue blazes sharply right and descend steeply for 0.5 mile through a fascinating series of rock chutes and slots. This trail meanders over ledges and through a boulder-strewn mountain laurel grove. It may again be the work of Will Monroe, whose eye for beauty was second to none.

Stay on the blue Hewitt-Butler Trail, passing an intersection with the white Macopin Trail. Make a left on the blue trail where it rejoins the yellow Mine Trail. The two paths coincide until they hit paved Snake Den Road at 2.6 miles. Turn right and follow the road 0.5 mile downhill to the Weis Ecology Center parking lot.

The ecology center, too, is a legacy of early trail-building days. It was the camp of the Naturfreunde (Nature Friends), a 1920s Austrian Socialist hiking group that maintained Wyanokie trails until the 1960s. Today, the Weis Ecology Center is run by the New Jersey Audubon Society.

🔎 THE 1,200-MILE MIRACLE

The legacy of trail building, born with groups like the New York chapters of the AMC, GMC and Naturfreunde, spread quickly throughout the New York metro area. In 1920 these and other tramping groups allied themselves as the New York–New Jersey Trail Conference. Led by Raymond Torrey, a Manhattan journalist and conservationist, volunteers built the first miles of the Appalachian Trail and snaked trail networks across the New Jersey and Hudson Highlands. Their close work with government also led to many new state and county parks.

The New York–New Jersey Trail Conference and its clubs continue as the dominant trail building organization in the metro area today, managing more than 1,200 trail miles. Volunteers paint blazes, cut brush, place rock steps and stone water bars (for erosion control), and lay down bog bridging. They maintain 73 miles of Appalachian Trail in New Jersey and are helping build the Highlands Trail, a 150-mile path connecting the Hudson with the Delaware River. The group has been instrumental in preserving parklands, especially Sterling Forest. The New York–New Jersey Trail Conference and its many hiking clubs welcome volunteers eager to give back to the trails the joy they've gained from them.

Hours, Fees and Facilities

Norvin Green State Forest trails are open during daylight hours year-round.

Getting There

Take I-287 north or south to Exit 57. Follow signs to Skyline Drive. Take Skyline Drive to end, then turn left on Route 511. Make the first major right on West Brook Road, crossing the Wanaque Reservoir on a viaduct. Bear left at an intersection with Stonetown Road, and in another 0.5 mile, turn left on Snake Den Road. Follow Snake Den Road signs to the Weis Ecology Center parking lot.

For More Information

Weis Ecology Center, 150 Snake Den Road, Ringwood, NJ 07456; 973-835-2160. New York–New Jersey Trail Conference, 232 Madison Avenue, Suite 802, New York, NY 10016; 212-685-9699.

17 Four Birds Trail

Splitrock Reservoir and Farny State Park

- 5.6 miles
- 4 hours
- Elevation gain 680 feet
- Challenging; rocky footing

Explore a secluded mountain and black bear habitat

The Farny Highlands is a rugged and wild, 35,000-acre watershed that lies only a few miles north of where Interstate 80 pierces the New Jersey Highlands. This jumble of Precambrian gneiss cliffs, scoured by the Wisconsin Glacier, rises above deeply etched, stream-washed valleys. Black bear, river otter, beaver, porcupine, and timber rattlesnake inhabit dense hardwood forests, while native brook trout populate small streams.

The region's rich veins of magnetite were tapped by eighteenth- and nineteenth-century iron miners. In the twentieth century, the Farny Highlands's widest valleys were dammed to form the Charlotteburg and Splitrock Reservoirs, which supply drinking water to Jersey City. Overlooking the reservoirs at the heart of this mountainous area is the undeveloped Farny State Park.

In 1996 the 19.5-mile-long Four Birds Trail became the first blazed hiking path to traverse the region. Running from south to north and built by volunteers of the New York–New Jersey Trail Conference, it crosses only one paved road along its entire length. The trail was named in honor of the wild habitats and avian inhabitants hikers may encounter: wild turkeys find shelter in deciduous forest, red-tailed hawks ride thermals above the cliffs, osprey hunt over the quiet reservoirs, and great blue heron fish secluded marshes.

This challenging 5.6-mile-out-and-back hike samples a portion of the Farny Highlands known locally as the Bumps. Here the white-blazed Four Birds Trail repeatedly climbs to stony summits and falls into shaded ravines. The walk rewards with aerial and shore-side views of Splitrock Reservoir, and promises with telltale signs of plentiful wildlife.

From the pull-off spot on Split Rock Road, walk 0.2 mile south and uphill along the road. The Four Birds Trail crosses the road just beyond the hill crest.

Four Birds Trail

FARNY STATE
PARK

Hibernia Road

Split Rock Road

scenic
shore
overlook

Sentinel
Oak

white-blazed

START

P

Splitrock
Reservoir

N

0.5 mile

Turn left, following the white blazes north. The trail immediately demands an energetic scramble to the top of a small stony outcrop (0.3 mile).

The thin soil of this ledge is host to remarkable plant diversity. Lowbush blueberry, maple-leaved viburnum, shadbush, black haw, scarlet hawthorn, black cherry, red and chestnut oak, mockernut and pignut hickory all grow here, feeding animals year-round. Shadbush is the first forest tree to bloom in spring. In early April, simultaneous with the Delaware River shad run, its five-petaled white blossoms appear like pearl white stars amid a gray universe of bare woodland limbs. In early summer shadbush wears purple, crab-apple-like fruit, a favorite of forty bird and mammal species. Look for shattered shadbush branches, a sign of feeding black bears (see sidebar). Black haw, a shrubby tree, also boasts white flowers (appearing later than shadbush). Its blue-black fruit sustains songbirds, gamebirds and mammals from autumn into winter.

This first outcrop gives limited views of Splitrock Reservoir's dam and water pumping station. The trail immediately descends and crosses a woods road at 0.4 mile, passing beneath a dense canopy of chestnut oak, sweet birch, beech, and sugar maple. American chestnut saplings and dogwood fill in the understory, while green fronds of Christmas fern, hay-scented fern, and cinnamon fern criss-cross the forest floor. Just beyond the woods road, at the ravine's bottom, a brook crosses the trail. It is surrounded by water-loving tulip trees and yellow birches with silvery, peeling bark and exposed snaky roots.

Now the trail starts a challenging climb, amid boulders topped by leathery olive-drab rock tripe and the delicate forest green fronds of polypody fern. The ledges form a small rock shelter which could serve as a hiker haven in a rainstorm. This climb leads to a cliff-top view of Splitrock Reservoir at 0.7 mile. From here we watched a kettle of turkey buzzards as they rode the boiling thermals above the reservoir.

As the trail descends from the vista over billion-year-old banded gneiss, notice that 350-million-year-old chunks of purple-hued puddingstone erratics have been dropped here like so many scattered marbles, left behind by the melting ice of the Wisconsin Glacier 15,000 years ago.

The path reaches a low area at 0.8 mile amid basswood, American chestnut, and yellow birch, then crosses another woods road. Near here we found downy lobelia. This relative of the crimson cardinal flower wears pastel blue blossoms in early autumn. In spring, a scattering of purple violets adorns the leaf litter.

The trail skirts left of a red maple swamp as it begins climbing again at 0.9 mile. Red maple flowers early in spring, creating a scarlet canopy above woodland swamps. Also in spring, walkers may be confused by a ducklike quacking rising from the swamp. This is not the cry of migrating waterfowl, but the massed voices of tree frogs giving their mating call.

Now comes the most athletically demanding climb of the walk, a 200-foot vertical rise over rocks and roots to a nameless, 1,100-foot peak (1.5 miles). Sitting atop this vista, we were perplexed by explosions reverberating over the hills. Later we learned of our proximity to Picatinny Arsenal, where the U.S. Army tests experimental artillery pieces by firing shells into a mountainside. Picatinny Arsenal was established in 1880 on the site of an eighteenth- and nineteenth-century iron forge that produced cannon and shot for Washington's army, the War of 1812, and the Civil War. The arsenal was razed in 1926 when a tree overhanging a powder magazine was struck by lightning. The rebuilt complex played a vital role in World War II and remains the nation's largest arms-research facility. The arsenal offers a mixed blessing to wildlife: much of the army's land is undeveloped and cloaked in forest, but toxic chemicals used in the past may affect water and land quality.

The Four Birds Trail leaves the vista and makes a few swift but challenging descents and ascents through rocky terrain as it passes among mountain laurel, chestnut oak and sweet birch. The path then undulates through an open forest of tulip tree, sugar maple, and hophornbeam, crossing several low rock ledges.

At 2.0 miles the path winds left around the Sentinel Oak, a four-foot-diameter red oak. The path continues descending through hickories. Walk quietly and you may see fleeing white-tailed deer as we did. Why, one wonders, do escaping deer fail to conceal themselves, and instead make a flashy show with their white tails? Some scientists speculate that this gesture is the animal's way of "thumbing its nose" at stalking predators. The defiant tail display informs predators that pursuit

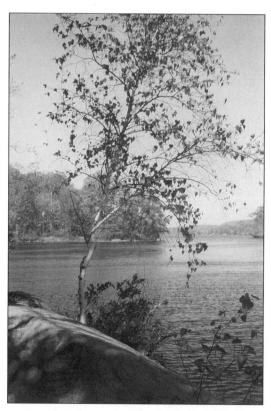

Splitrock Reservoir, where diving ducks, geese and swans flourish.

is futile once the deer has taken flight. (Fleet-footed deer can hit speeds of 35 mph and make thirty-foot horizontal leaps).

The trail descends through sassafras and gray birch to the reservoir, then makes its rocky way along the shore to a little island (2.8 miles). Hopping from boulder to boulder, you can easily put yourself out on the island, an ideal spot for lunch and from which to watch for diving osprey and waterfowl. From this point, you can continue following the trail north, exploring the reservoir shoreline. When you're ready, retrace your steps back to Splitrock Road.

🌰 THE RETURN OF THE BLACK BEAR

Native New Jersey black bears were hunted to extinction by the 1800s, but renewed oak and hemlock forests, mountain laurel thickets, rhododendron and blueberry bogs have brought them back. Migrating east from Pennsylvania's Pocono Plateau, black bears are now breeding in the Kittatinny Range and New Jersey Highlands. The state supports more than five hundred bears.

As you walk the Farny Highlands, look for signs of these lumbering omnivores. Overturned logs, branches torn from fruit-covered highbush blueberry and shadbush, clawed beech trees, and excavated anthills or rodent burrows all testify to hungry black bears foraging for twigs, roots, nuts, fruits, insects, and small mammals. The most recognizable sign are heaps of dark-colored scat containing undigested bits of berry in autumn.

Bears are shy and usually run from humans. If you meet one, use common sense. Never offer food or interfere with a mother bear and her cubs. If a bear won't run, don't make eye contact; take a nonaggressive stance and speak softly. If the animal still won't flee, whistle, wave your arms, speak loudly, or fire your camera flash. Don't run; a black bear can top speeds of 30 mph. Warnings aside, these magnificent animals deserve our wonder and respect.

Hours, Fees and Facilities

The Four Birds Trail is open dawn to dusk year-round.

Getting There

From I-80 take US 23 north to the Route 513, Green Pond Road exit. Follow Route 513 south for 5.3 miles to the town of Marcella, turning left on Upper Hibernia Road. In 1.1 miles turn left on Split Rock Road. In 0.6 mile look for a small pull-off parking place on the right. Trailhead is 0.2 mile farther up the road by foot.

For More Information

New York–New Jersey Trail Conference, 232 Madison Avenue, Suite 802, New York, NY 10016; 212-685-9699.

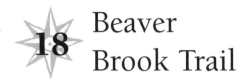

18 Beaver Brook Trail

Farny Highlands

- 6.2 miles
- 5 hours
- Elevation gain 700 feet
- Challenging; with climbing and rocky footing

A rugged hike to a beaver colony

Many people feel an affinity toward the North American beaver, perhaps because of a perceived similarity to human beings. Like us, these industrious animals cooperate to construct elaborate homes and, in the process, transform their environment.

Sixty million beaver controlled precolonial America's waterways, including most New Jersey streams. Unfortunately, the beaver's velvety soft pelts were their undoing. Lenape tribesmen were perplexed at the obsessive interest shown by Dutch traders in the furs. The Dutch offered cloth, iron tools, rum and brandy in trade for the pelts, which were processed into pricey felt hats for Europe's fashion elite.

By 1656 the New Netherlands was exporting 80,000 pelts a year. At this rate, the animal population quickly declined, as did the value of Native Americans to the Europeans. Colonist Johan Printz lamented the failure of the Lenape fur trade, declaring, "Nothing would be better than that a couple hundred soldiers should be sent here and kept here until we broke the necks of all of them." By 1750 the Lenape were gone, forced west, and by 1820 the last free-roaming New Jersey beaver were exterminated.

Not until 1900, when escapees from the New Jersey Rutherford estate reestablished a wild colony, did anyone give much thought to beaver. The state, encouraged by this success, imported more, until by 1952 limited trapping was again allowed. Today, New Jersey's beaver population thrives.

This rugged, 6.2-mile-out-and-back hike ascends to a beaver colony. While the animals are nocturnal, daytime visitors will be rewarded with proof of the beaver's engineering feats. The hike also climbs into a classic New Jersey Highlands environment characterized by rocky crags, sweeping vistas, and plentiful signs of shy wildlife, including bear and coyote.

The white-blazed Beaver Brook Trail is one of New Jersey's newest trails, completed in 1997. It extends for 6.5 miles from Morris County's Mahlon Dickerson

Lost
Lake

Split
Rock

power lines

beaver lodges
& dams

Beaver Brook

N

0.5 mile

Valley
View
Lookout

Berkshire Valley Road

white-blazed

Taylor Rd.

P

START

Beaver Brook Trail

Reservation into the state's Rockaway River Wildlife Management Area. This walk uses the southernmost trail section.

The path departs from the south corner of the trailhead parking lot, climbing quickly on a woods road through a mixed deciduous forest of sugar maple, oaks, hickory and ash. Steep becomes steeper as the gullied road shoots straight toward the top of the mountain. Watch the blazes. At 0.3 mile, the trail makes a sharp right, leaving the woods road and ascending a rock outcrop. Stop to catch your breath, and notice that the Highlands stone beneath your feet is black with iron, a fact that didn't go unnoticed by nineteenth-century entrepreneurs. These hills were heavily mined.

The trail rises less steeply now, as it hops from stony outcrop to stony outcrop, with views over Berkshire Valley and to Green Pond Mountain. The best vista comes at about 0.5 mile. You've now climbed 500 vertical feet from your starting point and are within the territory of Highlands wildlife. Standing here in November, we heard the screams of red-tailed hawks and found bear scat dotted with undigested partridgeberry. Bears put on a good supply of fat in autumn, preparing for a sedentary winter. While they don't truly hibernate, being easily roused from sleep, they won't eat again until spring.

The thin soil at these heights supports black cherry, shagbark hickory, oaks and cedar. Rock slabs are edged in maple-leaved viburnum and lowbush blueberry. Shadbush also grows here. With its nondescript simple-toothed leaf, this little tree blends in with the scenery most of the year. But in April, when the rest of the Highlands forest is still a tangle of naked branches, the shadbush blossoms with downy masses of white-petaled flowers. This blooming coincides with the spawning of shad in the Delaware and Hudson Rivers, explaining the tree's common name.

The Beaver Brook Trail next makes a steep 0.8-mile descent, departing the oaks and open ledges and entering deep forest dominated by sugar maples. The footing is rocky and a little treacherous, especially on slippery autumn leaves or in wet weather. The forest floor is adorned with cinnamon, hay-scented and Christmas ferns. Birds are plentiful. An immense dead hemlock stump has been pulverized by pileated woodpeckers, while tulip trees display the neatly drilled horizontal holes made by yellow-bellied sapsuckers.

Falling deeper into a shaded hollow, the trail crosses several major woods roads and passes through a disturbed area where Christmas ferns fill trenches that may have been dug as exploratory mining pits. Partridgeberry, striped pipsissewa, maidenhair fern, and rattlesnake root rise from leaf litter.

At about 1.2 miles the trail steadily climbs through mountain laurel, at first along a woods road and then making its own path. It weaves to the top of the Valley View Vista (1.5 miles), a reindeer-lichen-covered ledge. Here we found several trees with hickory nutshells tightly wedged into their bark. This was probably the work of woodpeckers or flying squirrels, who use the trees as a vice for holding the nuts while eating them.

After rising a little farther, the path levels off on a typical Highlands ridge, a rugged, undulating plateau marked by open forest and overlooked by low out-

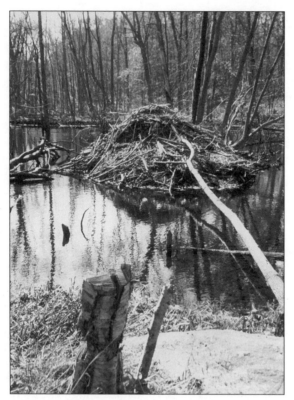

A beaver lodge at Beaver Brook provides year-round safety to these water-loving animals.

crops. This tableland is mantled in chestnut oak, sweet birch, sugar maple, shadbush and beech trees. Blueberries and polypody fern hug rocky spots. Rattlesnake plantain, with mottled snakeskin-like leaves, blooms white in summer. At 2.8 miles the trail enters a disturbed area with clay mounds topped by trees, evidence the area may once have been considered for development.

Just past these mounds, the path descends to Beaver Brook and a sight that never ceases to surprise. The stream runs down the center of a shallow valley crossed by a succession of beaver dams (see sidebar). Behind each dam, a glimmering pool gathers to protect a dome-shaped beaver lodge. Stream banks are clearcut, with stumps everywhere. Yellow birch logs, beaver's food of choice, lie on the ground stripped of bark. While this may seem like wanton destruction, beaver actually enrich their habitat. The ponds support insect growth, encouraging fish, which attract raccoons, great blue heron, belted kingfishers and other animals. Hawks hunt white-throated sparrows and other prey among the newly created forest openings.

The trail follows Beaver Brook upstream, then descends to a rocky place where it passes beneath a power line and crosses the brook on a rickety bridge. It climbs uphill, passing another beaver dam and lodge. Finally, at 3.1 miles, the path reaches Lost Lake, a wide marsh choked at its edge by phragmites. At least two more beaver lodges are visible from shore. The trail skirts the lake's west edge. We had lunch here and turned back at a lemon squeezer, a large boulder split by frost action through which the trail passes. Those wanting a longer walk may go farther before returning the way they came.

🪶 BEAVER: BORN TO BUILD

The beaver, a large rodent, is uniquely suited for its engineering role. Its shovel-shaped, scaly tail serves as a brace when the animal gnaws trees, as a balance when it carries building materials, and as a rudder when it barges heavy logs through open water.

Its incisors, each a quarter-inch wide, can cut through tree trunks; strip the cambium layer from trees; or nip leaves, buds and twigs. Beaver can roll branches between their nimble forefeet, chewing away bark as we would corn from a cob. Smaller trees (two to six inches in diameter) are cut for food and building materials (a five-inch willow can be downed in just three minutes), though sometimes beaver tackle immense trees. Awkward land animals, portly beaver do most onshore work at night, warily sniffing for coyote and river otter, their enemies.

The beaver is built for the water. When the animal submerges, valves close off ears and nostrils, while skin flaps seal the mouth, leaving front incisors exposed for work. Clear membranes, like goggles, protect the eyes. A beaver is an ideal swimmer, with webbed hind feet, waterproof pelt and thick fat layer to withstand icy winter streams.

Human engineers agree that beaver always know the best spot for dams. In fact, strong dam construction of interwoven branches packed with mud frequently foils park officials, who find trails or picnic groves flooded. Beaver foolers, disguised plastic pipes inserted into dams to drain off water, seem to fool no one. The mere sound of water flowing cues the animals to repair their work and plug the "fooler."

Hours, Fees and Facilities

The Beaver Brook Trail is open daily year-round.

Getting There

From I-80 take NJ 15 north for 2.0 miles. Turn right on Berkshire Valley Road. Trailhead parking is 2.0 miles north on the left just beyond the Rockaway River crossing and the junction with Taylor Road.

For More Information

New York–New Jersey Trail Conference, 232 Madison Avenue, Suite 802, New York, NY 10016; 212-685-9699.

19 Tripod Rock and Bear Rock

Pyramid Mountain, Morris County Park

- 3.0 miles
- 3 hours
- Elevation gain 400 feet
- Moderate; one steep ascent and descent

*A wildflower walk to New Jersey's
most celebrated glacial erratics*

Just north of Morristown's suburban sprawl, a series of low ridges rise to nine hundred feet above sea level. These Highlands summits, separated by narrow valleys, have remained sparsely settled for centuries. Native Americans once hunted and foraged here. Later, notorious outlaws used the region as a hide-out, while nineteenth-century charcoal makers and quarrymen came and went.

This rough country was long recognized for its freakish rock formations, glacial erratics that have since shaped local history. Native Americans may have utilized Tripod Rock (a two-hundred-ton boulder perched atop three basketball-size stones) as a celestial calendar. Nineteenth-century surveyors used house-size Bear Rock as a boundary marker. In the twentieth century, hikers laid out trails and made pilgrimages to both sites. Eventually, it was these two unique boulders that inspired conservationists to protect Pyramid Mountain.

By 1980, developers' bulldozers began probing lowland hollows, tearing up trees and replacing favorite trails with roads. In 1982, alarmed local resident Lucy Meyer determined that Tripod Rock and Bear Rock were too valuable to lose. She rallied neighbors, government, conservation groups and corporate interests to save an acre of ground at each site.

The Friends of Pyramid Mountain succeeded beyond their wildest hopes. Lucy's two acres grew to two thousand protected acres of Morris County parkland. Today, Pyramid Mountain and adjacent Turkey Mountain are an important stopover on the Atlantic flyway, attracting birds. Bear and bobcat populate rocky hills, as do two hundred native plants.

This 3.0-mile loop hike is celebrated for its spring and autumn wildflowers. It takes walkers to both Tripod Rock and Bear Rock, and to a Manhattan skyline vista.

Tripod Rock and Bear Rock

From the Pyramid Mountain Visitor Center, follow the blue trail into a low-land forest dominated by maple, beech and sweet birch. In late summer, tall blue lettuce grows ten feet high, while tiny woodland asters, among the most success-ful of all wildflowers, poke up from leaf litter (see sidebar).

In about 0.2 mile the blue-blazed visitor center trail ends at a junction with the blue-blazed Mennen Trail. Turn left on this trail (named for a major Pyramid Mountain corporate sponsor). The blue trail soon crosses Stony Brook on a bridge. Ignore a yellow-blazed trail branching right.

In autumn, woodland sunflowers, jewelweed and joe-pye weed blossom along this wet trail section. Native Americans squeezed juice from the pendant-shaped, yellow-orange jewelweed flower onto skin to soothe poison ivy rashes, a proven medical treatment. Joe-pye weed, a tall, spindly plant with a curly head of pinkish purple flowers, is named for a mythical Native American herbalist who, it is said, treated typhoid fever outbreaks in colonial times with the herb.

The trail starts an easy climb on stone steps and the first glacial erratics appear, some ten feet tall and all dropped by the melting ice of the Wisconsin Glacier more than 15,000 years ago.

At 0.4 mile the blue trail meets a white trail entering from the left beneath a power line, then makes a steep ascent under red and chestnut oaks to a vista at 0.6 mile. The scrub oak–cloaked view looks east over Turkey Mountain to Manhattan's World Trade Center and Empire State Building. An unseen quarry on Turkey Mountain once provided local carvers with green serpentine, a soft, waxy mineral that, when shaped and shined, is as beautiful as jade.

The blue trail ascends, then levels off, passing through chestnut oak, sweet birch and leggy growths of mountain laurel. This area is beautiful when the laurel blossoms in June with white and pink cup-shaped flowers.

Ignore a yellow-blazed trail entering from the right and exiting to the left. Just a little farther on (at about 1.0 mile), a blue-and-white-blazed side trail leads left over loose rocks to Lucy's Overlook (named for Pyramid Mountain crusader Lucy Meyer). This ledge looks west to Stony Brook Mountain and offers good birding. The hawk migration passes overhead in autumn and eagles have been spotted. Five types of owl, including the endangered barred owl, live on Pyramid Mountain.

Return along the side trail, continuing left on the blue trail. At about 1.3 miles the blue-blazed trail intersects with a white trail. Continue straight ahead on the white trail along the ridge top for another 0.1 mile to Pyramid Rock. Here, the retreating glacier capriciously balanced a minivan-size boulder atop three small stones. As precarious as the situation looks, it has remained unchanged for 15,000 years. Whether Native Americans really used this site as an observatory no one knows, but it has lately become a popular solstice celebration spot.

Return 0.1 mile to the junction of the blue-blazed and white-blazed trails. Turn right, following the blue-and-white combined trail as it plummets 150 verti-cal feet from Pyramid Mountain into the valley. Notice as you drop from the ridge-crest how quickly the chestnut oaks disappear, replaced by tall tulip trees, hicko-ries and red oaks. Virginia creeper and poison ivy wind viny tendrils around

Tripod Rock, a 200-ton boulder precariously balanced on three small rocks, has stayed in place since the passing of the last glacier 15,000 years ago. Photo credit: Jean LeBlanc

bottomland trees. The trail is flat and easy for the rest of the hike.

At 1.8 miles the blue-white trail crosses Bearhouse Brook, where bumblebees crawl headfirst into white-blossoming turtleheads and where cardinal flower blooms in late summer. This wetland flower, named for scarlet clergy robes, is a favorite with hummingbirds.

Just ahead is Bear Rock. This one-story-high boulder, dragged from nearby Stony Brook Mountain, is believed to be the largest glacial erratic in New Jersey. In front of Bear Rock, the blue-blazed Mennen Trail veers right. Go left on the white trail, as it follows a woods road edged by a stone wall and shaded by white ash, sugar maple and hickory. The stone walls and barberry (once forming a natural hedge) testify to ruined nineteenth-century subsistence farms.

At 2.1 miles the trail passes to the right of a tiny foundation, ruins of the Morgan Place. This was not so much homestead as hide-out. The Morgans were robbers who made regular raids on Boonton in the late 1800s. The stone cellar hole blooms with violets and wild geranium in springtime.

The trail crosses a bridge over Bearhouse Brook and enters a wet area with fine autumn wildflower displays. Joe-pye weed grows as high as your head, intermixing its soft purples with the reds of winged sumac. Common New England asters, white snakeroot and boneset mix with rarer closed gentians and lovely purple gerardia (the two best color pages in *Newcomb's Wildflower Guide!*). There is no deeper blue than that of the closed or bottle gentian, as it contrasts with yellowing wetland sedges. Trumpet-shaped gerardia blossoms are dotted with dark spots and yellow ribs on the inside of elegant throats.

Follow the white trail as it swings gently uphill around the south base of Pyramid Mountain back to the power line and the junction with the blue Mennen Trail (2.7 miles). Turn right and return the way you came to the visitor center.

🌺 LATE BLOOMERS: A RIOT OF FALL WILDFLOWERS

Most of us think of spring as the time for wildflowers. But late summer and early autumn offer displays of purple asters, yellow goldenrods and blue gentians that are just as dazzling and uplifting as are spring beauties.

This is the time when composites make their showiest appearance. Composites are one of the most recent developments in flowering plants and one of the most successful worldwide. They are flowers within flowers. Look at an aster, sunflower, goldenrod, daisy, thistle, white snakeroot or joe-pye weed and you'll discover that what appears to be a single central flower head is actually composed of a fused mass of many (sometimes hundreds) of tiny florets. Each floret contributes pollen for propagation.

Autumn wildflowers, along with plentiful berries and nuts, provide a last rich autumn harvest before winter descends. More than fifty varieties of goldenrod, for example, grace our meadows, each providing plentiful seeds for migrating birds, as well as nectar and pollen for monarch butterflies, wasps, hornets, beetles and bees. Goldenrod is often blamed for causing hay fever, a crime it doesn't commit. Its pollen is too heavy to float on the breeze. Other meadow flowers, like red clover, wild bergamot and bull-thistle attract insect pollinators with colorful displays before the first frosts turn the world golden.

Hours, Fees and Facilities

Trails are open dawn to dusk year-round. The visitor center is open Fridays and weekends.

Getting There

From I-287 north, take the Main Street, Boonton, exit. Proceed to Boonton Avenue (County 511). Turn right (north). The Pyramid Mountain Visitor Center is 3.3 miles on the left (opposite Mars Court).

For More Information

Morris County Park Commission, P.O. Box 1295, Morristown, NJ 07962; 973-326-7600.

Friends of Pyramid Mountain, Lucy Meyer, 2 Cook Terrace, Kinnelon, NJ 07405.

20 Black River and Kay Environmental Center

Morris County Park

- 3.6 miles (optional additional 1.5 miles to hemlock gorge)
- 3 hours (or 5 hours)
- Easy; mostly on woods roads

A river gorge and bountiful biological diversity

No hike in this book offers greater diversity of habitat, human history, and beauty concentrated within so few miles. Black River Park boasts a deeply etched river valley, a deciduous flood-plain forest, a hemlock-cloaked ravine, an upland forest with blooming rhododendron, and broad meadows planted in flowering dogwood. Hundreds of migrating bird and butterfly species are attracted to the park, as are diverse mammals, including coyote and black bear.

The Black River Gorge is just as significant historically. Starting in the eighteenth century, the valley was exploited for its resources: trees harvested, iron mines dug, mills and railroads built. In the 1920s, the area became the gentrified estate of the remarkable Elizabeth Kay (see sidebar). In the last half of the twentieth century, that estate was preserved as the crown jewel of the Morris County park system and as headquarters for the New Jersey Nature Conservancy.

This walk can be done as a 3.6-mile-out-and-back-hike, but can be lengthened to 5.1 miles to include the deepest part of the gorge (a free pass available at Cooper Mill or Kay Environmental Center is needed to enter this environmentally sensitive area).

Begin at Cooper Mill. Here the Black River abruptly changes from sluggish stream to roaring river as it begins dropping into the gorge. This was a prime location for water-powered industry. The first mill was built here in the 1760s. The present one, raised in 1826, is now a living history museum.

Walk behind the mill, past the sixteen-foot-high water wheel. This energy-efficient marvel is so well balanced that just two cups of water are needed in half the wheel's forty-eight buckets to make it spin. It grinds 400 pounds of flour per hour.

Cross over the mill tailrace beneath ornamental catalpa trees. A blue-blazed trail leads downstream into the forest, entering another world. The river roars between black boulders while trout rise in shaded, golden pools. Sweet birch, yellow birch, beech and tulip trees push arrow-straight trunks out of the gorge toward

N

Cooper Mill

24

P START

Black River

Blue-Blazed Trail to Kay Environmental Center

Kay's Pond

0.8 mi. to Environmental Center

Kay Environmental Center

Hemlock Ravine

(optional unblazed trails)

(optional side hike)

field

Kay summer house ruins

Black River & Kay Environmental Center

the sky. These are some of the tallest trees I've seen in New Jersey, and require the arms of two or three people to encircle them.

The trail traverses a flood plain where spring beauties, rattlesnake plantain and trout lily bloom in April. Asters, jewelweed and jack-in-the-pulpit spread across the forest floor in autumn. Jack-in-the-pulpit, with its characteristic green-striped hood (or spathe), has the ability to change sex with size. Bigger plants are female, while smaller ones are male. Easy sex change allows this herb to attune its propagation rate to match lean or plentiful growing seasons.

In a short distance the blue trail along the river becomes easier, seeming to follow an old road. This is really the remains of a nineteenth-century narrow-gauge railroad that served riverside iron mines. As the gorge walls rise around you, look for mine holes and trenches, plus ore tailing piles composed of rust-colored, fist-sized, magnetite-rich stones.

Tulip trees and red and white oaks rise higher now, while smaller American hornbeam and witch hazel trees huddle in the shade. Look for the American basswood, its bark pecked with neat rows of holes. This is the work of yellow-bellied sapsuckers, who tap the trees for their sweet sap. After drilling the trees and eating their inner bark, the birds return later to sip dripping sap and eat insects that have gathered to feast on the sticky flow. Ruby-throated hummingbirds also come to feed at sapsucker wells.

The stream broadens into a lily-covered pond (0.5 mile), backed up behind a stone dam. This nineteenth-century mill site became the electrical generating plant for Elizabeth Kay's self-sufficient estate in the 1920s. The pond is overhung with elm, black locust and sycamore, while escaped hostas dot the ground, attesting to Mrs. Kay's gardening skills.

At 1.2 miles the trail reaches a woods road junction where a sign informs hikers that the Kay Environmental Center lies 0.8 mile ahead on the blue trail. For those who favor a shorter, easier hike on blazed paths, continue on the blue-blazed trail as it leads away from the Black River into upland oak and ash forest to the Kay Center. From there, explore the surrounding meadows (see below).

For the more adventurous who wish to explore the Black River Gorge hemlock ravine, follow the unmarked but very obvious woods road to the right, entering the Environmentally Sensitive Area (free entrance passes available at Cooper Mill or Kay Environmental Center). At a major woods road fork in 0.1 mile, turn right, descending to and crossing Black River on a bridge. At stream's edge, shade-loving mountain laurel spreads beneath shagbark hickory, yellow birch and tulip trees. Follow the road on the stream's far side for 0.4 mile, as it climbs uphill, winding into the heart of the gorge under a canopy of Eastern hemlock and beech trees. Among fallen hemlock needles grows the amanita mushroom. Known as the Destroying Angel, it resembles some edible varieties, but is so poisonous it should never be touched. Follow the road until it descends back to the Black River and dead-ends at a turnaround spot.

Return the way you came uphill, looking for a set of concrete steps descending steeply right to the river. At the base of the steps you'll find a cement dam and the ruins of Elizabeth Kay's summer home with its huge fireplace. This spot was the scene of festive 1930s swimming parties.

Do not cross the dam, but return up the steps to the woods road, following it right, returning over the Black River bridge. After crossing the stream, climb uphill a short distance and turn right on a major woods road that leads out of the gorge into an upland forest with a lush understory of rhododendron. The road then emerges into open fields. Make a long, lazy sweep to your left, circling gradually north through the meadows to the Kay Environmental Center building (now within sight).

The Kay Center meadows, planted with dogwood trees, are a pleasure to the eye in any season. In spring, the trees wear a mantle of white blossoms. In autumn, they glow scarlet, as do Virginia creeper and poison ivy. All three plants exhibit fall foliar flagging: they blaze crimson to advertise ripening berries to birds who eat the fruit and disperse seeds on southward migrations.

The Kay Center meadows are the ideal place for bird- and butterfly watchers. Monarchs pause here to feed on milkweed on their way to Mexico. Two hundred bird species have been spotted in the Black River area (with an estimated hundred species nesting here). Look for magnolia and hooded warblers, scarlet tanagers, Baltimore orioles and eastern phoebes.

The open meadows of the Kay Environmental Center attract migrating birds and butterflies.

No matter which hike option you choose, after thoroughly exploring the meadows, walk to the environmental center, and follow the blue trail for 1.8 miles back to Cooper Mill.

🌰 THE AMAZING MRS. KAY

Elizabeth Donnell was born in 1894 to a prominent Philadelphia family and in 1918 married stockbroker Alfred Kay. The couple, like many wealthy urbanites, sought peace on a gentrified country estate. In the early 1920s, they moved to rural Chester, N.J., establishing their 233-acre Hidden River Farm.

Elizabeth Kay was a far-seeing naturalist and believer in self-sufficiency. She generated her own electricity, raised sheep and dairy cows, and grew organic fruits and vegetables decades before the hazards of chemical fertilizers and pesticides were recognized. Her guests dined on home-grown turkey, squab (pigeon), mutton, peaches, apples, butter and eggs at tables graced by her own exquisite flower arrangements. Local seniors flocked to Mrs. Kay for rejuvenating herbal cures.

When developers tried to buy the farm, Mrs. Kay declared, "I'll have no part in any bulldozers!" She and her husband bequeathed the entire tract to Morris County as an environmental center so that "each day would bring a new wonder and challenge to learn."

Natural New Jersey has long profited from such benefactors. The Kusers and Worthington families donated extensive tracts in the Kittatinny Mountains, while the Hewitts, Farnys and Greens offered up their Highlands acreage. Today, the New Jersey chapter of the Nature Conservancy works with landowners large and small who wish to sell or donate ecologically significant lands. The group's 28,000 members have preserved nearly 40,000 wild New Jersey acres.

Hours, Fees and Facilities

Trails are open dawn to dusk year-round. Cooper Mill is open weekends May to October, and Friday through Tuesday in July and August. Kay Environmental Center, headquarters for the New Jersey chapter of the Nature Conservancy, is open daily year-round.

Getting There

Take I-80 east or west to US 206 south for 8.0 miles to Chester. Turn right on NJ 24 west for 1.2 miles to Cooper Mill on the left.

For More Information

Cooper Mill, Route 24, Chester, NJ, 07930; 908-879-5463.

Kay Environmental Center, 200 Pottersville Road, Chester, NJ, 07930; 908-879-0566.

Nature Conservancy at Kay Environmental Center; 908-879-7262.

Schooley's Mountain

Morris County Park

- 2.9 miles
- 3 hours
- Elevation Gain: 300 feet
- Moderate; with one hand-over-hand descent

Highland hardwoods and a waterfall

Early European map makers labeled the uncharted emptiness of our continent simply as "The Great Forest of America." And great it was. Stretching from tropics to tundra, from the Atlantic Ocean to Midwestern grasslands, it covered a million square miles and a third of what was to become the United States.

The Great Forest was a stately cathedral and treasure house. Old-growth trees grew 10 feet around and rose 150 feet high. Europeans were staggered by forest diversity. Today, even after centuries of ecosystem disruption, parts of the Appalachians still claim 130 species of native trees and 1,300 flowering plants.

The Great Forest provided timber, tools and fuel to the first immigrants. It offered lumber for homes, shops and ships; charcoal for iron furnaces; and rich soils on which to plant crops. Woodlands offered fruits and nuts for food and herbs for medicine. The forest was a primary resource on which the first settlers depended for survival, and on which America built its wealth.

Today, the Great Forest of America has been shattered into fragments, cut into national, state and county parks. Preserved for us are pale reminders of the magnificent whole. And in our time, when plastic and metal often replace wood, it's easy to forget how much we once relied on trees—and still do.

The forests of Schooley's Mountain Park, like most of the Great Forest, have been used and abused since the first settlers. The land, named for the Schooley family who owned it in the 1790s, has been logged, farmed, quarried, and used as a resort and estate. The rejuvenated woods inspired Girl Scouts in the 1920s. Today, the park's third- and fourth-growth trees attest to both Great Forest resilience and threats to its future.

This 2.9-mile loop hike, on obvious but unblazed trails, starts at the lower, larger parking lot. Walk west toward the boathouse and cross Lake George on a floating dock. Red maple and knapweed line the near shore, while mallard ducks and Canada geese glide the lake. Waterfowl were so plentiful in colonial times as to inspire comparisons to Eden. The birds were diminished by unlimited hunting and a loss of wetland habitat. Alarmed hunters lobbied for laws to protect their sport, and waterfowl have seen a comeback. Today, 10 million mallards populate North America, while the Canada goose is so numerous it has become a pest in suburban parks.

On the far shore, turn left and pass along the lake shore where multiflora rose forms a hedge beneath black cherry and red cedar trees. Multiflora rose was introduced by the state of New Jersey to farmers as a "living fence." Unfortunately, the prickly bush drives out native plant species. But the news isn't all bad: the fast spread of multiflora rose has helped the northern mockingbird expand its range. It feeds on rose hips and nests amid the plant's thorns.

At the end of the lake (0.3 mile), turn left and pass over the Lake George Dam. On the far side of the dam, turn right on an obvious trail and enter the forest. The trail descends into a deepening gorge, paralleling Electric Brook and passing a powerhouse ruin. The power plant once generated electricity for a stone quarry.

Today, a rich mix of canopy and understory trees stretches hungrily up from the ravine to claim a share of sunlight. Every species was native to the Great Forest and valued by first settlers. White oaks, like those standing beside this brook, were milled into impenetrable hulls for America's navies, including the unsinkable Old Ironsides, the U.S.S. *Constitution*. Hophornbeam, known as ironwood, was once crafted into sled runners and wagon parts. Witch hazel was endowed with magical powers and used by dowsers to locate water. Sassafras makes an aromatic tea and was useful as a colonial pain reliever.

Many of these trees are still important today. Sugar maples, like those along Electric Brook, are tapped for sugar, a New England cash crop. Beeches provide wood flooring and bentwood furniture. Basswood is a source of gourmet honey, crates and berry baskets. Tulip tree, made into dugout canoes by Native Americans, is a valuable commercial hardwood utilized in furniture making. It also provides pharmaceutical companies with a heart stimulant.

The trail follows the brook's falling cascades, which are edged by Christmas fern. The path becomes more difficult, descending over a sloping rock face to the base of one of the prettiest waterfalls in the Highlands (0.7 mile). The bottom of this thirty-foot falls is a fine place to sit, but avoid swimming. Sadly, this pretty stream has been polluted and supports little life.

As you rest, meditate on the immense diversity of the Great Forest fragment surrounding you. Early immigrants were equally amazed. While Europe claims just dozens of native tree species, North America boasts hundreds. Geography is the reason. European mountain ranges stretch east and west, while American ranges stretch north and south. When the glaciers advanced, European trees were backed against a solid mountain wall and driven extinct. American trees simply retreated, propagating southward along valleys. When the glaciers melted, the forests again spread north.

The trail continues briefly along the stream, then climbs steeply left through sugar maples, sweet birch, beech and tulip trees. The tulip tree, its distinct leaves shaped like a child's drawing of a tulip flower, is our tallest eastern tree and one of the most ancient. Fossil specimens 70 million years old have been found, but most of the world's many tulip tree species were wiped out by the Ice Age. Only an American and Chinese variety survive today.

At 0.8 mile, the path arrives at a rocky vista framed by black cherry trees. It looks over a ravine through which Electric Brook flows. Black cherry offers another example of forest value: it feeds 200 butterfly species and 70 bird species, plus bear, raccoon and deer. Native Americans brewed the inner bark as tea. Today, its workable wood is made into fine-grained furniture.

The trail continues to the right through a typical Highlands forest, with chestnut oak, red oak, beech, and pignut and mockernut hickory trees rising overhead. In early spring the ground is dotted with purple violets. The hickory, so prominent here, has a hundred uses, serving as lumber, furniture, tool handles and sporting equipment. American hickories are also survivors of the Ice Age. All of Europe's hickories were lost in the last glacial advance. Even the common violet has its uncommon uses: it is now being researched for its positive effects on skin cancer.

At 1.3 miles a short side trail leads right to a rock outcrop without a view (an interesting short detour), while another major trail turns left, leading back to the parking lot. Continue straight ahead on a wide trail that descends to a T at 1.6 miles. Turn left. At 2.1 miles, this path swings left, entering open meadows. These fields are edged in gray birch (used for barrel hoops and toothpicks) and quaking aspen (a leading pulpwood tree). Native Americans ingested aspen bark as an effective painkiller; it contains salicin, a modern aspirin ingredient. The Great Forest supplies many modern medicines and holds the hope of future cures, should we choose to preserve its fragments.

Walk straight ahead through the meadows back to the parking lot.

ODE TO THE GREAT FOREST

In 1680, Mahlon Stacey wrote a letter to his brother in England proclaiming New Jersey as "a country that produceth all things for the support and sustenance of man... It is my judgment, by what I have observed, that fruit trees in this country destroy themselves by the weight of their fruit."

Today, we must measure forest health not only by what has been saved, but what has been lost. While we can be proud of our parks, half of the Great Forest's million acres are gone. The American chestnut and elm have been decimated by imported pests, while Eastern hemlocks, beeches, and sugar maples may suffer similar fates. Woodland wildlife may never recover. In 1697, New Jersey offered twenty shillings to any "Christian," and half that sum to "Negroes or Indians" for wolf pelts. Gone today are the state's wolves, panthers, elk and passenger pigeons (which once darkened our skies).

The future health of our forests is uncertain. While awareness and preservation efforts grow, scientists fear that the Great Forest may be too fragmented and disease threatened to be perpetually preserved.

Hours Fees and Facilities

Schooley's Mountain Park closes at twilight.

Getting There

From I-80 East or West take US 206 south 8.0 miles to Chester. Turn right on NJ 24 West 5.0 miles to Long Valley. Turn right on Route 24 and climb Schooley's Mountain. Turn right on Camp Washington Road, and right again on East Springtown Road. In 0.3 mile, turn right into the park.

For More Information

Morris County Park Commission, PO Box 1295, Morristown, NJ 07962; 973-326-7600.

Piedmont Province

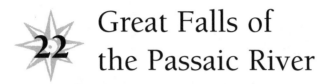

22 Great Falls of the Passaic River

Paterson

- 1.5 miles
- 2 hours
- Easy

View the cataract that inspired America's industrial revolution

Two hundred million years ago lava surged out onto the surface of the earth in eastern New Jersey, burying Piedmont sandstone and tropical jungles. That forty-story-high magma wall cooled into erosion-resistant basalt and hardened as the First Watchung Ridge. A weakness in the columnar joints of that basaltic ridge helped shape the future of New Jersey and America.

The powerful Passaic River was the first force to capitalize on the weak basaltic zone. The river cut a gap through the First Watchung Ridge, plunging over igneous cliffs, and seeking sea level. Of all eastern waterfalls, only the Niagara's thundering water volume is greater than the raging torrents of the Passaic River's 280-foot-wide, 77-foot-tall Great Falls.

Alexander Hamilton was the second to exploit the gap in the basalt. A picnic enjoyed with George Washington at the Great Falls in 1778 inspired Hamilton to harness the river's 2,000-horsepower and to declare American industrial independence. In 1792, Hamilton's Society to Establish Useful Manufactures (S.U.M.) hired Pierre L'Enfant (architect of the nation's capital) to design the raceways, water wheels and mills of a new industrial-age Mecca.

The planned city of Paterson, which sprang up at the falls, became an epicenter from which technology rippled forth over the world. Paterson mills manufactured clipper ship sails and Holland submarines to master the oceans, Colt revolvers and steam locomotives to win the American West, and the Curtis-Wright airplane engine, with which Charles Lindbergh conquered the air. Finally, howev-

Great Falls of the Passaic River

er, terrible working conditions at Paterson mills resulted in labor unrest, the flight of industry elsewhere, and decline of the city along the Passaic.

The first Dutch visitors to the Great Falls in 1680 declared it "a sight to be seen in order to observe the power and wonder of God." This 1.5-mile hike shows off that wonder, while demonstrating how people can both wisely use and abuse nature's power.

Exit the Harry S. Haines Overlook parking lot, turning right onto McBride Avenue. The sidewalk immediately passes the Captain Graupe veteran's monument, which sits astride a basaltic outcrop. Notice how the black igneous rock has solidified into characteristic five- or six-sided polygonal columns.

Just beyond the Graupe monument, turn right into a cinder parking area and walk straight ahead, crossing a footbridge over a small arm of the Passaic River. Mulberry trees are common here. They were cultivated in a scheme to provide silkworms and raw silk to Paterson's textile industry. While silk manufacturing flourished, the silkworms did not. They succumbed to hard New Jersey weather. Raw silk had to be imported from Asia, then twisted and warped into fabric at Paterson mills. So successful was the business that the town was nicknamed Silk City.

Walk straight ahead to a second footbridge spanning the Passaic River. Just before crossing the bridge, look right where a large elm and hackberry tree (identified by its warty bark) cling to a basalt outcrop. Hackberry trees are air pollution resistant and often planted in cities. Watch for robins, flickers, and squirrels feeding on the tree's autumn seeds.

The gracefully arching footbridge over the Passaic gives spectacular views of the football field–wide falls and narrow gorge. In wet times, waves of white water tumble from above, crashing among broken basalt blocks far below. On sunny afternoons, a rainbow arcs up from the bottom of the gorge through the foam and mist. In dry times, the black basaltic cliffs are divided by multiple sheets, chutes, and trickles of falling water. As beautiful as this scene may be, it seems not to have impressed nineteenth-century urbanites. They often dumped trash from the cliff, using the Passaic River as an open sewer. Today, the Passaic is polluted with agricultural runoff and industrial and suburban effluent.

Beyond the bridge, walk along a wrought iron fence, descending left on steps to another impressive Great Falls overlook. Mulberry, hickory, and black locust trees (with deeply etched bark) shade the shore. Black locust grows well on depleted soils, such as those of industrial waste places. Like other legumes, its root nodules support nitrogen-fixing bacteria, which enrich nutrient poor soils.

Continue circling left around the Passaic River pool above the falls, passing by neat, nineteenth-century brick industrial buildings. The noise of the powerful falls drowns out city sounds. Huge sycamores, silver maples, and pin oaks overhang a paved bike path which swings up to Wayne Avenue.

Turn left on Wayne Avenue and follow it back over the river. Mallard ducks and herring gulls find safe haven at the pool above the falls. Both species have adapted to humans. Scavenging herring gulls feed at mid-Atlantic landfills.

After crossing the stream, swing left back onto McBride Avenue and then cross the street. Just before reaching an intersection with Spruce Street, turn right and enter a path along the Upper Raceway. Here the Society for Establishing Useful Manufactures harnessed the waters of the Passaic River. They channeled the stream's flow into a three-tiered system of raceways, turning water wheels and running mill machinery. Today, aquatic water marigolds and duckweed bloom in pools overlooked by Norway maple, elm, and hackberry.

In a few hundred feet turn left, cross a bridge over the Middle Raceway, and follow a path back to McBride Avenue. Just before reaching the street, a man-made waterfall topples from the upper raceway into the middle one. In summer, the pool beneath this artificial cascade blooms with white arrowhead.

Cross McBride Avenue and return to the Haines Overlook parking lot. Descend the stairs past the Alexander Hamilton monument to the Passaic River shore at the base of the Great Falls. From this vantage point walkers look along the 280-foot length of the gorge. We once watched a great cormorant resting on a piling here, and viewed English sparrows and starlings flitting over the water.

Pressed against the basalt cliff is the 1914 hydroelectric plant. This church-like brick building with its gracefully arched windows and steeplelike tower attests to the reverence with which American industry once regarded itself. Today, the plant has been renovated to provide electricity to local residents. From here, return to your car or take a side trip to the Paterson Museum (see sidebar).

Paterson once offered hope to rural America as it sought to grow into a world power. Today the Passaic River, which has suffered years of exploitation, proclaims a new hope. It could become a clean river at the heart of a fine urban park, where the power of the Great Falls could again be viewed in all its glory.

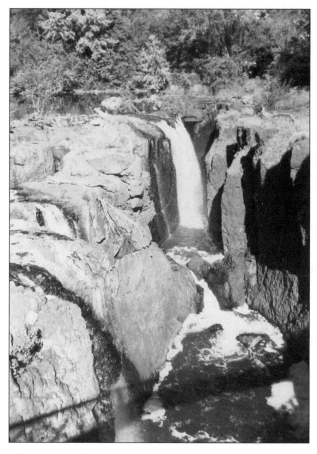

The Great Falls topple over the First Watchung Ridge at Paterson.

🪶 A SIDE TRIP TO THE PATERSON MUSEUM

At the Great Falls walkers learn why New Jersey's Piedmont, which covers just 20 percent of the state's land area, supports more than 60 percent of its population. The Piedmont's sudden elevation drops and waterfalls at places like Paterson and Trenton along the Passaic, Delaware, Black, and other rivers challenged the imagination of Yankee mill builders and attracted settlers.

Walk from Haines Overlook Park across McBride Avenue along Spruce Street. Turn left on Market Street and enter the Paterson Museum to see products born of the Great Falls and a great city. The red-brick factory housing the museum once manufactured Rogers locomotives. Paterson made 12,000 train engines for America's railroads. The museum also exhibits Colt revolvers and Holland submarines, which this teacher-turned-inventor modeled after swimming porpoises.

Most beautiful is an exhibit of basaltic minerals found at only two spots on the globe, in Paterson and India. These zeolite minerals resemble fantastic sea coral formations, white and green crystals with showy fanlike and fibrous projections. Pectolite, natrolite, apophyllite, and other mineral crystals formed within gas bubbles of cooling basalt.

An exhibit of nineteenth-century patent medicines, including Doctor Hand's Colic Mixture, Lydia E. Pinkham's Sanitive Wash, and Ayer's Sarsaparilla, is fascinating. Most are herbal remedies containing such locally gathered ingredients as yellow dock root, buckthorn bark, burdock root and gentian blossom. Some ingredients have medicinal value recognized today, some do not. Other medications packed a real wallop, containing 18 percent alcohol and morphine.

Hours, Fees, and Facilities

The falls are open dawn to dusk year-round, except when mist freezes on the footbridge, making walking hazardous. The Paterson Museum is open Tuesday through Friday 10:00 A.M. to 4:00 P.M., Saturday and Sunday 12:30 P.M. to 4:30 P.M., and closed Mondays. Suggested donation is $2.00 for adults, children free.

Getting There

From the east, take I-80 west to the 57C Paterson Main Street exit. Go left two blocks to Grand Street. Turn left and drive four blocks to Spruce Street. From the west take I-80 east to the 57B Downtown Paterson exit. Pass under I-80 to Grand Street. Turn left and drive one block to Spruce Street.

Turn right on Spruce and drive three blocks. At the intersection of Spruce Street and McBride Avenue, turn right and then immediately left into the Haines Overlook parking lot.

For More Information

Great Falls Visitor Center, 65 McBride Avenue Extension, Paterson, NJ 07501; 973-279-9587.

Paterson Museum, Thomas Rogers Building, 2 Market Street, Paterson, NJ 07501; 973-881-3874.

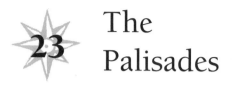

The
Palisades

Shore Trail and Long Path

- 5.5 miles
- 4.5 hours
- Elevation gain 500 feet
- Challenging; steep climb

Explore a botanical melting pot

Visitors to Palisade picnic groves in 1910 could shut their eyes and enjoy a symphony of immigrant voices. Scents of boiled cabbage, sauerbraten, and falafel floated on summer air beside the Hudson. Today trees cloak the shore, though they too represent the world. This exotic "multicultural forest" holds specimens from Europe, Asia, and beyond.

The Palisade cliffs formed about 190 million years ago when a magma wall or sill intruded between beds of Piedmont shale and sandstone. This molten rock cooled and hardened underground into diabase, contrasting with the fast-cooling surface basalts of the nearby Watchung Mountains. Like the basalts, the igneous diabase formed thin polygonal columns. It was these pillars, rising five hundred feet above the Hudson River, that caused settlers to name these cliffs the Palisades after their resemblance to wooden stockades.

The Hudson shore "under the mountain" was settled by the Dutch, who farmed its narrow bands of rich soil and sailed round-bottomed river sloops. Later settlers pitched timber from cliff tops, providing fuel for steamships.

Nineteenth-century citizens were environmentally awakened by dynamite as quarrymen blasted Palisades diabase into paving stone. The New Jersey Federation of Women's Clubs led a fight to close those quarries and save the Palisades. In 1900 these women, who had yet to win the right to vote, triumphed. They preserved fourteen miles of cliff, forming the core of Palisades Interstate Park.

The Palisades Shore Path (13.5 miles in length) parallels the cliff base, while the Long Path (which one day will run from the George Washington Bridge to the Adirondacks) follows its top. This 5.5-mile loop hike samples both trails in a strenuous but scenic walk.

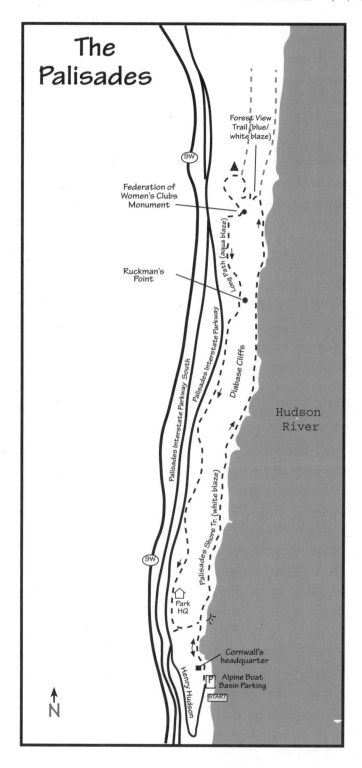

The Palisades

Forest View Trail (blue/white blaze)

9W

Federation of Women's Clubs Monument

Ruckman's Point

Long Path (aqua blaze)

Palisades Interstate Parkway

Palisades Interstate Parkway South

Diabase Cliffs

Hudson River

Palisades Shore Tr. (white blaze)

9W

Park HQ

Henry Hudson

Cornwall's headquarter

Alpine Boat Basin Parking

START

N

An ornamental Norway spruce at the far end of the Alpine Boat Basin parking lot provides a first indication that you're not in a typical American forest. This European native is easily identified by its drooping, or weeping, limbs.

Walk straight ahead past Cornwallis's headquarters (0.1 mile). The British general paused at this tavern before he and 5,000 troops climbed the cliffs in a failed attempt to headoff Washington's army in its 1776 retreat to Trenton.

A small concrete-lined stream flows into the Hudson here. Note the change in water level between the start and end of your hike. The Hudson River channel was gouged below sea level by the Wisconsin Glacier. Tidal for the lower 150 miles of its length, it is a fjord. This estuary, where fresh and salt water mix, is rich in life. Ocean shad and striped bass migrate far upriver to spawn. Once a great commercial fishery, the Hudson is now polluted with carcinogenic industrial PCBs. Pete Seeger and his Hudson River Sloop Clearwater group are leading the PCB cleanup effort.

Just past Cornwallis's headquarters, look for the white blazes of the Palisades Shore Trail as it follows a cobbled road uphill. The path enters what we called a "mixed up" deciduous forest, where native and exotic tree species rub elbows. Native hackberry, black locust, and oaks mix with Norway maple (a smog-tolerant European shade tree), ailanthus (a fast-growing Chinese species and invasive pest), and Japanese maple (a pretty Asian ornamental).

The understory also holds an erratic mix of native plants (poison ivy, joe-pye weed, and jewelweed), plus exotics (Japanese knotweed, garlic mustard and multiflora rose which drive out less hardy natives). A naturalist writing in 1959 found that 40 percent of all Palisades plants were European in origin.

At 0.2 mile ignore the blue-blazed Alpine Approach Trail leading steeply left on a cobbled road (this will be your return route). Continue on the white-blazed trail past a usually trickling waterfall, along a picturesque stone wall that offers intermittent but inspiring views of the Hudson.

The bird mix is also eclectic. Tufted titmice, warblers, and European starlings share the trees. "Bird-brained" Eugene Scheifflin deserves blame for the aggressive starling, which drives out native birds. In the 1890s, he released a hundred starlings in New York's Central Park in an attempt to introduce all the bird species mentioned in Shakespeare's plays to America. That mere hundred launched a starling takeover of the continent. Coincidentally, the pesty starling helped stem the spread of Japanese beetles, another destructive exotic. The starling invasion led to laws curbing the import of exotic species (see sidebar).

The white-blazed Shore Path leaves the cobbled road behind, rising and falling between the cliff base and the river. It alternates between difficult walking on uneven igneous diabase and easy walking on an earthen path.

The trail continues through an exotic vegetation mix. A weird topiary of clinging grape and poison ivy vines lines the riverbank. Native sweet gum and ash are joined by two odd immigrants, the royal paulownia tree and Mexican alvaradoa. The royal paulownia from China blossoms with clusters of purple flowers. The shrubby Mexican alvaradoa (with small, rounded, pinnately compound ailanthus-like leaves) should only grow south of the Rio Grande. How it found its way to the Hudson's shore is anybody's guess.

A riverside clearing amid tumbled down diabase blocks provides a spectacular view to the cliff tops at Ruckman's Point (2.2 miles). Here the five- and six-sided columnar jointing of the stone is plainly visible.

At about 2.5 miles, look for the blue-and-white blazes of the Forest View Trail leading left. This path switchbacks steeply for 500 vertical feet to the top of the cliff. Near the top, the blue-and-white trail intercepts the aqua-blazed Long Path (2.8 miles). Follow the combined trails left and south back toward Alpine.

The path rises along a shallow ravine over glacially scratched diabase slabs. Manhattan lay under the Wisconsin Glacier just 15,000 years ago. You know you've made it to the top when you get to the New Jersey Federation of Women's Clubs monument, a castle turret with views of the Hudson River (3.0 miles).

The cliff has served as a barrier to the invasion of exotics found below. On the flat, even walk south a more traditional forest of beech, red oak, hickory, and maple muffles the sound of nearby Palisades Parkway.

Follow the Long Path's aqua blazes now, ignoring the right turnoff of the blue-and-white blazed trail (3.1 miles). Short unmarked paths regularly lead left to cliff views. One of the best paths comes just past a wooden bridge and leads to Grey Crag, a mass of diabase pillars separated from the main cliff by a ravine and reached by a footbridge.

The Long Path exits the woods at the New Jersey Palisades Interstate Park Commission headquarters (5.0 miles). Follow the paved road 0.1 mile past the

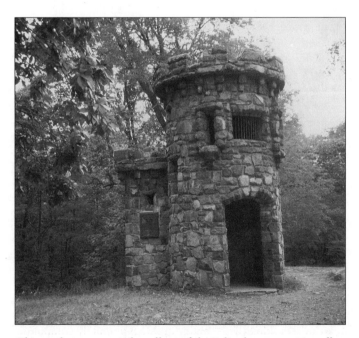

This castle turret reminds walkers of the Palisades preservation effort won by the New Jersey Federation of Women's Clubs in 1900.

building and turn left at a sign that reads Path to River. Walk straight ahead on the blue-blazed Alpine Approach Trail as the aqua Long Path turns right through a stone arch. Descend steeply to an intersection with the white-blazed Shore Trail (5.4 miles). Turn right, returning to the Alpine Boat Basin parking lot.

♦ GLOBAL DISASTER OR GLOBAL ECONOMY: THE THREAT OF EXOTIC SPECIES

The largest mass extinction since the dinosaurs is underway in Africa's Lake Victoria, as ravenous Nile perch, stocked for sport fishing, hunt 150 fish species out of existence. Birdsong has ceased on the Pacific island of Guam, where 300,000 native birds have fallen prey to the brown tree snake, unwittingly imported by our military. In 1845, a fungus accidentally imported from the U.S. doomed Ireland's potato crop and a million people in the Irish potato famine.

Exotic species are plants and animals transported beyond their home ranges, usually by people. Unopposed by predators, exotics can wreak ecological and financial havoc. At least 4,500 exotics have been established in the U.S. since Columbus landed. Some, like soybeans or the European honeybee, are beneficial to us. But about 15 percent of known U.S. exotics—more than 600 species—cause severe ecological harm.

Who is to blame? Round up the usual suspects: a population that craves imported consumer goods, from rare tropical plants to parrots and piranhas. Also blame global corporations that maximize profits by manufacturing abroad and shipping in bulk: aliens ride free on planes, boats, and trains. Also blame the globetrotting U.S. military that transports aliens on equipment.

No study has been done to estimate the number of exotics introduced worldwide. But as the distance between places shrinks and the tide of global commerce swells, the exotic species problem deepens. A 1993 congressional study declared that, if unchecked, "by the mid-21st century, biological invasions will become one of the most prominent ecological issues on Earth."

Hours, Fees and Facilities

Palisades hiking trails are open dawn to dusk.

Getting There

From the George Washington Bridge go north on the Palisades Interstate Parkway, and take Exit 2. Go east past the Palisades Park Commission headquarters and then downhill to the Alpine Boat Basin.

For More Information

Palisades Interstate Park Commission; P.O. Box 155, Alpine, NJ 07620; 201-768-1360. If interested in the Hudson River cleanup, contact Hudson River Sloop Clearwater, Inc., 112 Market Street, Poughkeepsie, NY 12601; 914-454-7673.

24 Hackensack Meadowlands

DeKorte State Park and Trash Museum

- 1.5 miles
- 1.5 hours (not including museum)
- Easy; flat

*The revival of an urban estuary within
sight of Manhattan skyscrapers*

The emblem of DeKorte State Park is the egret. It could just as appropriately be the phoenix. This wetland park—today a haven for flocks of migratory birds—arose from the ashes of terrible environmental degradation.

Fifteen thousand years ago, New Jersey's Meadowlands lay beneath the chilly waters of glacial Lake Hackensack. As the climate warmed, the ice melted, the lake drained, and the ocean rose to encircle Manhattan. By 1492 the Meadowlands were transformed into a lowland maze of meandering streams and fresh- and saltwater marshes. Vast tracts of Atlantic white cedar with trunks four feet in diameter grew to more than a hundred feet tall. The estuary supported a fabulous wealth of waterfowl, mammals, and shellfish, upon which Lenape Native Americans feasted.

Enter the Europeans. Dutch settlers arrived on the banks of the Hackensack River in 1626, driving out the Lenape. Settlers grazed cattle on salt hay and used marsh reeds as roof thatch. White cedars, covering a third of the Meadows, were cut for ship timber, fencing, casks, and churns. By the 1800s, demand for dry land led to wetland "reclamation" projects. Drainage ditches and dikes were built in endless wars against tides and muskrats. Homes and factories steadily encroached on the marsh.

By 1900, the sunken meadows and tidal creeks had become a dumping ground for raw sewage and industrial pollutants. Wildlife diversity plummeted. In the 1950s, flocks of sea gulls lurched over mountains of noxious urban garbage. Bulldozers buried tons of filth in landfills. Drainage projects and pesticide spraying temporarily controlled mosquito populations. Railroads, roads and power lines crisscrossed the dying land.

In 1968, a new sort of reclamation project was launched. With the creation of the Hackensack Meadowlands Development Commission, the rebirth of the 20,000-acre wetland began. Snap a photo at DeKorte State Park today and it's possible to capture a great egret within the same frame as the World Trade Center. This natural and man-made juxtaposition perfectly symbolizes the miracle of this urban preserve.

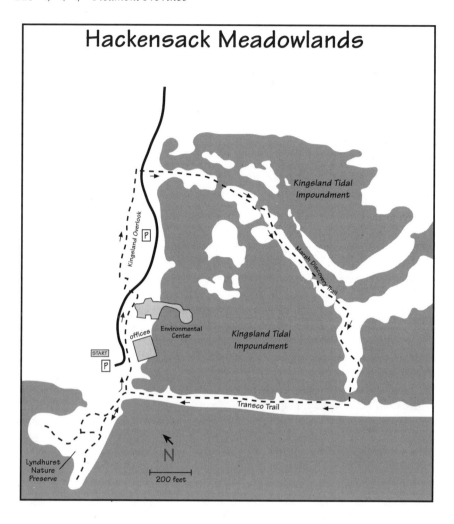

Hackensack Meadowlands

Begin this 1.5-mile walk across the parking lot from the environmental center. Follow the trail as it gently climbs a man-made mountain. The six-acre Kingsland Overlook represents a high-tech solution to the landfill reclamation problem. Tons of household waste were capped by a waterproof fabric made from 400,000 recycled soda bottles. The skin of this artificial hillside was then covered with topsoil, sewage sludge, and decomposed leaves rich in nutrients. Today, native and nonnative plants blanket the area. Kingsland Overlook is a miracle of carefully nurtured diversity.

A 0.25-mile stroll along the trail takes you on a tour of natural succession from butterfly meadow through eastern coastal grassland prairie, late woody field, young woodland, and evergreen forest. Wildflowers carpet the knoll. Flower-of-an-hour (pale yellow blossoms with a purple center), rugosa rose, morning glories, day lilies, honeysuckle (with white tubular flowers), and common mugwort (exuding a pleasant kitchen herb smell) offer up a varied pallet of rich colors and sweet scents. Sit on a bench and sniff the air while taking in the view of Manhattan.

Monarch butterfly larvae (yellow-black-and-white–striped caterpillars) browse on milkweed. This plant is toxic and unpalatable to many animals, as is the monarch butterfly. Its bright red-brown color warns would-be predators of a disagreeable meal. The nonpoisonous viceroy butterfly mimics the monarch in color and pattern in an attempt to fool feeding birds.

Kingsland Overlook is also graced by red cedar, shining sumac, gray birch, and bigtooth aspen (representing early successional trees), plus pin oak, ash, and spruce (representing later growth stages). Blue grosbeaks, mourning doves, and mockingbirds flit amid dense foliage.

The Overlook Trail descends gently, crosses a road, passes through a gate, and enters the Kingsland Tidal Impoundment on the Marsh Discovery Trail. This 0.4-mile path connects the mainland with a series of dredge-spoil islands via a wide, floating plastic boardwalk. Handrails, trash cans, and benches are made from recycled material. Explore several short side trails to bird blinds.

This estuary, where Kingsland Creek flows into the brackish Hackensack River, is a tidal wetland. Estuaries provide the lifeblood of the world's oceans. As fresh water streams mix with salt water, nutrients and oxygen are added while pollutants are removed. Estuaries offer food and shelter to two-thirds of all commercially important fish. Of the more than 12,000 square miles of salt marsh that once lined the eastern seaboard, less than 50 percent remains. New Jersey alone has lost a million wetland acres. These facts explain just how valuable the revitalized Hackensack Meadowlands ecosystem is to the world.

More than 260 migrating bird species already know the worth of the marsh. In spring, waterfowl and shorebirds stop off on their flights to northern breeding grounds. In summer, wading birds and songbirds arrive. In autumn, shorebirds stop over on their long migrations to South America. Many raptors, especially red-tailed and rough-legged hawks, and sea gulls winter in the Meadowlands.

Listen for the laughing cackle of common moorhens (marsh chickens or gallinules) as they move among the reeds. Endangered pied-billed grebe and ruddy ducks nest in dense cover. Sandpipers gather on the mud flats to feed. Snowy and great egrets stalk fish upon stiltlike legs (see sidebar). Look for raccoon, muskrat, mouse and shrew tracks along the shore at low tide.

Bird and beast seem blissfully unaware of overflying jets and the roar of Route 3 and Pulaski Skyway traffic. There's something very calming about the presence of wild animals here at the very heart of industrial civilization.

Phragmites is a dominant marsh plant. This reed propagates quickly via rhizomes, underground runners which sprout into new plants and so displace other wetland plant species. Phragmites offers scant seed to wildlife and limited nesting material and cover. Switch grass and groundsel trees (with leathery, coarsely toothed leaves and cottonlike fruit in autumn) thrive.

Visible too in the estuary are the blackened stumps of Atlantic white cedars. These trees are so rot resistant that submerged stumps have endured in Meadowlands muck hundreds of years after cutting.

About 0.8 mile into your walk the Marsh Discovery Trail intersects with the Transco Trail, a dike in which a transcontinental gas pipeline is buried. Turn right and follow a wide flat road for 0.5 mile back to the mainland. Milkweed, phlox and campion, overshadowed by black locust trees, line the Transco Trail. The showy rose mallow, a hibiscus family member, blooms in late summer.

At the end of the Transco Trail, pass through a gate and turn left into the Lynd-hurst Nature Preserve. This 3.5-acre reclaimed garbage island holds diverse habi-tats: salt marsh, beach, upland holly woodland, and pine-oak forest.

At the end of the trail, backtrack to the parking lot and environmental center. Check out the kid-friendly exhibits inside featuring VIBs (very important birds), a living salt marsh diorama, and the Trash Museum, an indescribable display that turns household waste into art.

🖋 AMONG THE GREAT EGRETS

A great egret poses statuesque in ankle-deep water. In one smooth motion it unfolds a powerful S-curved neck, dips a sharp-pointed yellow bill beneath the ripples, and snaps up a fish. In an instant it again stands utterly still. Fishing great egrets are among the most public of birds at DeKorte State Park.

These majestic all-white birds are much more private when they breed on bar-rier islands and in marshes along the Jersey coast in summer. There's a real peck-ing order to claiming the best nest sites. Great egrets bully their way into the high-est trees, bushes and reeds, pushing smaller herons and ibis into lower, places exposed to mammal and snake predators.

Parents take turns sitting on bright blue eggs, protecting them from gulls and crows, while a mate flies off in search of food. In autumn the birds migrate as far as the Gulf coast, though some winter in the Garden State.

We're lucky to have these beautiful animals. Like other wading birds, great egrets were hunted nearly to extinction by nineteenth-century plume hunters seeking to beautify ladies' hats.

Hours, Fees and Facilities

Trails are open 8:30 A.M. until dusk. They may be closed in inclement weather. The environmental center and Trash Museum are open 9:00 A.M. to 5:00 P.M. weekdays, and 10:00 A.M. to 3:00 P.M. weekends.

Getting There

From Route 3 west, take Route 17 south (Lyndhurst exit). Follow the ramp to a traffic light, and make a left on Polito Avenue for 0.6 mile to its end. At the stop sign, turn left onto Valley Brook Avenue and follow for 1.5 miles to HMDC Environmental Center. From Route 3 east, take Route 17 south (Lyndhurst—Service Road exit). At the bottom of the exit ramp is a traffic signal. Go straight through the intersection onto Polito Avenue. Follow directions above.

For More Information

Hackensack Meadowlands Development Commission Environmental Center, 2 DeKorte Park Plaza, Lyndhurst, NJ 07071; 201-460-8300.

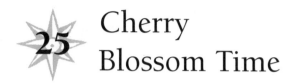

Cherry Blossom Time

Branch Brook Park, Newark

- 2 miles
- As many hours as you wish!
- Easy

Cure cabin fever with a million spring blossoms

In Japan, winter's passing is celebrated with *hanami*, literally translated as "flower looking," a few sweet, fleeting days when raucous friends and romantic couples gather to eat, drink, laugh, and sing beneath a white and pink cloud of cherry blossoms. This is a time not only of great joy, but also of spiritual rebirth.

Most Americans imagine cherry blossom time to be celebrated only in Asia or along the Tidal Basin of the Potomac River. In fact, Newark's Branch Brook Park boasts 2,700 cherry trees, and it out-blossoms Washington, D.C. every year. In mid-April, while winter still holds upland New Jersey in its fierce grip, Newark enjoys a profusion of spring color and renewed life.

Branch Brook Park itself is the product of several remarkable rebirths. In 1895, this former Civil War training ground was a tenement-encircled marsh. Old Blue Jay Swamp simultaneously supplied drinking water and sewage disposal to the city's poor. By 1900, the area was transformed into America's first county park, with a new lake and formal gardens. In that same year, John Charles Olmsted (stepson of Frederick Law Olmsted, designer of New York's Central Park) redesigned Branch Brook's landscaping along more natural lines.

In 1927, Caroline Bamberger Fuld (heir to a Newark retail fortune) donated 2,000 Japanese cherry tree seedlings to Branch Brook. But as the trees grew to maturity, Newark itself suffered from devastating urban blight. In the 1980s, the park enjoyed another rebirth, as its waterways, walkways, and playing fields were fully renovated. Today, meticulous groundskeepers spend a thousand annual hours preparing the park's cherry trees for their spring display.

Unlike most of the woodland hikes in this book, this walk requires no sturdy hiking boots or attention to trail blazes. It is best enjoyed as an aimless ramble amid the first bounties of spring.

This seasonal walk *does* require perfect timing. Arrive too early in April and you'll be greeted by bare limbs. Arrive too late, after heavy rain or wind, and you'll find only fallen blossoms. The cherry trees usually flower in the second and third

113

Branch Brook Park

weeks of April but make their showiest display for just two or three days. In Japan, weather forecasters give daily predictions of progressing cherry blossom peaks. In New Jersey, a call to the Essex County Park Commission (973-621-7199) provides the same information.

Most of the ornamental cherry trees are located in the northernmost section of the park, extending between Heller Parkway and Belleville Avenue, called the Extension Division. To begin your walk, face the visitor center and turn left, heading north along a paved pathway paralleling Park Road.

Venerable eastern deciduous trees line the way and contrast dramatically with woodland counterparts. A solitary black oak, for example, seen at a Y in the pathway next to a baseball diamond, has no need to grow tall to compete for light. This stocky tree has a short, thick trunk, above which it spreads outward in a wide, rounded crown. Sycamores (with mottled, light and dark green camouflage-style bark) and beeches (with smooth, bluish gray bark) are two of the easiest trees to spot at Branch Brook before leaves appear.

Fork left at the Y mentioned above. You immediately encounter your first Japanese cherry trees. There are six subspecies of ornamental cherry in the park. While these hybrid trees produce spectacular blossoms, they've had most of their sexual and reproductive traits bred out of them (see sidebar). Sterile flowers often produce little scent to attract pollinators and no fall fruit. They are, however, a welcome treat for winter-weary eyes.

The absence of foliage makes bird-watching easy. Look for juncos (slate gray snowbirds that winter in New Jersey's urban parks), chickadees and English sparrows. A trickle of spring warblers sometimes arrives at cherry blossom time. Palm, yellow-rumped, and pine warblers are the first to appear in April, the vanguard of a flood of songbirds arriving in May. The park boasts more than 130 bird species, including 24 types of warblers.

Robins, rooting out earthworms, are prominent on the park's greening lawns starting in March. While these red-breasted thrushes are known as harbingers of spring, global warming may be changing that. Warming trends have resulted in robins wintering not in southern states but deep within northern forests. Experienced birders have seen the birds in New Jersey Highlands woods as late as December first.

Many of the earthworms upon which robins feed in springtime are European imports. The Wisconsin Glacier froze out many New England and mid-Atlantic species. Night crawlers, large and powerful earthworms, arrived in the potting soil of European settlers and quickly colonized our highly compacted glacial soils. Besides serving as a meal for robins, the worms revitalize and aerate topsoil, moving eighteen tons of earth to the surface per acre per year.

About fifteen minutes into the walk, you arrive at Second River. Make a right and wander along the many looping pathways that play tag with this walled-in urban stream. Now you are truly in what Newark has dubbed "cherry blossom land." At peak times, a white-blossom cloud creates the illusion of a bizarre blizzard's aftermath. Tree limbs appear to be blanketed by fresh snow, while tufts of lush green grass rustle in the breeze beneath them.

The Higan cherry, or weeping Japanese cherry, with pale pink flowers and gracefully weeping crown, is one of the showiest varieties. The origin of the Yoshino cherry, one of Japan's favorite cultivated trees, is shrouded in mystery. This beautiful tall hybrid was discovered growing in Tokyo in 1872. Kwanzan, Shirofugen, Amanogawa, and Cornelian cherry trees bloom with clusters of pink-and-white flowers. The stone walls of Second River are draped in yellow cascades of forsythia, while clumps of daffodils bloom in scattered beds.

When you reach Mt. Prospect Avenue or Broadway, turn back. Cross to the north side of Second River to enjoy cherry trees and beeches on the hillside above the stream in Belleville Park. As you walk, you may encounter the Lenape Trail (blazed with a green arrowhead on a yellow background). This thirty-six-mile urban trail connects Essex County parklands between Branch Brook Park and South Mountain.

When you intersect Franklin Avenue on the west side of the park, turn left and meander back to your car at the visitor center parking lot.

❀ *A NATIONAL PASSION FOR FLOWERS*

Since ancient times, the Japanese have fostered a deep reverence for and sensitivity to nature and the changing seasons. The Shinto religion inspired peaceful gardens, where ornamental bonsai and cherry trees were cultivated for their aesthetic and spiritual value. Flower arranging became a national obsession, with each arrangement seen as a mirror of the soul.

In southern Japan (on the same latitude as Georgia), people stayed attuned to the unfolding seasons with a floral calendar. New Year's Day came in February and coincided with the first appearance of the plum blossoms. March marked the blooming of ornamental peach and cherry trees. The following months saw the appearance of wisteria, iris, lotus, hibiscus and chrysanthemum blossoms.

Patient Japanese gardeners with a keen eye for selection nurtured many ornamental flowering varieties. Fruit trees, they learned, could be cloned from a single branch, sucker, or cutting of a parent tree. Thousands of years before Gregor Mendel's studies in heredity, the Japanese employed sophisticated grafting techniques. A cutting was fastened to the stem of a tree, resulting in hybrids selected for the very showiest display of blossoms.

Today the *sakura* cherry blossom, is Japan's national flower, and the ephemeral blossoms remain a favorite of Japanese poets:

> What a strange thing!
> to be alive
> beneath cherry blossoms.
> — Kobayashi Issa (translated by Robert Hass)

Sit upon the grass beneath a Branch Brook cherry tree and pen your own haiku celebrating the miracle of spring.

Hours, Fees and Facilities

Branch Brook Park is open dawn to dusk. To avoid crowds, try to walk on a week day during cherry blossom time (usually the second or third week in April). The park sponsors a very popular Cherry Blossom Festival and run.

Getting There

From I-280 east, take the First Avenue, Newark, exit. Turn left on First Avenue, then right at the second traffic light onto Park Avenue. Make an immediate right, following signs into Branch Brook Park. Turn left on Park Road, passing around a lake and heading to the north end of the park. Visitor center parking is on the right.

For More Information

Essex County Park Commission, 115 Clifton Avenue, Newark, NJ 07104; 973-621-7199.

Cherry blossom poem credit: *The Essential Haiku: Versions of Basho, Buson & Issa,* edited by Robert Hass. Hopewell, NJ: Ecco Press, 1994. p. 156.

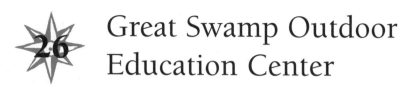

Great Swamp Outdoor Education Center

Morris County Park

- 1.5 to 3 miles
- 1 to 3 hours (avoid mosquito season in July and August)
- Easy; flat

Walk the bottom of forme glacial Lake Passaic

Like so many of America's most prized parks, the Great Swamp's 7,500 acres were only preserved due to a close brush with oblivion. Its townless and roadless inaccessibility (so loved by outdoors people today) nearly doomed it. This tangle of hardwood swamp, marsh, upland timber, river, and brook just thirty miles from Manhattan was viewed in 1959 as the ideal site for a jetport.

Some 160 million years ago, dinosaurs roamed these acres, while an impermeable layer of clay and silt was laid down. Twenty thousand to 40,000 years ago, the Wisconsin ice sheet covered northern New Jersey. Meltwater trapped between the glacier to the north and the basaltic Watchung Mountains to the south, formed glacial Lake Passaic. This thirty-mile-long and ten-mile-wide lake was 160 to 240 feet deep near the spot where you'll be hiking.

As the glacier receded 15,000 years ago, the lake drained slowly through the Watchung Mountains via the Passaic River at Paterson (see Chapter 22, p. 99). It is still draining today. Colonists skirted these wet acres, entering only to graze livestock and to harvest trees as fuel and as timber for railroad ties, fruit baskets, shingles, and Morris Canal boats.

To jetport planners this blank spot on New Jersey maps appealed. What they failed to see were the Great Swamp's 200-plus bird species (about a quarter of those found in the U.S.), 600 plant species, 18 amphibian species, 24 fish species, and 33 mammal species, including mink and river otter. A grassroots army of citizens rallied to rescue the swamp. The battle raged until 1964, when the Great Swamp National Wildlife Refuge was dedicated.

The Morris County Outdoor Education Center, with its 3.5 miles of easy trails, provides access to the easternmost section of the national refuge. Begin the hike by leaving the center and following the Orange Loop Trail.

Note immediately how water level determines plant life in the Great Swamp. A variation of a few feet in elevation means the difference between pond, swamp,

117

Great Swamp Outdoor Education Center

marsh, or dry woods. The rich former lake-bottom soil here at the swamp's edge supports tall oaks, tulip trees, hickory, and beech. Beneath their leafy canopy, mountain laurel and blueberry bushes thrive. Only about 40 percent of the Great Swamp is actual wetland.

To the right is a red maple swamp. Such wetland forests support many species of migrating birds, including Canada warblers, yellow-rumped warblers (identified by the unique golden splash atop their tails), ovenbirds, and catbirds. The slender, gray catbird lives in the deep thickets of edge environments, but it is curious and often pops into the open to get a better view. It is identified by its jumbled succession of musical and mechanical-sounding phrases, mixed with a catlike mewing call. It successfully mimics more than thirty other birds. The catbird is valuable to farmers for its voracious consumption of insect pests.

A boardwalk leads to an observation platform which looks out over a pretty pond. In springtime, painted turtles line up on logs to sun themselves (see sidebar). Beside the boardwalk, poison ivy vines climb maple saplings. In April, tussock sedge, skunk cabbage, unfolding fern fiddleheads, and cattails are renewed.

Cattails are ecologically vital to marsh health. Swamp sparrows, marsh wrens and red-winged blackbirds nest amid cattail stalks. Goldfinches line their nests with cattail down. Muskrats feed on the plant, as do painted turtles and many birds and insects. The plant had many uses among Native Americans (as bandages, dolls, and pillow stuffing), and has many more among modern people (as a source of flour, ethyl alcohol, burlap, adhesive, and rayon).

At the end of the boardwalk, the trail enters another wooded upland. Turn right on the Blue Loop Trail, passing through an understory of mountain laurel. Look to the right at the start of this trail for a swamp chestnut oak. This tree, with wavy-edged oblong leaves, was once nicknamed for its particular uses: basket oak (because its fibers were easily woven into baskets) and cow oak (for its sweet edible acorns preferred by cows).

The Blue Loop Trail curls around several open pools of water, which in springtime are filled with flitting pollywogs. The Great Swamp provides New Jersey amphibians with fine breeding habitat. The endangered blue-spotted salamander, for example, is found almost exclusively in the Great Swamp. It spends most of its year underground but emerges to breed in seasonal ponds during the first March thaw.

A tapestry of woodland wildflowers, including starflower, rue anemone, and Canada mayflower blossom here. The moisture-loving Canada mayflower, with its glossy, heart-shaped leaves and delicate cluster of white flowers, spreads via underground runners (called rhizomes) from which many clones sprout, colonizing the forest floor.

When the Blue Loop Trail returns to the Orange Loop Trail, turn right on the branch of the Orange Loop Trail that begins closest to the boardwalk. This inner loop skirts the edge of the wetlands. The trail crosses a disturbed area beneath a power line where phragmites, topped by seed-covered plumes, are taking over the swamp. Phragmites, a plant with little nutritional value, drives out native cattails and other marsh plants, forming a monoculture and destroying wetland diversity.

The path now goes onto another boardwalk over a wet area lined with horsetail rushes, Virginia rose, cinquefoil, skunk cabbage, and sensitive fern. If you are here in May, this is the place to stop and enjoy spring beauties. These tiny, pinkish white flowers speckle the swamp.

The Orange Loop Trail returns to the outdoor center. You've now walked about 1.5 miles. If you want to extend your walk, follow the red-blazed Pioneer Loop to your right just before reaching the center. This trail, named for the AT&T corporate volunteer group who built it, wanders through a wet woodland where we saw ribbon snakes (resembling garter snakes, but with narrow heads and bodies), a great blue heron taking wing, and blooming Mayapple.

As the Pioneer Loop Trail returns to the Outdoor Education Center, follow the Green Loop Trail right as it passes through a drier upland forest where white-tailed deer have left tracks in soil that once lined the bottom of glacial Lake Passaic. Back at the parking lot, walk out to the bird blind that overlooks the pond. As you sit, try to imagine the irrevocable loss if the flight patterns of migratory songbirds had been sacrificed to those of Boeing 747s.

❧ *TURTLE TALK*

A turtle's shell is an ancient structure; turtles witnessed the rise and fall of the dinosaurs. Fused with vertebrae and ribs, the shell can never be shed the way a lobster, for example, molts its exoskeleton. Instead, the shell grows outward and thickens as the turtle grows.

The bird blind at the edge of the pond is the perfect place from which to observe turtles. Painted turtles regularly bask in the sun atop logs and rocks. With binoculars, look for red and yellow stripes on the sides of these turtles' heads and necks. These reptiles have good vision; the slightest movement on shore will prompt them to slide into open-water safety.

Snapping turtles also inhabit this pond, though they mostly stay submerged. In early summer, female painted turtles and snappers lay eggs in holes they excavate on dry land. Heat from the sun incubates the eggs. A cool summer (averaging below 88°F) will result in most of the eggs developing into males; warmer temperatures produce mostly female hatches. A late-season clutch of eggs, or even the hatchlings, may spend the winter underground.

Mostly vegetarian, painted turtles occasionally eat decaying animal matter. Snappers are mostly carnivorous, but will occasionally have a salad of aquatic vegetation. In winter, both species burrow into the mud and hibernate. Breathing ceases, and the turtle's heart may beat only once every ten minutes. In spring, when the water becomes warmer than the mud at the pond's bottom, the turtles awaken from their suspended animation.   —sidebar by Jean LeBlanc

Hours, Fees and Facilities

Trails are open dawn to dusk year-round (though insects are fierce in July and August). The center is open daily from September to June and has nature walks and other environmental activities.

Getting There

From I-287 south in Morristown take the Madison Avenue exit, turning left at the end of the ramp onto Route 124. From I-287 north take the South Street exit, go left and immediately right onto Route 124. Follow Route 124 east into Madison. Go under a small railroad bridge, and at the second light turn right onto Green Village Road. Continue straight ahead through three lights, then go another mile. The Great Swamp Outdoor Education Center is on the right

For More Information

Great Swamp Outdoor Education Center, 247 Southern Boulevard, Chatham, NJ 07928; 973-635-6629.

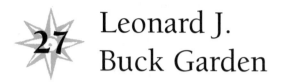

27 Leonard J. Buck Garden

Somerset County Park

- 1.5 miles
- 2 hours
- Easy

*Explore lava flows and an extinct waterfall landscaped
by a fantastic garden*

Interstate Route 287 shoots through a gap in the Second Watchung Mountain near Far Hills. The highway pursues the path of least resistance, a low spot in the igneous basalt ridge. During the last Ice Age a mighty river took advantage of the same gap as it rushed out of glacial Lake Passaic, tumbled over a great waterfall, and surged out to meet the Raritan River on the Piedmont plain.

The mile-high Wisconsin ice sheet melted away 15,000 years ago, no longer damming the 200-foot-deep Lake Passaic. The lake found a new outlet, flowed south into the Passaic River, looped northeast, and passed through the Watchungs at the Great Falls of Paterson (see chapter 22). The thirty-mile-long glacial lake eventually drained, becoming the Great Swamp (see chapter 26). The spectacular waterfall at Far Hills faded into prehistory, its dry riverbed a landmark only in the lore of New Jersey geologists. A tiny stream, Moggy Brook, zigzagged among the igneous outcroppings that once marked the falls.

In the 1930s the magic of Moggy Hollow was rediscovered by Leonard J. Buck. This mining engineer purchased the old riverbed as part of his estate. When he discovered the land's fascinating geological roots he resolved to turn the spot into one of the Northeast's premier rock gardens. Buck and landscape architect Zenon Schrieber used high-powered hoses to clear away stony debris and dynamite to expose and sculpt the relict waterfall. The unique garden they nurtured among the basalt lava flows offered a sensuous contrast between native plantings and exotics gathered from around the world. In 1976, Buck's widow donated the garden to Somerset County.

Today, Buck Garden is a thirty-three-acre pleasure garden where groomed paths meander between rock outcrops, around lily-pad-covered pools, over rainbow bridges, and amid woodland wildflowers, bulbs, azaleas, ferns, and heathers. This is also a fine place to learn trees, since most are labeled.

Leonard J. Buck Garden

Begin your walk at the upper parking lot. A deeply furrowed black locust rises in the courtyard of the visitor center (once the Buck family carriage house). This Appalachian native tree was almost wiped out by the Wisconsin Glacier. With human help it has more than reclaimed its range. Black locusts are planted as ornamentals from Maine to California. They were also exported to France in the 1700s and are now one of Europe's most common American trees.

Pass through the visitor center and walk straight ahead into a rhododendron grove where Virginia bluebells and shocking-pink bleeding hearts show off their drooping blossoms in springtime. The path quickly reaches the top of Big Rock. This basalt outcrop forms one wall of Moggy Hollow and is the northern remnant of the extinct waterfall. A small, grassy vista looks over the Lower Pond. To the left of the pond are Reno Rock, New Rock, and Horseshoe Rock which once formed an island at the center of the great cataract. Opposite the pond is Polypody Rock, the former southern side of the falls.

Continue straight ahead beneath towering hemlocks. Native Christmas fern thrives amid cultivated plum-leafed azalea and Japanese painted fern (with its alternate leaflets).

Turn right just before reaching Reno Rock and walk among Japanese jack-in-the-pulpit, which sports green berries in autumn instead of the red of our American variety. Native Solomon's seal, hay-scented fern, early saxifrage, and white snakeroot adorn the ground, while witch hazel, chestnut oak, and mockernut hickory fill out the canopy above. Legend has it that Mr. Buck jokingly named Reno Rock after the Nevada "divorce capital" when his wife warned him that she would not tolerate another landscaping dynamite blast.

Pass beneath New Rock and Horseshoe Rock (you're now at the base of the prehistoric falls) and curve left into the Azalea Field, with its many seasonal planting beds. Buck Garden is renowned for its early plantings of spring bulbs, big drifts of purple-spiked salvia, and winter aconite, blooming in late March and early April. The garden is also acclaimed for its display of woodland flowers in May, when trilliums mix with the pinks and whites of native and hybrid azaleas. The summer and fall boast a steady progression of colorful blossoms.

Bordering the left side of this little meadow is a small copse of trees. Look for a shagbark hickory, white ash, Hercules'-club, and rare Franklinia tree. A single grove of Franklinia (named for Benjamin Franklin) was discovered growing wild in 1765 near Georgia's Alatamaha River. Botanists collected seeds before the grove disappeared around 1790. The Franklinia now exists only in cultivation and is valued for its showy white, cup-shaped blossoms, appearing in autumn.

Just past a small shed on the left is a red buckeye tree. This North Carolina native grows this far north only when planted here. Its bright red flowers caused it to be nicknamed the "firecracker plant." Its polished bronze-colored seeds are poisonous and were ground up by Native Americans into a powder which, when dumped into still water, stunned fish, making them easy to catch.

At the far end of the Azalea Field a wide path called the Big Walk leads past a tall white oak and into a deciduous forest. The trail parallels Moggy Brook for a

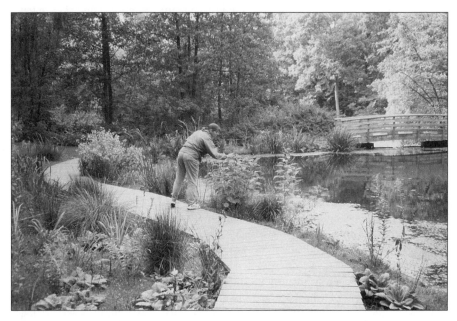

The Lower Pond provides a wet micro climate for river birch and cardinal flower.

short distance, then sweeps uphill in a lazy S curve. Opposite a bench at the first turn is a large basswood tree. Also called the American linden, the basswood can grow to 100 feet tall and has long served humankind with sweet honey made from its flower nectar, a soothing tea steeped from its dried blossoms, and carvings made from its workable, light-colored wood.

A stone wall beside the Big Walk is covered in Kingsville box, looking like a furry green "Chia Pet." Asters and goldenrod spot the open forest floor in autumn. The exposed basalt of the Second Watchung Mountain also lines the path. This material burst from the earth about 200 million years ago as immense waves of molten lava, which then hardened into tough igneous stone. Notice how the basalt fractures into polygonal columnar shapes. Long quarried for paving stone, this igneous rock often forms natural staircases, possibly explaining why it is some-times called traprock. *Trappen* is Dutch for "step."

After about 0.3 mile, the Big Walk reaches a dead end. Return the way you came, cross the Azalea Field, then turn left and pass over Moggy Brook on a wood-en bridge. Another left leads up onto Polypody Rock, where bloodroot and rue anemone bloom in spring. Spreading Canadian hemlock (looking like a bonsai-ed Eastern hemlock) grows just two feet tall.

Circle completely around the Lower Pond to enjoy the moist micro climate created by Leonard Buck. River birch (with its acne-like flaking bark) and cardinal flower (with scarlet blooms in late summer) flourish at the edge of the pond, while water shamrock (an aquatic fern that looks like a floating four-leaf clover) rises from the bottom of the pool.

Take the Primrose Path past Fern Rock and beneath Big Rock back toward the visitor center. Enjoy the contrasting textures of the Fern Garden. Japanese toad lilies with star-shaped blooms, ostrich fern with graceful plumelike leaves, and English lady fern are planted here.

Before climbing the wooden stair back to the visitor center, notice the stately conifer with feathery needles growing beside the path. This tree is Buck Garden's greatest treasure. It is a dawn redwood, or metasequoia. This majestic tree was once the most abundant conifer in western North America, then was devastated by Pleistocene glaciers. Thought to be extinct, only fossil evidence of the dawn redwood was known until the 1944 discovery of a single tree enshrined by the people of the remote Chinese village of Mo-tao-chi. A 1948 expedition to China located one grove of a thousand metasequoias, the last remnant of the species. Seedlings sent to the Arnold Arboretum in Boston, Massachusetts, were distributed worldwide. Today, this living fossil again grows on the North American continent where its ancestors ruled, and at Buck Garden where an extinct river and waterfall once drained the now vanished glacial Lake Passaic. Thus, this pleasure garden preserves the treasures of an ancient age.

Hours, Fees and Facilities

Buck Garden is open from 10:00 A.M. to 4:00 P.M. Monday through Friday, 10:00 A.M. to 5:00 P.M. on Saturday, and noon to 5:00 P.M. on Sunday. It is closed during December, January, and February on weekends and major holidays. A $1.00 donation is requested.

Getting There

From I-287 take Exit 22 if approaching from the north, or Exit 22B if approaching from the south, onto US 202/206 north. Stay right on US 202, following signs for Morristown and Far Hills. At the Far Hills train station turn right just before reaching the railroad tracks onto Liberty Corner–Far Hills Road. In 0.9 mile turn right onto Layton Road. Buck Garden is on the left.

For More Information

Buck Garden, Somerset County Park Commission, Horticulture Department, 11 Layton Road, Far Hills, NJ 07931; 908-234-2677.

28 Delaware and Raritan Canal State Park

Kingston to Rocky Hill

- 4 miles
- 3 hours
- Easy; flat and rock-free

Hike into history along a shady canal towpath

The red shale, sandstone, and argillite formations of the Piedmont, stretching between Trenton and New Brunswick, rise to a mere 57 feet above sea level. This so-called "narrow waist" of New Jersey—just 44 miles wide—long tempted entrepreneurs as a potential canal shortcut between Philadelphia and New York City.

While William Penn may have dreamed of a water crossing of the narrow waist, it wasn't until 1830 that the project got launched. By then, the Erie Canal had shown the way, and canal building was all the rage in America.

Three thousand Irish immigrants, many brought to the U.S. by the canal company, were paid a dollar a day to hand-dig the Delaware and Raritan (D&R) Canal. They shoveled from dawn to dusk, cutting through forest and farmland little changed since colonial days. Long hours, inadequate sanitation and poor food led to an 1832 Asiatic cholera epidemic that killed hundreds of these laborers.

The unsung, unmarked graves of Irish immigrants contrasted sharply with the triumphal canal opening of 1834. Governor Peter Vroom and friends sailed their official barge along the canal, hailed by cheering crowds. Their trip ended with a twenty-four-gun salute at New Brunswick. The D&R Canal boomed. Mule-drawn boats gave way to steam tugs. Civil War gunboats passed through, heading south. In 1871 the canal hauled nearly 3 million tons of freight, surpassing the Erie Canal.

Railroad competition finally killed the D&R in 1932. Today the "big ditch," once the pride of American industrialists, is a fifty-eight-mile-long greenway and state park where Piedmont flora and 200 bird species flourish. The park includes a thirty-six-mile stretch beginning near Bordentown and ending at New Brunswick, plus a twenty-two-mile feeder canal on the Delaware River (see chapter 29).

This 4.0-mile circuit hike passes along both sides of the tree-shaded D&R Canal between the sleepy towns of Kingston and Rocky Hill, and explores the flood plain of the Millstone River.

126

Delaware & Raritan Canal State Park

D&R Canal

ROCKY HILL

518

rock outcrop

canal towpath

old railroad bed

Millstone River

river flood plain

START

P

KINGSTON

27

N

From the Kingston parking lot, follow the path north through a tunnel beneath Route 27. A short, unmarked side trail leads left to the Millstone River. Be careful if you decide to venture down the unmarked path. This is a "look but don't touch" forest. Flood plain silver maples and red maples are draped with light-loving poison ivy vines (see sidebar). Leaves of three, let it be!

Follow the main trail as it swerves right, uphill, onto the wide canal towpath. Here, teenage boys and girls in bare feet once led mule teams pulling boats loaded with tons of coal. Each canal boat was guided by a tillerman who blew on a conch shell horn to notify lock and bridge tenders of his approaching boat. Wives typically lived on board in cramped quarters with their families.

The canal towpath plays tag with the Millstone River for the next 1.8 miles. The flood plain to your left is covered in a classic northern deciduous flood plain forest. Black cherry, black locust, red and silver maple, elm and ash trees are nourished by the seasonal spill of water and rich silt overflowing the Millstone's banks. Each tree finds its particular niche, depending on how much moisture it can stand. The forest floor is a tangled vine community. Poison ivy, Virginia creeper, Asiatic bittersweet, greenbrier, wild grape, and climbing hemp weed are resilient vines which recover quickly from annual floods.

Black oak, black locust, and sycamore trees hang over the canal, making a grab for sunlight and forming a cool green tunnel. The canal didn't always look like this. In the 1800s trees were cut from banks to allow passage of mules and boats. Canalers endured sun and rain six days a week, sunrise to sunset.

This habitat is a boon for wildlife. In the canal, bluegill, pumpkinseed, and red-breasted sunfish dodge largemouth bass and chain pickerel. Shad sometimes wander into the D&R from the Delaware River. Mallards, cormorants and herons patrol quiet waters. Dead flood plain trees provide hollow cavities for raccoons, opossums, kingfishers and woodpeckers. The dense flood plain undergrowth contrasts drastically with the open farmlands that surround the greenway, offering shelter for mammals and birds in winter.

Just before reaching Rocky Hill, the canal again approaches the Millstone, where open rock slabs overlook the river. This is a fine, sunny lunch spot. Here we found broken freshwater clamshells, the remains of a favorite meal of seagulls and raccoons. In springtime, the Millstone rises and becomes one of New Jersey's most enjoyable canoeing rivers.

At 1.9 miles, the towpath passes through a gate into the town of Rocky Hill. Turn right, cross the canal on Route 518, then turn right again, following a wide path south along the far side of the canal back toward Kingston.

Just to the left of the Rocky Hill canal towpath gate is a large sycamore or buttonwood tree, with its camouflage-style bark. Sycamores grow quickly (seventy feet in seventeen years) and display greater girth than other American deciduous trees. A Belvidere, New Jersey, specimen is eight feet in diameter. The core of older trees sometimes rots out, leaving a deep hollow at the base of the still living tree. Such cavities can hold several people standing up. Native Americans once made sycamores into huge dugout canoes.

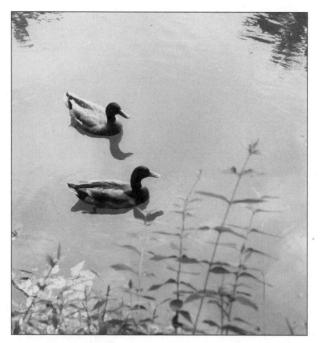

Mallard ducks frequently patrol the D&R Canal in search of succulent vegetation.

The tranquillity of this portion of the hike is marred by the noise of the near-by Traprock Industries quarry (which provided the trail corridor on this side of the canal). The quarry exploits an underground diabase seam that rises to overlook the Hudson River as the Palisades (see chapter 23). This igneous rock was first dug here in the 1860s, providing crushed paving stone for Jersey City and Newark. If you have time, explore Rocky Hill, a nineteenth-century village that supported farmers with its gristmill, sawmill, taverns, and general stores.

You are now following the abandoned right-of-way of a spur of the Camden and Amboy Railway, built in 1864. Note that the fields and forest to your left are much drier. The canal's embankments have artificially defined the boundary between Millstone River flood plain and surrounding upland ever since its construction in the 1830s.

The trail passes through disturbed quarry lands populated by native plants (black locust, speckled alder, and red cedar saplings) and exotics (ailanthus, catalpa, and royal paulownia trees). This open land is slowly progressing through field succession as it returns to forest.

At 2.5 miles, the old railroad bed enters a woods where black willow and locust trees overhang the canal, shading smaller river birches and tickseed sunflowers. To the left, an upland forest of mulberry, pignut, and mockernut hickory shades Asiatic dayflower, goldenrod, and evening primrose.

The path reaches the parking lot of the John W. Flemer Preserve in Kingston at 3.9 miles. Turn right and cross the canal on Route 27, returning to the parking lot and your car on the left (use the tunnel to avoid traffic).

🌰 *POISON IVY: OUR BANE AND NATURE'S BOON*

While New Jersey long ago eliminated or controlled many woodland "enemies"— wolves, panthers and rattlesnakes—one perceived pest persists. Poison ivy abounds as creeping ground cover; low leafy shrub; and frayed, ropelike vine. This hardy plant grows in all kinds of soil, and is shade tolerant but comes into its own in bright sun, making it a common trailside companion. Its red rash and persistent itch (caused by people's allergic reaction to a chemical called uroshiol) have ruined many hiker sojourns.

But as you spread on the calamine lotion or jewelweed juice (a soothing Native American remedy), consider that poison ivy is extremely valuable to the forest community.

More than sixty bird species feast on the plant's autumn white berries. In fact, it is believed that poison ivy leaves turn bright red as a bold announcement of this bounty (called "fall foliar flagging" by botanists). Feeding grouse, pheasants, warblers and flickers pass the seeds straight through their digestive systems, spreading poison ivy plants out over the landscape. Insects feed actively on poison ivy foliage and pollinate its flowers. Rabbits browse the plant in winter, a pruning that causes it to branch out ever more luxuriant each spring.

Hours, Fees and Facilities

The park is open year-round.

Getting There

From I-287 at Bridgewater, take US 206 south to Princeton, then go left (north) on NJ 27 to Kingston. Parking is on the right, just before the canal crossing.

For More Information

Delaware and Raritan Canal State Park, 625 Canal Road, Somerset, NJ 08873; 732-873-3050. To volunteer in the restoration of the state's canals, contact the Canal Society of New Jersey, P.O. Box 737, Morristown, NJ, 07963; 908-722-9556.

29 Delaware River at Prallsville

Delaware and Raritan Canal State Park

- 6.5 miles (3.3 miles with a car shuttle)
- 3 to 4 hours
- Moderate; level

A canal and railroad walk along and over the Delaware River

Before there were roads, there were rivers. People traveled upon their flood, rafting raw materials to market and sailing home with manufactured goods. Farmers relied on alluvial soils for fertile cropland. Industrialists depended on water power to spin mill wheels, grind grain into flour, and saw timber into lumber. America's first towns, cities, canals, and railroads rose along its rivers.

The Delaware River, in its seeming disdain for topography, made a fine early American road. In its 280 miles the stream shoulders its way across all five New Jersey physiographic provinces: gouging through the Ridge and Valley region at the Water Gap, cutting across Highland cliffs at Riegelsville, pushing through the Piedmont at Trenton Falls, spreading over the Inner Coastal Plain at Philadelphia, and widening into a bay on the Outer Coastal Plain.

Native Americans canoed the Delaware's waters, commuting from coast to interior. The Swedes settled at its mouth in the 1650s, while William Penn colonized its middle reaches in 1681 and the Dutch its upper valley by 1700.

Daniel Skinner was the first to bring a timber raft down the Delaware in 1764, converting its pine logs into ship masts and a pretty profit at Philadelphia. Immense arks, laden with anthracite coal, followed in 1806. The Delaware and Raritan (D&R)Canal bypassed the risks of river navigation in 1834. Shore-hugging railroads and highways came later, penetrating the Delaware Water Gap by the 1860s.

Bruce Stutz, writing of these years in his book *Natural Lives, Modern Times*, declares that "the Delaware grew into one great river village that went upstream to fetch the wood, fuel, and water to build its downstream industries." Many river towns blossomed. "It was a world of local mills, local foods, local parades...of village philosophers and immigrant inventors with big ideas."

This 6.6-mile-out-and-back walk begins at one of these nineteenth-century river villages. The hike also passes along two canals and a railroad and crosses the Delaware River on a scenic footbridge.

Delaware River at Prallsville

Begin by exploring Prallsville, the epitome of an old river town. Wickecheoke Creek flows into the Delaware here, and the stream's tumbling waters offered power to the first gristmill, built in 1711. Later water-powered Prallsville businesses cut lumber, quarried stone, made linseed oil, harvested river fish, and traded with local farmers. An 1877 mill and other buildings still stand at this spot, and the Delaware River Mill Society offers occasional tours.

The Delaware and Raritan Canal also ran through Prallsville, crossing the Wickecheoke Creek on an aqueduct. After 1834, raw materials and finished goods flowed through this feeder canal, which ran for 22 miles from Bull's Island to Trenton, and then across New Jersey for 44 miles to New Brunswick (see chapter 28). The railroad came to town in 1850.

After exploring the town, walk north, crossing Wickecheoke Creek on a bridge and following the roadbed of the Belvidere and Delaware Railroad. The crushed-stone treadway offers smooth, easy footing. Pay attention; you'll be sharing this multi-use trail for the entire walk with bicyclists and joggers. This is also a good cross-country ski trail in winter.

A moisture-loving forest of sycamore, black locust, sassafras and silver maple immediately closes in. Most noticeable are river birches, their flaky, peeling, cinnamon red bark looking like a terminal case of acne. This southern tree supports a southern bird, the yellow-throated warbler, which is at the northern limits of its range. Yellow-throated and cerulean warblers use the river birch's shredded bark for nesting material.

The right side of the rail bed is edged by a neatly cut stone wall. This Stockton Formation sandstone was quarried nearby and makes fine building stone. Princeton's Nassau Hall and Rutgers's Old Queens building are both faced with this Triassic brownstone. To the left, there are good canal views.

The wide path alternates between a well-shaded green tunnel and an open corridor. The forest to the left is an impenetrable jungle of Virginia creeper, poison ivy, wild grape, honeysuckle, and Asiatic bittersweet. Note the vine scars on large sweet birch and white ash trees. These deep etchings, alternating with thick bulges, wind around trees in barber-pole spirals and show where vines once climbed the trees seeking sunlight and support.

As the forest becomes drier, white ash, black walnut, bitternut, and shagbark hickory rise above flowering dogwood and box elder trees. The fast-growing box elder is in the maple family and produces high-quality syrup, which Native Americans made into sugar.

In late summer the trailside herbaceous layer is a colorful embroidery of purple-flowering raspberry, knapweed, evening primrose, and zigzag goldenrod with its characteristic stem twist at each yellow flowering cluster.

The railroad bed crosses a major stream (1.4 miles), from which you can look past large elms down to the D&R Canal and Delaware River. It's easy to climb down to the stream and find a quiet lunch spot. Watch for poison ivy.

Now the path runs much closer to Route 29 than it does to the D&R Canal. The bothersome road noise made me wish that the state would restore the overgrown canal towpath, creating a more secluded riverside hiking trail.

At 3.0 miles the old railroad bed arrives at a gate. Turn left on the paved road and pass over the canal onto Bull's Island. The flood guard lock here marks the northern terminus of the D&R Canal.

In 0.1 mile you arrive at the pedestrian bridge over the Delaware River. On your left, just before you cross the bridge, stands a large silktree (also called mimosa). This Asian ornamental, growing with native oaks and hickories, has delicate, feathery leaves and pink flowers in summer. Young leaves in spring shrink away at a person's touch.

The pedestrian bridge takes you high above the Delaware, offering spectacular river views. This ancient stream once hosted migrating giant sturgeon and still welcomes spawning shad each spring. This river, so rich in history, continues to be vital to the region. Its water slakes the thirst of 20 million people, with 700 million gallons alone going to New Yorkers every day.

As you cross the suspension bridge, look for a thousand silken threads glistening in the sun. Spiders fasten their wheel-shaped orb webs to bridge cables. Each tiny protein thread possesses greater tensile strength than steel. The webs not only catch unwary insects, they also act as dish antennae, magnifying and communicating vibrations to spiders, which have poor eyesight.

Wickecheoke Creek where it flows over a dam into the Delaware River.

On the far shore, the footbridge passes over Pennsylvania's Delaware Canal (completed in 1834), then puts you on firm ground inside the picturesque hamlet of Lumberville. The Lumberville Store (left 100 feet on Route 32) has fresh deli sandwiches and sodas, collectibles, and local artisan jewelry. For those desiring more elegant fare, the Black Bass Hotel serves sea scallops with wild mushroom compote and champagne vanilla sauce. Beginning as a hotel in 1745, this establishment regularly welcomed Grover Cleveland, who sneaked away from his presidency for fishing trips.

Return the way you came, across the bridge into New Jersey and to Prallsville. For those wishing to use a two-car shuttle to shorten this hike, there is a trail parking lot located at Bull's Island just off Route 29.

Back in Prallsville, take the time to stroll a few yards south of the mill and to enjoy a beautifully maintained nineteenth-century herb garden where coneflower, flax, wormwood, thyme and patchouli grow. Such gardens once provided settlers with spices, teas and tonics. The plants grown here still extend the hope of cures. Modern health-food stores stock coneflower as echinacea, an immune system booster. Flaxseed (known as linseed oil) is purported to lower cholesterol, wormwood to kill parasites, and thyme to ease the digestive system. Patchouli is a mainstay of aroma therapy and claimed to establish calm and balance. The little garden at the end of your walk, with its fluorescent purple plumes of amaranth, is also likely to bring about calm.

Hours, Fees and Facilities

The Delaware and Raritan Canal State Park is open dawn to dusk year-round. The Prallsville Grist Mill is leased by the Delaware River Mills Society and is open occasionally in summer for tours. Call for times. There is state-park camping at Bull's Island; first come, first served. Advance camping reservations can be made with the park by mail or in person (two-night minimum, fourteen-night maximum, $10 per night and $7 prereservation fee). Call for information.

Getting There

Take I-95 south to NJ 29 north at the Delaware River. The Prallsville Grist Mill is about 4 miles north of Lambertville on the left. Bull's Island is three miles farther north and also provides trail parking on the left.

For More Information

Bull's Island State Recreation Area, 2185 Daniel Bray Highway, Route 29, Stockton, NJ 08559; 609-397-2949.

To volunteer with the Delaware River Mills Society, write P.O. Box 298, Stockton, NJ 08559; 609-397-3586.

Inner and Outer Coastal Plain Provinces

30 Holmdel Park and Longstreet Farm

Monmouth County Park

- 4.1 miles (plus 1.0 mile for farm and arboretum)
- 3 hours
- Moderate; some hilly terrain

Enjoy the sights, sounds, and smells
of nineteenth-century farm life

New Jersey's coastal plain was born out of a dance between land and sea. Starting about 135 million years ago, ancient rivers dumped sediments brought from eroding uplands. The ocean then rose, covering the sediments and leaving behind clay, silt, sand, and gravel. This process of sediment deposition and ocean encroachment was repeated many times over millions of years. Today, the plains have again risen above sea level.

Dividing the Inner from the Outer Coastal Plain are the *cuestas*, low, gravel-capped ranges of hills rising a few hundred feet above the otherwise flat landscape and running in a diagonal line from the Atlantic Ocean to Delaware Bay. You can follow the cuestas by tracing town names on a road map southwesterly from Atlantic Highlands through Hillsdale, Mount Holly, Mount Laurel and Mullica Hill. These hills, capped by peanut-colored pebbles, are more erosion resistant than surrounding clay and sand lowlands.

Sitting astride a cuesta in Monmouth County is Holmdel Park, the site of Longstreet Farm. Established in 1775 as a subsistence farm growing all its own produce, it had by 1890 shifted to the harvesting of potatoes as a cash crop. In the twentieth century it flourished as a dairy farm. In 1967 Monmouth County purchased and preserved the farm as Holmdel Park.

136

wooden
bridge

marsh
viewing
area

High Point Trail
(blue-blazed)

Marsh Trail
(yellow-blazed)

program
building

lawn

tennis courts,
playground,
and picnic area

P3

Ridge Walk Trail
(green-blazed)

Ridge Walk Trail
(green-blazed)

Beech Glen Trail
(green-blazed)

START

P2

Longstreet Road

upper
pond

shelter
building

P1

Longstreet
Farm

lower
pond

Arboretum

Arboretum

Roberts Rd.

N

TO
RTE. 34

Holmdel Park & Longstreet Farm

This 4.1-mile loop walk circles through hilly deciduous woods which once served as the croplands, pastures, and orchards of Longstreet Farm. The hike ends with a tour of the farm complex, where interpreters dressed in period costume demonstrate 1890s agricultural life (see sidebar).

Begin at parking lot #2, which is lined by sugar maple and Norway maple. It's easy to differentiate these two trees in autumn. The Norway maple, a European shade tree, stays green long after the sugar maple has gone golden.

Leave the parking lot at the corner farthest from where you drove in. Head uphill through a meadow toward treeline. In 0.1 mile you'll pass the Fitness Trail. Continue to the left along a road lined by a split-rail fence and passing a sign that says Trails Straight Ahead. Follow the green-blazed Beech Glen Trail into deep woods.

This beautiful forest trail passes among stately stands of pignut and mocker-nut hickory, tulip tree, sweet birch, and oak. Dogwood, sassafras, shrubby arrow-wood and sweet pepperbush compose the understory.

The sandy path sinks deep into the glen and parallels a brook (0.3 mile). The highlight of this stroll is a magnificent stand of American beech, the favorite tree of tufted titmice, Acadian flycatchers and red-shouldered hawks. Mammals feast on beechnuts, and you'll find plentiful gray squirrels here. Look, too, for the broad beech fern, with wide triangular leaves.

Beech trees, with their smooth tombstone gray bark, unfortunately have attracted graffiti carvers for centuries (the Anglo-Saxon root for "beech" and "book" is the same word, points out John Eastman in his fine field guide *The Book of Forest and Thicket*). This vandalism, common at Holmdel, is not only ugly, it allows the easy introduction of wood-rot fungi into the trees.

Farm life at Longstreet Farm, circa 1890.

Beeches primarily propagate through cloning. Mature trees send underground runners called rhizomes out from their base, from which genetically identical replicas sprout. In winter, young beeches hang onto their leaves, which shrink into rice-paper-thin rolls and rustle eerily in icy winds.

The trail crosses bridges over intermittent streams, then turns right and climbs uphill. At 0.6 mile the Beech Glen Trail ends at a paved road. Walk straight ahead, crossing both the road and the blue-blazed Cross-Country Ski Trail. In a few yards you intersect the green-blazed Ridge Walk Trail. Turn left.

The Ridge Walk Trail follows the crest of a *cuesta*, a Spanish word for a hill with one gently sloping and one steep side. This *cuesta* forms the divide between two watersheds and between the Inner and Outer Coastal Plains. The trail parallels the paved road and passes among more beech trees, black tupelo, white oak and chestnut oak.

At 0.9 mile the Ridge Walk Trail reaches a parking lot and turns right, passing a playground and tennis courts. As the green-blazed Ridge Walk Trail continues straight ahead, turn left on the blue-blazed High Point Trail (1.1 mile).

The High Point Trail follows a treeline past light-loving shining sumac, sassafras and bigtooth aspen. Here we saw autumn witch hazel trees in full bloom, with their yellow flowers looking exactly like shredded cheddar cheese.

The trail re-enters the beech forest and descends on a sandy path. It levels off and swings right at 1.5 miles to parallel a deeply etched stream bed. Take a brief detour left onto a large wooden bridge crossing the stream. This is a nice spot for a snack or water break. The area is blanketed by wood aster, wild rose, partridge-berry and Indian cucumber-root. In spring look for pink lady's slippers.

Continue on the blue-blazed High Point Trail as it veers sharply right away from the stream and climbs gently. Watch closely for the yellow-blazed Marsh Trail at about 1.9 miles. Turn left. The Marsh Trail quickly feeds into a boardwalk which passes through a wetland where the spindly trunks of speckled alder rise above jewelweed, joe-pye weed, sensitive fern and tickseed sunflower. A viewing platform gives birders a chance to study songbirds and waterfowl.

A short dead-end trail leads left going deeper into the wetland. The Marsh Trail continues on a boardwalk, passes briefly over dry land, then emerges onto another stretch of boardwalk. Spicebush, its leaves giving off a spicy fragrance, surrounds you. Its fall fruit is savored by wood thrushes and veeries.

The Marsh Trail leaves the wetland, climbing on steep steps at 2.6 miles (to your left, a park entrance road passes over a stream). The Marsh Trail ends as it exits the woods onto an open lawn. Walk straight ahead, passing the Holmdel Park Program Building on the right (2.7 miles) and the Activity Area. Follow the green-blazed Ridge Walk Trail leading to the right.

Ignore the first small wooden bridge you come to on your left. Turn left and cross a second bridge at 3.0 miles. You are now following the combined green blazes of the Ridge Walk Trail and blue diamond blazes of the Cross-Country Ski Trail. Stay to your left as the trail passes through a beech forest, a spruce grove, and more hardwoods. At 3.8 miles the trail bursts from the woods into open meadows. Walk straight ahead on a well-worn dirt path back to the parking lot (4.1 miles).

From the parking lot continue straight ahead 0.3 mile to the Longstreet Farm, which is within sight. After strolling the farm, enjoy the meditative Holmdel arboretum with its dawn redwood from China.

🌰 LIFE DOWN ON THE FARM

In the 1890s the Longstreet Farm prospered. This old-style farm relied on horse-power and muscle power to harvest produce at a time when others were mechanizing. Tenant farmers planted potatoes for resale, plus hay to feed draft animals and corn for hogs and chickens. Farm wives used "butter and egg" money to purchase mail-order goods from the Sears and Roebuck catalog.

The choice of potatoes as a cash crop was determined by geography and inexpensive transportation. By the 1890s, vast midwestern farms were cheaply meeting most of New York City's produce needs. But spuds were too weighty to haul profitably cross-country by rail. Nearby Longstreet Farm shipped their potatoes to hungry Manhattanites.

While New Jersey's Coastal Plain farmers didn't benefit from the fertile soils found in Kansas, they enriched the earth by both ancient and modern means. They spread locally plentiful marl, or greensand, on their fields. Greensand is made of the mineral glauconite, the fecal pellets of ancient marine filter-feeding organisms. Nineteenth-century South Jersey farmers also imported tons of horse manure from a surprising source: the carriage-covered streets of Manhattan.

Today Longstreet Farm interpreters educate visitors year-round. In spring they disk, harrow and plant the fields, while caring for newborn lambs and chicks. In autumn they share their knowledge of harvesting and cider making.

Hours, Fees and Facilities

Holmdel Park is open 8:00 A.M. to dusk. Longstreet Farm is open 9:00 A.M. to 5:00 P.M. from Memorial Day to Labor Day, and 10:00 A.M. to 4:00 P.M. the rest of the year. The farmhouse is open weekends and holidays, March through December, from noon to 3:30 P.M. or by reservation. Both are free.

Getting There

Take the Garden State Parkway to Exit 114. Go west on Red Hill Road to the first light and turn right on Crawfords Corner Road. Turn left on Roberts Road and right on Longstreet Road. Immediately turn left into the Holmdel Park main entrance. Stay right at the Y and pull into parking lot #2.

For More Information

Longstreet Farm, Longstreet Road, Holmdel, NJ 07733; 732-946-3758. Monmouth County Park System: 732-842-4000.

Poricy
Park

Middletown Township

- 2.5 miles
- 2 hours (plan additional time for fossil collecting)
- Easy; several flights of wooden stairs

72 million years of nature on New Jersey's Coastal Plain

Poricy Park exemplifies dedication. The historic farm located here was built by Joseph Murray, a bold Revolutionary War militiaman murdered on this land by Loyalists in 1780. For nearly two hundred years, intrepid farmers tilled the fields. Then in 1969, a determined group of Monmouth County residents formed the Poricy Park Citizen's Committee to preserve the area's environmental integrity. Today at this 250-acre park owned by Middletown Township, staff members are committed to environmental, cultural and historical education.

The staff's enthusiasm enlivens the nature center. Check out the displays, marvel at the live iguana, and pick up copies of the park map and self-guided nature trail brochure. Plan to spend a couple of hours walking Poricy Park's trails, and then return to the nature center to rent screens and trowels for another couple hours of fossil hunting (see sidebar). A brochure entitled "The Fossils of Poricy Brook" will tell you what to look for and how.

Begin your walk past two weeping willow trees to the left of Alberts Annex (a tan house near the parking area). The grassy trail is mowed in a wide swath to keep walkers away from the ticks that lurk in tall vegetation.

Multiflora rose is common throughout the park and lines the trail. This invasive species redeems itself as excellent songbird nesting habitat. Birds eat the rose hips throughout winter. Because of this abundant food source, mockingbirds—once only southern in range—are now common in the Northeast, including Poricy's meadows.

Edging the field, the trail turns left at a six-trunked box elder. Ignore the little path to the right. Small trees such as staghorn sumac and wildflowers such as evening primrose abound. These plants provide winter seeds for birds. The meadow ecosystem and meadow/woodland ecotone are rich bird habitats. More than 100 species of birds have been observed within park boundaries.

Keep bearing right on the grassy trail, ignoring left turns toward the nature center and farmhouse. After 0.5 mile of this field-edge walk, the trail splits. Turn right toward the Caution: Steep Steps sign. A dead-end side trail leads down to the marsh dock. Dead ailanthus trees litter the forest floor on your right. This obnoxious invasive species, unlike multiflora rose, has no ecological benefit here.

The marshy edge of Poricy Brook is a contrast to the meadow ecosystem you just left behind. Where a short boardwalk crosses a wet area, a large tulip tree graces the forest. Skunk cabbage emerges from the marsh in early spring; actually, skunk cabbage flowers overwinter and then undergo a growth spurt while snow still blankets the ground in February. The flowers can grow despite freezing temperatures because they release heat, thus creating their own temperate microclimate.

This marsh reveals even more of Poricy's wildlife. Watch and listen for osprey, also called fish hawks. Near the top of the steep stairs, a fox has excavated her den at the base of a red oak. Coastal Plain geology also becomes apparent along this deep stream cut: peanut stone and bog iron reveal Poricy's affinity with the Pine Barrens (see chapter 39).

Ascend the stairs back to the mown trail. The farmhouse is directly ahead. Just before the farmhouse, bear right. You will now descend into a small ravine, at the bottom of which you cross the winsomely named Troll Bridge. Jewelweed thrives in the sandy bottomland. As you climb the stairs on the other side, notice the beech and sweet birch on the hillside.

At the top, bear right. The trail soon passes through woodland. A grove of locust trees attests to this tree's ability to clone from underground shoots. Black cherry also grows in this bright forest. Many of the trees are festooned with multiflora rose. Poison ivy also thrives here, so don't stray from the trail.

Ignore left-hand turns; keep bearing right, walking the perimeter of the park along Poricy Brook. Hickories, beeches, and maples line the trail. A side path on the right leads down to the edge of the wetland again, where you can observe more stately beeches. Arrowwood greens the marsh edges. Back up on the trail, observe Poricy Brook from above. In early spring, bright yellow marsh marigolds line the stream.

One mile into the walk, another sign warns of steep steps. This is the "dock that leads to nowhere" on Poricy Pond. Canada geese and elegant swans feed amid the aquatic vegetation. Beeches loom on the bank above, while a boardwalk takes you out through ferns and cattails to a dead-end.

Re-ascend this side trail and turn right on the wide grassy main trail (ignore the narrow dirt path that bears sharply right at the top of the steps). Take the first right-hand turn, posted with yet another steep-stairs warning. An immense, 200-year-old tulip tree stands guard at the top of the steps, while another can be seen at the top of the stairs on the opposite rim of the ravine.

After emerging from the ravine, bear right. Trout lilies with their speckled leaves and yellow spring blooms carpet the forest floor. Tulip trees line the trail. Wooden stairs through a mini-ravine bring you up to a patch of false rue anemones. These spring flowers, members of the buttercup family, have six or more white petals forming cup-shaped blooms.

At 1.5 miles, a dropoff overlooks the pond, a good spot to watch for osprey. The trail makes a hairpin turn left, away from the pond. It is about 1.0 mile back to the nature center. Bear left at the next T; the railroad track is to your right. When you see the railroad overpass, the trail bears left. This short section of trail leads back to the ravine; note the magnificent tulip trees along the trail. Bear right at the wooden stairs that take you back through the ravine. At the top of the steps on the other side, cut straight across the field on the grassy, wide trail. The nature center becomes visible ahead, slightly to the right. At another T, bear right through more meadows. Ignore a left over some boardwalks. The trail will turn left onto a dirt road that leads to the farm. You can explore the farm or keep bearing to the right along the grassy trail back to the nature center (its roof is visible as your guide).

🪨 THE PORICY PARK FOSSIL BEDS

Seventy-two million years ago, dinosaurs still ruled the land. Mesosaurs and plesiosaurs terrorized the sea. The first flowering plants were evolving in the fern and conifer-dominated swamps. New Jersey's Coastal Plain lay below a warm shallow sea, closer to the equator than it is today.

Rivers deposited eroded materials from land into this ocean, burying the remains of marine creatures. Today these Cretaceous sediments, 145 million to 65 million years old, are exposed in a wide arc from Martha's Vineyard to Philadelphia. Poricy's 72-million-year-old outcrop offers a fascinating glimpse into the life of this ancient sea.

To sift for fossils in Poricy Brook, call first and check with Poricy Park personnel; a large school group may be fossil hunting that day. Then check in at the nature center, where you can rent a screen and trowel for $1. After exploring Poricy's nature trails in the morning, a wade in the cool brook will be refreshing as well as geologically educational.

In two hours of sifting, we found several of the species illustrated in the park's fossil brochure. Large oyster shells seemed to be the most common fossil; we even observed these shells emerging from the still-compressed, bedrocklike marl on the bottom of the stream. We also found delicately curved and toothed oyster shells, graceful brachiopods, glasslike squid guards (an internal shell of these extinct animals), and worm tubes.

Hours, Fees and Facilities

Nature center: Monday through Friday, 9:00 A.M. to 4:00 P.M., Sunday 12:30 P.M. to 3:30 P.M. The park is open for walkers even when the nature center is closed.

Getting There

From the north: Garden State Parkway to Exit 114 (Holmdel-Middletown); at end of ramp, make a left at the light onto Red Hill Road. After 0.4 mile, at second light, make a right onto Dwight Road. After 1.5 miles, make a left onto Middletown-Loncroft Road at the first light (you will pass the Poricy Park Fossil Beds on this road; note the gravel parking area on your right just after the road crosses the brook). After 0.25 mile, turn right at the first light onto Oak Hill Road. The entrance to the park is immediately before the second railroad crossing.

From the south: Garden State Parkway to Exit 114 (Holmdel-Middletown); at end of ramp, make a right. At the next light, turn left onto Dwight Road and proceed as above.

For More Information

Poricy Park, Oak Hill Road, Middletown, NJ 07748; 732-842-5966; poricypark@monmouth.com.

—chapter and sidebar by Jean LeBlanc

32 Shark River

Monmouth County Park

- 2.5 miles
- 2 hours
- Easy; stair-climbs and some wet footing

A birder's delight along one of New Jersey's little rivers

Shark River isn't much of a stream where it meanders between the gravel-capped sand hills of Monmouth County toward the sea. A world-class long jumper could leap it without getting wet. But in a very short distance the river broadens into a mile-wide tidal basin, then briefly constricts into a narrow channel at Belmar before emptying into the Atlantic Ocean.

This small coastal stream offers a big draw for birds and birders. The region's habitat diversity—upland forest, riverine lowland, salt marsh, and protected tidal bay—attracts waterfowl, shorebirds, and songbirds.

In winter, duck and geese flocks are ogled by birder caravans. In spring, the sand hills upstream attract returning migrants. In May, as oaks and sweet gums leaf out, warblers arrive on cue from their winter ranges in Mexico, Central America, the Caribbean, and South America. In summer, trees become animated with cardinals, robins, titmice, and nuthatches as they nest and raise families. The temperate Jersey Shore is also the winter home for some yellow-rumped warblers, brown thrashers, kinglets and white-throated sparrows.

The 587-acre forest that was to become Shark River Park was nearly lost. In the 1960s it was slated to become a housing project. The contractor had already cleared the development's roads when Monmouth County decided to buy the land. In 1967 Shark River was established as the county's first park, and the developer's sand roads became its trails.

This 2.5-mile circuit walk utilizes the Cedar Loop Trail, Hidden Creek Trail, and River's Edge Trail to circle through upland oak and pine forest, cross open meadows, and weave along a river flood plain. Bring your binoculars; the birds will be waiting.

From the parking lot entrance, cross the street and follow the red-blazed Cedar Loop Trail into the woods. Stay right and avoid taking two trails that exit to the left within 300 feet of each other. After passing Fitness Trail Stops #4 and #5, turn sharply right at a sand road fork, following the right branch of the red-blazed Cedar Loop Trail (0.2 mile).

This open woodland of pitch pine, black tupelo, and white oak supports Northern flickers. This brown-and-black-speckled, red-naped, jay-size woodpecker thrives on insects. It is a ground feeder and in summer may be caught in the act of probing anthills with its long, sticky tongue. In autumn the bird switches to a diet of plentiful berries.

The understory here is a tangle of greenbrier, blueberry, mountain laurel and sweet pepperbush. These shrubs, especially the thorny greenbrier, provide cover to songbirds from prowling raptors. Pepperbush is an excellent nectar source for ruby-throated hummingbirds. Mountain laurel is home to scale insects eaten by chickadees and kinglets. Greenbrier and blueberry fruits offer a feast to ruffed grouse and thrushes.

Where the red-blazed Cedar Loop Trail goes to the left through a sand pit at about 0.4 mile, turn right on the sand road which is the blue-blazed Hidden Creek Trail. For those unable to make a long trip from the New York metro area into the vast Pine Barrens, this sandy trail through pitch pine and scrub oak offers up a mini-Pinelands habitat. Scarlet oak and black oak fill in the forest mix. Bracken fern, with its woody stem, covers the ground.

At about 0.5 mile, follow the blue-blazed trail left as it leaves the sand road. Pay close attention to the trail markers, since, oddly, the park has paint-blazed only the opposite side of the wooden posts marking the trail.

The path passes beneath black tupelo, sassafras and pitch pine and amid high-bush blueberry and bracken fern. Kinglets, tiny birds with boundless energy, flit among the greenbrier like a swarm of atoms in autumn. It's hard to imagine that the kinglets gather enough aphids, beetles, wasps and spiders to fuel their intense dance. Magnolia warblers (males are black-and-white streaked above and bright yellow below) are also found along this secluded stretch of trail in the spring and fall. These birds are somewhat misnamed, for though the first specimens were collected in southern magnolia trees in the 1800s, the birds typically breed in northern conifers.

Continue following the blue-blazed trail as it passes over a small brook on a bridge (0.9 mile), then climbs gently to a gravel-capped knoll topped by blackjack oak and pitch pine. The trail skirts the edge of a clearing, then swerves left on a sunken sand road (1.1 miles).

This sand road, eroded about five feet below the forest floor, provides a peek underground. The complex sand and clay strata of the Outer Coastal Plain go a half-mile deep in some places before touching bedrock. These sands were deposited by the sea that repeatedly covered this area in the past 350 million years. Some deposits were also made in the last million years by glacial outwash, flooding meltwater from the ice sheet in north Jersey.

The sunken sand road leads downhill to a mowed meadow (1.3 miles). Turn sharply left along the wooded edge of the meadow. At the far corner of the meadow you intersect again with the red-blazed Cedar Loop Trail. Turn sharply right and follow it along the treeline (1.4 miles).

The meadow-edge environment is drastically different from the pitch pine and oak forest. The treeline is composed of light-loving black cherry, bigtooth aspen, sweet gum, and gray birch. This is a great place to watch for hawks. We heard a red-tailed hawk screech as it circled this open country in search of prey.

The trail leaves the meadow (1.4 miles), descends a steep set of stairs and crosses a small swamp on a boardwalk. Here we saw a brown creeper in October spiraling up a tree trunk in a meticulous search for insects. Unlike the nuthatch, which can descend a trunk, the brown creeper can only ascend, then must fly back to the base of the tree to resume its bug search.

At 1.6 miles the red-blazed trail reaches a T. Turn right on a sand road, the green-blazed River's Edge Trail. The sand road ends and the green-blazed trail descends on steps to the Shark River at 1.7 miles. Reaching the stream, the path turns left. For the last 0.8 mile of the walk the River's Edge Trail plays tag with the stream. Look for raccoon, skunk and snapping turtle tracks in soft sand.

According to local legend, Shark River's name dates from the 1800s when a doomed shark was swept into fresh water by incoming tides. The stream is aptly named, since 40-million-year-old shark's teeth are regularly recovered from its banks, which once formed the ocean floor.

The river shore is lined by red maple, sweet gum, sassafras, and American hornbeam (also called musclewood for its smooth bark resembling flexed muscles). Native arrowwood and sweet pepperbush, plus exotic barberry and Japanese knotweed fill in the understory.

Continue following the green blazes upstream. Straight ahead, Schoolhouse Road crosses Shark River on a bridge (2.4 miles). Swing left on the trail and up the stairs. Stay inside the guardrail, then cut back into the woods, following the green arrow. Where the green trail intersects the red trail, turn right, returning to Schoolhouse Road and the parking lot. At the end of your walk you can enjoy lunch at the picnic shelter or fish the small pond for bass.

▲ WHERE HAVE ALL THE SONGBIRDS GONE?

Rachel Carson feared that our songbirds would disappear, poisoned by pesticides, leaving us with a silent spring. Today, the woods grow quieter each year. But pesticides may not be the only culprit. Deforestation and fragmented habitat are also threatening these sweet singers.

Warblers, flycatchers, vireos and thrushes winter in the tropics, then migrate thousands of miles into North America to nest and raise their young. Our insatiable hunger for beef has caused the conversion of tropical rain forest into grazing land, while suburban development has cut our northern forests into smaller and smaller pieces. Many songbirds require deep forest to thrive. Edge habitat leaves them vulnerable to nest-robbing domestic cats, blue jays, and brown-headed cowbirds. Cowbirds parasitize nests, substituting their own eggs for the songbirds to raise.

The loss of the world's songbirds reminds us of Earth's seamless ecological web. The hamburger we enjoy today may rob us of song tomorrow.

Hours, Fees and Facilities
Open daily 8:00 A.M. to dusk. Free.

Getting There
From the Garden State Parkway take Exit 100 onto Highway 33 east. Turn right on Schoolhouse Road. Shark River Park is on the right in 0.5 mile.

For More Information
Monmouth County Park System: 732-842-4000.
Shark River Park, 1101 Schoolhouse Road, Neptune, NJ 07753.

Wells Mills

Ocean County Park

- 6 miles
- 4 hours
- Moderate; many small hill-climbs

A hike through a secluded tract of
Pine Barrens forest, swamp, and bog

Cloaked in pitch pine and oak, the hills at Wells Mills seem wild and changeless today. But the forest resources of this ancient Pine Barrens ecosystem were heavily exploited by people for two hundred years before finally being preserved in the mid-1970s.

These rugged sand hills, cedar swamps and freshwater bogs were owned first in colonial times by zealous Tory Elishia Lawrence, who backed the wrong side in the Revolutionary War. A vengeful American government confiscated his property. Elishia Lawrence's loss was James Wells's gain.

In the late 1700s, James Wells dammed Oyster Creek, creating a thirty-seven-acre lake. He built a sawmill and harvested old-growth stands of Atlantic white cedar. Woodcutters and charcoal makers crisscrossed the Wells Mills tract, clearing pine and oak. Some pitch pines were bled for oleoresin, which was distilled into turpentine, while the stumps of cut trees were burned to extract tar and pitch (used to caulk ship hull seams). Quarries provided sand-rich clay for firebrick, terra cotta ceramics, and redware pottery. Sphagnum moss gatherers prowled swamps collecting the sterile, super-absorbent plant. It served as surgical dressings through World War I and as floral packing material.

By the twentieth century these natural resources, as elsewhere in the Pine Barrens, had either been exhausted or ceased to be of commercial value. In the 1930s the Conrad family built a rustic cabin retreat here and used the tract for hunting. The New Jersey Conservation Foundation, recognizing the land's natural value, bought it in the 1970s. Ocean County purchased its first Wells Mills acreage in 1985, establishing this fine county park.

Today the sugar-sand roads that once guided woodcutters and sphagnum moss gatherers are a well-blazed and meticulously maintained sixteen-mile trail system. This 6.0-mile loop hike utilizes both the white-blazed Penns Hill Trail and yellow-blazed Ridge Road/Cooks Mill Road.

N↗

Laurel Hill

Penns Hill

1996 Area of Prescribed Burn

TO
BOYSCOUT
CAMP

Laurel Ridge

Raccoon
Ridge

Ridge Rd. (sand)

Raccoon Branch

Oyster Creek

Penns Hill Trail
(white-blazed)

Field Branch

Wells Mills

Wells Mills
Lake

Wells Mills
Swamp

Cooks Mill Rd. (sand)
(yellow-blazed)

Penns Hill Trail

Nature
Center

START

P

532

Stage Branch

Oyster Creek

Old Brook

Wells Mills Road

Due to the high incidence of Lyme disease in the area, take precautions against ticks before starting your walk. Tuck pants into boots and wear insect repellent. Check yourself thoroughly after the hike. In an effort to curb the tick population, Wells Mills employees recently tried releasing guinea fowl, what they called the "hunt and peck" method of tick control. Sadly, the birds were curbed themselves, providing easy meals for local foxes.

The first white blaze of the Penns Hill Trail is placed on an extremely tall sassafras tree, the largest I've ever seen. The medicinal power of sassafras tea has been acclaimed for centuries. Sassafras bark was the first forest product exported to the Old World. Aromatic sassafras was once used to flavor and scent root beer, mouthwash, gum, toothpaste, and soap.

The first 0.4 mile of the white-blazed Penns Hill Trail edges the shore of Wells Mills Lake, threading between the pillarlike trunks of Atlantic white cedar. In precolonial times this majestic tree blanketed Pine Barrens swamps, growing to four feet in diameter and a hundred feet tall. The wood's straight grain, rot-resistance, and slowness to burn made it ideal for shingles, barrels, boats and fences and doomed the great cedar forests. Botanist Peter Kalm, writing in the mid-1700s, noted that all of Philadelphia's homes were roofed with white cedar shingles. He feared the tree would be clearcut into extinction. Conservationists have achieved a limited white cedar comeback in recent years.

At about 0.4 mile, the white-blazed trail veers right, leaving water and cedars behind. It climbs gently through a woods of white oak, blackjack oak, pitch pine, sassafras, and blueberry. Blackjack oak, with its three-lobed, thick, leathery leaves, is a small contorted tree that, like pitch pine, flourishes in barren, dry, sandy soils. It is one of the most common oaks of the Coastal Plain.

At 1.0 mile the trail tops Raccoon Ridge, then enters an extensive burned-over area. The blackened pines and oaks were part of a twenty acre prescribed burn set by park foresters in winter 1996. Such controlled burns prevent the buildup of duff: dry pine needles and leaf litter which lead to wildfire. They also rejuvenate these woodlands (see sidebar). When we walked here in 1997 trunks and limbs were scarred black and a faint odor of smoke still hung in the air, but most trees wore crowns of fresh green needles or leaves.

Descending Raccoon Ridge through the burned area we spied a northern flicker, a ground-feeding woodpecker, as it searched for ants and beetle larvae. The flicker, a cavity-nesting bird, benefits from plentiful dead and hollowed trees left by fire.

The white-blazed trail climbs Penns Hill (2.6 miles), descends and crosses a sand ditch, and leaves the burned area behind. Such ditches, called plow lines, are cut as firebreaks. In the unburned forest we found a luxurious undergrowth of mountain laurel, sweet pepperbush, and wintergreen amid stands of blackjack oak, post oak, chestnut oak and pitch pine.

The trail next crosses Laurel Hill (2.9 miles) and Laurel Ridge (3.4 miles). These ridges are broken repeatedly by small gullies with streams and trail bridges. While each gully is less than seventy-five feet deep, the land's ruggedness offers an unexpected workout in the usually flat Pinelands. These gravel-capped hills were created during the million-year-long Ice Age. While glaciers never reached South Jersey, raging rivers of meltwater did surge over the Coastal Plain, depositing sand and gravel mounds. Subsequent rising and falling sea levels submerged the area and left behind more sand and silt, plus marine fossils. These hills and surrounding swamps protect the endangered Pine Barrens tree frog, timber rattler, horned snake, rare orchids, swamp pink, Pine Barrens gentian, and bog asphodel.

The trail passes through a small Atlantic white cedar swamp, then turns sharply right on Ridge Road at 3.7 miles. The path is now blazed both white and yellow. In a few hundred feet follow the combined white and yellow blazes and turn sharply left (don't continue straight on Ridge Road into the Boy Scout Reservation).

From here on, the walk is easy and flat. The trail, now a wide sandy road, shoots between growths of pitch pine, oak, and sassafras. This old road, eroded about two feet below the surrounding forest, was once used by nineteenth-century wagons, woodcutters and hunters.

The combined white and yellow trails pass over Oyster Creek at 4.1 miles, then reach a trail junction at 4.3 miles. Do not diverge left on the white-blazed Penns Hill Trail, but continue straight ahead, following the yellow-blazed Cooks Mill Road. The road slowly curves left back toward the nature center.

Look for Pine Barrens heather, also called golden heather, edging the sand road. The trail crosses Stage Branch Creek (5.7 miles) and Oyster Creek (5.8 miles), offering nice views into a white cedar and red maple swamp. The yellow-blazed Cooks Mill Road crosses the top of the dam forming Wells Mills Lake and arrives back at the nature center.

● FIRE AND THE PINES

While people view forest fires as destructive, such infernos have been a part of the natural cycle in south Jersey for thousands of years. Fire fosters unique Pine Barrens plant and animal communities.

Pitch pine and short-leaf pine are well adapted to the cycle. They possess thick bark which resists high temperatures; they also respond automatically to fire by quickly putting out sprouts from scorched trunks. In fact, specialized pitch pine cones can open *only* during intense heat. Pine seeds also need cleared ground and sunlight to germinate. Without regular fires, oaks would replace pines as the dominant Pine Barrens forest tree.

Repeatedly burned areas support such rare flora as Pickering's morning glory and sickle-leaved golden aster, rare moths and butterflies including the Pine Barrens dagger moth and Attalus skipper, and rare reptiles like the pine snake and corn snake. Cavity-nesting birds such as the eastern bluebird and great crested flycatcher benefit by finding homes in dead trees.

Pine Barrens wildfires, unlike the small prescribed burns lit by foresters, can be destructive and terrifying. Crown fires burn with white-hot intensity, advancing with frightening speed through the forest canopy. Windborne embers quickly carry the blaze over the heads of firefighters, endangering lives. In 1995, wildfires

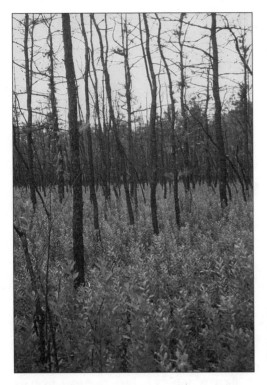

Ground cover enjoys plentiful light and a spurt of growth after a 1996 prescribed burn. The burning off of leaf litter reduces the possibility of wildfires.

fanned by 60 mph winds ravaged thousands of forest acres. The staff at Wells Mills watched the wildfire with fear, praying the wind wouldn't blow their way. Luckily the park was spared.

Hours, Fees and Facilities

The park is open dawn to dusk year-round. Nature center exhibits are open year-round from 7:30 A.M. to 4:00 P.M.

Getting There

From the Garden State Parkway southbound take Exit 67. Turn right onto Route 554 (West Bay Avenue) and proceed to Route 72, then 0.25 mile farther to Route 532. Turn right and go three miles to Wells Mills County Park entrance on the right. From the Garden State Parkway northbound take Exit 69. Turn left onto Route 532 west and proceed about 2 miles to the park entrance on the left.

For More Information

Wells Mills County Park, Box 905, Wells Mills Road, Waretown, NJ 08758; 609-971-3085.

34 Pakim Pond

Lebanon State Forest

- 6.8 miles
- 4.5 hours
- Moderate; minor elevation change

Explore the subtle, understated beauty of the Pine Barrens

The heart of the Outer Coastal Plain has been known as the Pine Barrens since colonial times. In the public imagination the 1.4-million-acre region was viewed as a dreary wasteland of impassable sugar sand, treacherous cedar swamp, and scraggly pitch pine.

In the nineteenth century, urbanites unjustly labeled the region's people "pineys" and painted them in the stereotype of Ozark hillbillies. One 1800s New Jersey state governor smeared the rural folk as a "race of imbeciles, criminals and defectives." In the 1900s the Barrens were viewed by most vacationers as a blank spot on the map through which one sped as quickly as possible to the Jersey Shore.

Starting in the 1960s, environmentalists and writers such as John McPhee recognized the area's cultural, biological and botanical richness. Conservationists, attempting to shed past stereotypes, even tried renaming the region the "Pinelands." While the new name sweeps aside old pejoratives, it lacks the air of strange, wild beauty conjured by the old one. No matter what you call this vast forest, it remains the last bastion of the primitive in New Jersey.

A fine Pinelands (or Pine Barrens!) sampler hike is a 6.8-mile loop to Pakim Pond. It begins on the Batona Trail, which weaves through an oak-pine upland to tiny Pakim Pond. It returns via the Cranberry Trail, a series of well-blazed sand roads offering a glimpse into an Atlantic white cedar swamp. To avoid crowds of people and mosquitoes, walk here in spring, fall or winter.

Begin at the Lebanon State Forest headquarters parking lot. This 32,000-acre park is named for the Lebanon Glassworks (1851–1866), which benefited from plentiful sand for silica and charcoal for fuel in the making of windows, fancy bottles, and glass walking canes. All that remains of the enterprise is an earthen mound southeast of Pakim Pond.

Walk from the entrance of the state-forest parking lot across paved Shinns Road and past a sign that reads Batona Trail. A blue-blazed access trail leads gen-

Pakim Pond

N

cranberry bog

Pakim Pond

Batona Trail (pink)

Cranberry Trail (red)

Cedar Swamp

Jersey Devil sighting

Shinns Branch

Shinns Road

Batona Trail (pink)

Lebanon State Forest office

START

P

Four Mile Rd.

Access Tr. (blue)

TO NJ 70

tly uphill through woods, connecting with the pink-blazed Batona Trail in 0.1 mile. Turn left on the Batona Trail atop a low sand-and-gravel ridge.

The Batona Trail was built by volunteers of the Batona (ba-to-na—back to nature) Hiking Club of Philadelphia in the 1960s. The fifty-mile trail runs from a northern terminus at Ongs Hat south to Bass River State Park. Camping is allowed at designated sites along its length.

This is the hike of many oaks. The path threads between species of the white oak family (chestnut oak, post oak and white oak with rounded leaf lobes) and red oak family (black oak, scarlet oak, blackjack oak, and scrub oak with pointy bristle tips at each leaf lobe). White pine and pitch pine join the mix. Oaks would dominate the Pine Barrens climax forest if it weren't for the regular fires giving the flame-resistant pitch pine and short-leaf pine their advantage (see chapter 33).

At about 0.7 mile the Batona Trail crosses a sand road. The path now undulates up- and downhill from about 150 feet to 110 feet above sea level as it crosses many unmarked sand ditches and paths. Watch blazes closely!

The Pine Barrens is not known for in-your-face beauty. It boasts no craggy vistas or waterfalls. But the understated splendor can catch you by surprise. On this walk I discovered slender ladder lichen growing beneath a shaggy mountain laurel bush, tiny bluish gray goblets perched one atop another like the fantastic multitiered flora of a Dr. Seuss children's book. Gray-green reindeer lichen with jumbled intertwined "antlers" sprawled in clumps amid fallen butterscotch-colored oak leaves and golden pine needles.

At 1.7 miles the forest scenery begins to change. Pitch pine (three stiff needles in a bundle) and short-leaf pine (usually two needles per bundle) become dominant, though blackjack and post oak are still present.

The Batona Trail veers sharply left at 2.0 miles and descends out of the upland, crossing Shinns Road at 2.1 miles. The trail threads its way through a swampy lowland over a boardwalk amid sheep laurel, cinnamon fern, red maple and much pitch pine.

At about 2.5 miles the Batona Trail turns sharply right and intersects with the red-blazed Cranberry Trail entering from the left. Note this turning point, as it marks your return route.

Continue on the pink-blazed Batona Trail for another 0.5 mile along gravel roads which twist their way into a picnic area at the near end of Pakim Pond. This is a fine spot for lunch and a swim. The pond's "cedar water," as everywhere in the Pine Barrens, is stained rust brown with iron and tannin (a mild acid derived from tree bark and leaves).

Follow the pink blazes along the left shore of Pakim Pond beneath young Atlantic white cedars. Survey the water for sunning painted turtles and study the shore at your feet for the purple-veined leaves of insectivorous pitcher plants. We found one pitcher plant with a live bee trapped inside (see sidebar). To the left of the trail is an abandoned cranberry bog. Pakim Pond (the name means "cranberry" in the Lenape language) once served as the bog's reservoir.

At 3.4 miles the trail reaches a small bridge at the far end of the pond. Look in the boggy area to the right for wild American cranberry. This diminutive trailing bog shrub has tiny waxen evergreen leaves and is the forerunner of hybridized cultivated cranberries.

Backtrack along the pond, through the picnic area, and return to the junction with the red-blazed Cranberry Trail (4.3 miles into the hike). Follow the red trail straight ahead on a sand road as the pink-blazed Batona Trail turns left. Watch the red blazes closely, since there are several unmarked turnoffs.

Walking the Cranberry Trail on a rainy day, I heard great wings stir from high atop a pitch pine. An immense dark shadow swept overhead and vanished in the fog before I could even look up. I first thought it was an eagle, then maybe a turkey vulture. But as eerie silence resumed, a new sinister thought took hold: Jersey Devil. This spawn of Satan with leathery wings, horse's head, razor-sharp teeth, talons and serpent tail feeds on sheep and small children. It has held a profane place in the pantheon of Pine Barrens mythological fauna since the early 1700s. The beast personifies all the irrational fears that race through a lone walker's mind while traveling these weird woods. Fortunately, the more common winged crea-

The veined open lips of the insectivorous pitcher plant beckon to unwary bugs.

tures sighted along the Cranberry Trail are brown thrashers and great crested fly-catchers.

At 5.5 miles turn left, following red blazes onto a major sand road, which passes over Shinns Brook and through a magnificent and mysterious Atlantic white cedar swamp. At 5.7 miles the Cranberry Trail turns right on another sand road. The trail turns sharply left on still another red-blazed road at 6.3 miles.

At 6.7 miles the path exits the woods onto a paved road. Follow the road to the right, and in a hundred feet turn left on an unblazed trail into the state-forest headquarters parking lot (6.8 miles).

🌰 PITCHER PLANTS

In nutrient-poor acidic bogs, plants must find a way to obtain nitrogen, potassium and phosphorus other than through their roots. Insects are an abundant source of nutrients, and pitcher plants (like sundews and Venus flytraps) have evolved into passive hunters. Within a pitcher plant's pale green, red-veined tubular leaves lurks a strange brew. An insect, trapped by the leaf's downward-pointing bristles and slick walls, will drown and be digested in this mix of rainwater, bacteria and enzymes.

Ah, but co-evolution works in mysterious ways. Some insects have adapted to life within pitcher plant leaves. Several types of flies and mosquitoes lay their eggs in the leaves, and the larvae thrive in this wetland within a wetland. A veritable zoo of micro-organisms also inhabits this mini-ecosystem, and the waste products of these protozoans may be another nutrient source for the plant. The flowers of the pitcher plant—tall, deep-purple nodding spheres that look like life forms from another planet—are pollinated by bees. The complex relationships between pitcher plants and insects chronicle the workings of evolution and the many special adaptations to life in the bog. —sidebar by Jean LeBlanc

Hours, Fees and Facilities

Lebanon State Forest trails are open dawn to dusk. The headquarters office has maps and rest rooms and is open 8:00 A.M. to 4:30 P.M. seven days a week.

Getting There

From the NJ 70 and NJ 72 traffic circle, follow NJ 72 east 1.0 mile and turn left at a sign for Lebanon State Forest. The headquarters office is 0.3 mile ahead and to the right on Shinns Road.

For More Information

Lebanon State Forest, P.O. Box 215, New Lisbon, NJ 08064; 609-726-1191.
    To volunteer with the Batona Trail Club: 215-659-3921.

35 Whitesbog

Lebanon State Forest

- 2.5 miles
- 2 hours
- Easy

Explore cranberry bogs and the birthplace of the commercial blueberry, and enjoy fine birding

Wild cranberries and blueberries have thrived in sodden, acidic Pine Barren bogs since the end of the Ice Age. The tasty fruit of both these hardy heath-family plants were savored by Lenape Indians and early settlers. Native Americans made a staple winter food called pemmican by pounding nourishing dried blueberries and cranberries onto venison strips. Colonial sailors stowed cranberries loaded with vitamin C aboard ship as protection against scurvy.

But it wasn't until 1816 that New Englanders grew the first commercial cranberries in the bogs of Cape Cod, Massachusetts. Colonel James Fenwick followed their lead, harvesting the nutritious red berries at Skunk's Misery in the New Jersey Pine Barrens in 1854. Fenwick's daughter Mary married J. J. White, a cranberry entrepreneur. The couple launched a venture scoffed at as "White's Folly," an attempt to dig bogs and cultivate cranberries where they didn't already grow. The couple succeeded beyond their wildest hopes. By 1900 Whitesbog was a thriving agricultural community with 600 workers.

In 1911 the Whites' daughter Elizabeth allied with Dr. Frederick Colville to develop the first commercial blueberry. Elizabeth rode horseback throughout the Pine Barrens, meeting with locals and collecting bushes with the plumpest berries. Hybridization experiments led to the world's first commercial crop in 1916.

Modern agricultural techniques utilizing immense tractor-driven harvesters eventually made small, irregularly shaped bogs obsolete. Today, Whitesbog (part of Lebanon State Forest) offers a 3,000-acre window through which walkers can look back to the year 1900 and view bog agriculture as it was practiced in the Pine Barrens. Abandoned bogs also abound with wildlife. Where cranberries were once harvested, tundra swans, gull-billed terns, whip-poor-wills, white-tailed deer, and fox flourish amid wetland and woodland flora.

This 2.5-mile walk explores the Whitesbog company town, traverses a forested nature trail, then loops through the bogs. A word of caution: there is little

Whitesbog

shade. Wear a hat, carry plenty of water, and avoid this hike on humid summer days when mosquitoes rule.

Tour the town first. Worth a look are the 1900s-vintage cranberry packing and storage buildings, water tower, a boardinghouse for unmarried workers and an entomologist's home (insect control was crucial to the bog!). The general store and post office from which Elizabeth White mailed blueberry bushes to farmers world-wide is now the Whitesbog Preservation Trust office. While all these buildings have been stabilized, they are not yet open to the public.

Begin the walk by following the numbered posts of the Old Bog Nature Trail (you can get an informative Nature Trail guide, driving tour, and Tree Trail guide mailed to you by contacting the Whitesbog Preservation Trust at 120-24A Whites-bog Road, Browns Mills, NJ 08015).

From the front of the general store, walk straight ahead across the street and circle right around to the back of what in 1910 was a lily-covered pond. Walk left along the edge of this former pond, now a seasonal wetland overgrown with marsh plants. Near the far end of the pond (at Nature Trail post #4), sphagnum moss grows in a thick mat while cinnamon fern rises to the right.

At post #7 on the Nature Trail (about 0.2 mile into the walk), park officials have fenced off several pitcher plants. Stoop down and peek within their cupped leaves. You may see a bug struggling to escape. These native Pine Barrens plants, along with insectivorous sundews, grow in nutrient-poor soils and supplement their diets with nitrogen-rich insects (see chapter 34).

The Nature Trail now twists through a pitch pine lowland where this dominant tree is joined by red maple and black tupelo. The black tupelo, also called black gum, is among the first South Jersey trees to turn color in autumn and the first to shed its brilliant scarlet leaves. Ruffed grouse and wild turkeys enjoy its bluish black berries.

The forest deepens as the trail passes between young Atlantic white cedar, pin oak, and sweet gum. Pin oak and sweet gum (with its easily identified star-shaped leaves) were introduced to Whitesbog as ornamentals.

At post #13 the trail passes through the Old Bog, an original cranberry bog from the 1850s. Forest succession has filled in the bog with trees. This change only hints at the metamorphosis undergone by this land over the past three hundred years. What began in precolonial days as a lowland cloaked in pitch pine and Atlantic white cedar was logged over by the 1790s. Whitesbog was then dredged for bog iron, which nearby Hanover Furnace turned into War of 1812 cannonballs. Only in the mid-1800s was the much-disturbed earth with its high water table recognized as the perfect spot for water-loving cranberries.

The Nature Trail ends as it exits the woods onto a sand road at 0.4 mile. Turn right and follow the unblazed sand road past Elizabeth White's home, Suningive. This little house was once surrounded not by a conventional flower garden, but by Ms. White's arboretum of acid-loving Pine Barrens plants, including rare orchids and insectivorous sundews. Plans are in the works to restore the now overgrown garden.

Make a right turn off the main sand road onto a second major sand road at 0.6 mile, out into the open bogs. A variety of possible routes are now available as you move along the unblazed sand roads and dikes marking the edges of roughly rectangular bogs and ponds. We suggest that you complete your loop walk by ignoring the next two lefts (at 0.9 mile and 1.1 miles). Take a third left at 1.4 miles. Then at 1.5 miles, turn left again, following the main sand road back into Whitesbog village, reaching the general store and the end of your walk at 2.5 miles.

The abandoned and cultivated bogs, reservoir ponds, and swamps, plus the pitch pine, oak, and Atlantic white cedar woods you see surrounding you are a very compatible land use with wildlife needs. For every acre of active cranberry and blueberry bog, ten acres of upland watershed are needed to provide clean water for the bogs. That means that the Pine Barrens' 11,000 active acres of bog require the preservation of 100,000 acres of forested upland!

We found fox scat and white-tailed deer and raccoon tracks. Four hundred tundra swans (also called whistling swans) winter at Whitesbog. In fact, the swans so love the tubers of a cranberry bog weed called redroot that active bogs must be armed with propane cannons to spook the birds. We heard the thunderous boom of these guns as we walked here in November. Fortunately, the whistling swans find plenty to eat in nearby abandoned bogs.

This is an ideal haven for wading birds and waterfowl. Blue herons, green herons and great egrets fish the bog reservoirs. Green-winged teals, wood ducks, black ducks and northern pintails migrate through. Most unusual are flocks of gull-billed terns arriving in late summer. This shorebird normally feeds in salt marshes, but feasts on Whitesbog insects, tadpoles, and frogs. More than 200 bird species have been observed here. As you walk these life-giving bogs, it becomes clear that the Pine Barrens is far from barren.

🌲 ALL ABOUT BERRIES

While neither cranberry nor blueberry plants seem to resemble each other, botanists tell us that their flower anatomies are closely related. These heath-family plants also sometimes share the same wetland habitat, though cranberries require a more acidic environment.

Nourishing cranberries are food for ring-necked pheasant, ruffed grouse and mourning doves. Among humans, the tart autumn-harvested fruit only graced Thanksgiving and Christmas dinner tables until the cranberry juice craze put "cranberry cocktail" in American refrigerators year-round.

While Elizabeth White's plump commercial blueberries in their cellophane-covered berry boxes are known to every shopper, hikers who are willing to brave bog and swamp know that the taste of the commercial fruit pales by comparison with wild varieties. The Chippewa tribe may have developed the strangest use for the plant. They burned its flowers and inhaled the smoke to calm and cure the crazy. For those of us who relish the peace and solitude of berry picking, the belief rings true.

Hours, Fees and Facilities

The sand roads are open to hikers dawn to dusk. The general store office is open 9:00 A.M. to 3:00 P.M., but has no rest rooms or public facilities.

Getting There

From the NJ 70 and NJ 72 traffic circle, follow NJ 70 east for 7 miles and turn left on Route 530. In 1.2 miles turn right at a sign for Whitesbog. In 0.4 mile park in the large lot in front of the general store.

For More Information

Lebanon State Forest, P.O. Box 215, New Lisbon, NJ 08064; 609-726-1191. Whitesbog Preservation Trust, 120-24A Whitesbog Road, Browns Mills, NJ 08015; 609-893-4646.

36 Dot and Brooks Evert Memorial Nature Trail

New Jersey Conservation Foundation

- 1.5 miles
- 1 hour
- Easy; very wet in winter and spring

A secluded walk amid a profusion of spring warblers

John McPhee, in his classic 1967 Pine Barrens profile, tells how he was lucky enough to go walking with Dot and Brooks Evert. He relates how Brooks reverently scooped up an insectivorous sundew in a handful of soggy sand, showed it to McPhee, then gently returned it to the spongy ground. Dot Evert intoned, "As a rule we take nothing, and we leave nothing."

The Everts, gone from the Earth now, did leave something significant behind. When McPhee walked with them the future of nature in the Pine Barrens was gravely in doubt. A 32,500-acre jetport and 250,000-person "city of the future" had been proposed by the Pinelands Regional Planning Committee. The airport, covering fifty-one square miles, was to be four times larger than Kennedy, Newark and LaGuardia airports combined. A would-be developer told McPhee, "This area of the pinelands simply begins to jump out at you if you're going to go for urbanization. It's magnificent."

But Dot and Brooks Evert saw a different kind of magnificence in the Pines. They found splendor in a tiny sundew, in the bog asphodel and corn snake. It was their vision which gained ascendance. Today, preservation of much of the Pine Barrens for future generations looks assured (see sidebar).

The Everts left behind a second legacy: their reverence for the region's botanical and biological diversity. The New Jersey Conservation Foundation, a statewide, private nonprofit land trust of which they were both active members, has created a preserve and a 1.5-mile nature trail in their honor.

This little 170-acre preserve straddles the border between the Inner and Outer Coastal Plains and is cloaked in a mature red maple, sweet gum, and holly swamp forest. It is split by Stop-the-Jade Run, a small stream meandering westward out of the Pine Barrens. Its waters eventually blend with Rancocas Creek (see chapter 37), the Lower Delaware River, and the Atlantic Ocean.

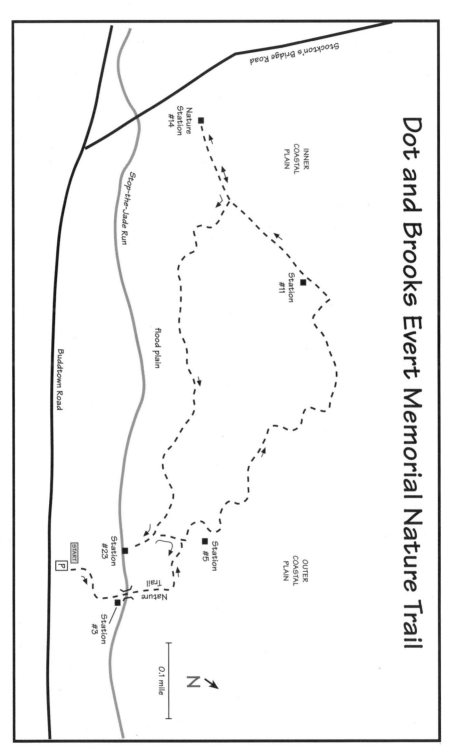

Dot and Brooks Evert Memorial Nature Trail

The ecology of the Dot and Brooks Evert Memorial Nature Trail has been described in wonderful detail in a nature guide written by Emile DeVito of the New Jersey Conservation Foundation. Be sure to pick up one of these fine Pine Barrens primers at the trailhead.

From the parking area, follow the 1.5-mile loop Nature Trail into the woods. The solitude immediately impresses. Sweet gum, black tupelo (sour gum), willow oak, red maple, and sassafras form a loose canopy overhead. In the 1980s the invasive gypsy moth caterpillar caused extensive damage to these woods and to much Pine Barrens acreage. Stripped of foliage, trees died, opening the forest floor to sunlight and inviting a riot of shrubby growth. Here, a viny tangle of Virginia creeper entwines tree trunks in a struggle to rise above an impenetrable jungle of greenbrier and sweet pepperbush.

Nature Trail station #3 (at 0.1 mile) puts you on a small bridge over Stop-the-Jade Run. This sluggish stream is copper colored with iron absorbed from the soil and with mildly acidic tannins found in leaves and tree bark. This pure "cedar water" is common to Pine Barren streams.

The natural diversity of the preserve is enhanced by two factors. The forested stream corridor is wet, providing plentiful moisture to the flood-plain species that flourish here (much of the trail is elevated on boardwalk). The preserve is also located within an ecotone, a transition zone between two habitats, fostering species richness. It straddles the older, richer soils of the Inner Coastal Plain and Delaware River Basin, as well as the younger, acidic soils of the Outer Coastal Plain and Pine Barrens.

Walk here in springtime and you stand a good chance of sampling ecotone diversity firsthand. The New Jersey Audubon Society believes that there may be a greater diversity of breeding songbird species in these woods than in all the rest of South Jersey.

The Nature Trail brochure asks walkers to listen for the *sweet-sweet-sweet-sweet* song of the prothonotary warbler or the *weetee-weetee-wee-tee-o* of the hooded warbler. It suggests that you may be the first to hear a Kentucky warbler in the preserve. This is no longer the case; this rarely detected warbler was recently discovered along the trail, as was the worm-eating warbler. These migratory species, more common to the Delaware River Basin than the Pinelands, are joined by many Pine Barrens birds. Prairie warblers, pine warblers and yellow-billed cuckoos nest here.

Just beyond the footbridge the trail splits (0.2 mile into the walk). Take the right fork. Near station #5, holly and sweet bay magnolia trees mix with the sweet gums, black tupelos and red maples. The undergrowth is still dense here, encouraging a large population of small mammals (mice, shrews, and voles) and nonpoisonous snakes (northern black racers and black rat snakes), which feed on the rodents. What you're unlikely to find are red-shouldered hawks or barred owls, which are less able to hunt the hidden mammals in the dense thickets.

As the land rises slightly, becoming drier, chest-high mountain laurel fills in the understory. One of the most versatile plants in the state, this acid-soil-loving heath thrives from the Highlands to the Pine Barrens. This gnarly shrub is a favorite nesting place of worm-eating and hooded warblers.

As you reach station #9 (0.5 mile), notice that pitch pine and a diversity of oaks (southern red, blackjack, willow, white, northern red, swamp white, and scrub oak) become prominent and that the canopy is less dense. Pitch pine needs much light to survive. It relies on regular forest fires to prevent the closure of the canopy by dense deciduous foliage.

At station #11 you cross from the acidic, sterile soils of the Outer Coastal Plain into the nutrient-rich soils of the Inner Coastal Plain. Notice how tall the American holly, sassafras, willow oaks and red maples are here. Persimmons grow too, bearing a sweet fruit tasting much like dates and used to flavor puddings, cakes and beverages and consumed by birds, opossums, skunks, and raccoons. Just after station #13, a short trail branches right for 0.1 mile to station #14, your deepest penetration into the Inner Coastal Plain.

Backtrack from station #14 and turn right to reach station #15 (1.0 mile). Water along this trail section can get shin deep from November through April. If you would rather stay dry, return the way you came. The last 0.5 mile is through a climax red maple hardwood forest dotted with large holly trees. A short trail spur leads right at station #23 for a view of Stop-the-Jade Run. The main path closes the loop. Just past station #24, turn right and return to the parking lot.

Luxuriant growths of cinnamon fern. ·

🌑 *PINE BARRENS PRESERVATION*

The outrageous jetport and "city of the future" proposal that would have paved much of the Pine Barrens may have spared it. This attempted land grab spurred South Jersey residents like Dot and Brooks Evert to organize and act. A vigorous grassroots coalition was led by the Pine Barrens Conservationists, Citizen's Committee to Preserve State Lands, New Jersey Conservation Foundation, New Jersey Audubon Society, and the Nature Conservancy.

A proposal for a Pine Barrens National Monument failed, but the Pine Barrens Coalition (an umbrella of environmental organizations) championed the creation of the federal Pinelands National Reserve in 1978. Today, the Pinelands Commission, a state agency, is charged with managing, preserving and protecting 935,000 wild acres at the heart of the region. In 1983 the United Nations recognized the uniqueness of the Pine Barrens, designating it an International Biosphere Reserve.

A 1995 attempt by conservative politicians and developers to abolish the national reserve fell on deaf ears. While the reserve seriously controls development, many local people heartily defend it, seeing the protection of species like the bog asphodel as a means for maintaining their own quality of life.

The New Jersey Conservation Foundation, born in 1960, continues to play an active role in keeping New Jersey green. They've preserved more than 70,000 acres of woodland, wetland, and farmland statewide.

From 1995 to 1998 the New Jersey Conservation Foundation preserved 4,230 acres in the Forked River Wilderness, while the Nature Conservancy protected another 3,578 acres. This Pine Barrens locale lies at the heart of the proposed 1960s megadevelopment. Instead, these wildlands will continue to ensure the survival of the endangered Pine Barrens gentian, curly grass fern and globally rare kniesekern's beaked rush.

Hours, Fees and Facilities

The trail is open dawn to dusk.

Getting There

From US 206 in Vincentown, take Route 530 east to Pemberton. Turn right on Magnolia Road, then right on Ongs Hat Road. The Dot and Brooks Evert Memorial Trail is on the right, before reaching Stockton's Bridge Road. Other nearby walks are the north end of the Batona Trail at Ongs Hat, and at the New Jersey Conservation Foundation 4-Mile Springs Preserve (call for trail info).

For More Information

New Jersey Conservation Foundation, Bamboo Brook, 170 Longview Road, Far Hills, NJ 07931; 908-234-1225.

Rancocas Nature 37 Center of the New Jersey Audubon Society

Rancocas State Park

- 1.5 miles
- 1 hour
- Easy

Hike from field to forest to river flood plain

In colonial times the marshes of the Inner Coastal Plain along the Lower Delaware River and its tributaries such as Rancocas Creek supported waterfowl by the hundreds of thousands. "I have nowhere seen so many ducks together," declared Jasper Daenckaerts in 1679, "When they flew up there was a rushing and vibration of the air like a great storm coming through the trees and even like the rumbling of distant thunder."

Over the next three centuries the thundering wings were silenced. Sportsmen launched flat-bottomed skiffs, laid out decoys and gunned for the "reed birds," slaughtering uncounted flocks. Blackbirds were also massacred in cattail marshes. Muskrats were relentlessly trapped and catfish netted.

New Jersey's Inner Coastal Plain also had the misfortune of perfectly coinciding with the vital transportation corridor connecting Washington, Baltimore, Philadelphia and New York. By the late twentieth century most forest and marsh had vanished beneath the New Jersey Turnpike; Routes 130 and I-295; or condominiums, subdivisions, factories, malls, gas stations, and golf courses.

State parks are spread thin along the overdeveloped Inner Coastal Plain. But one struggling park, Rancocas, has allied itself with the nonprofit New Jersey Audubon Society. When budget cuts in the 1970s forced the 1,100-acre park to close, the New Jersey Audubon Society stepped in. It established a fine nature center in an old farmhouse and built a Nature Trail exploring a portion of the park's fields, lowland deciduous forest, freshwater streams and marshes. The New Jersey Audubon Society is a privately supported group that has preserved 2,200 acres statewide within thirty nature sanctuaries, all open to the public.

Rancocas Road

Nature
Center

START
P

Willow
Oak

open
field

open
field

forest

forest

Woods Road

Rancocas Creek

N

1000 feet

Rancocas Nature Center

Begin your 1.5-mile loop walk at Rancocas State Park with a look at the Rancocas Nature Center exhibits housed within the hundred-year-old farmhouse. The informed volunteer interpreters will tell you about their terrarium-housed northern pine snake, corn snake, and spotted turtle. The endangered corn snake is a constrictor feeding on mice and rats. Be sure to pick up a copy of the excellent numbered interpretive Nature Trail guide before starting your walk.

The Nature Trail begins behind the farmhouse at the end of the driveway. A large graceful willow oak rises to the left of the trailhead. With its slim, lance-shaped leaves, it may look like no oak you've ever seen before. The tree does bear acorns, however, one of the defining characteristic of the oak (*Quercus*) genus. Willow oaks are to the southern U.S. what American elms once were to the north, a top choice for a handsome shade tree with which to line city streets.

The first hundred yards of the nature trail provide a vivid lesson in field succession. As you move past the numbered posts, pause and imagine that the forest is slowly growing toward you: it is! Eventually the surrounding woods will completely overgrow this abandoned farm field.

The field dotted with red cedar to your left (last cultivated more than twenty years ago) supports at least a hundred different plants. Some have names perfectly describing their appearance. In late summer, nodding foxtail grass sprouts a bushy green top resembling a fox's drooping tail, goldenrod possesses an erect stalk encircled by bright-yellow blossoms, and Queen Anne's lace is topped by an ornate creamy white crown of florets resembling an old-fashioned doily. St. Johnswort also flourishes. This plant, with showy five-petaled yellow flowers blooming in July, was used in old England to ward off evil spirits, and is currently in vogue as an organic treatment for depression.

Light-loving plants edge the field. Black cherry, red maple, black locust and arrowwood trees serve as scaffolding for viny tendrils of frost grape, multiflora rose and Asiatic bittersweet. Shrubby arrowwood has arrowhead-shaped leaves, but it was named for its strong straight stems, fashioned by Native Americans into arrows. Its juicy blue-black berries are a fall favorite of birds.

At Nature Trail post #5 you walk into the future of the abandoned farm field: the forest closes in around you. Vines and red cedars, starved for light, are dying out. These young woods are composed of red maple, black locust and tulip trees, all reaching for the sun and competing for light.

At post #7 you enter a planted pine plantation of native white pine, Austrian pine (easily confused with American red pine) and Norway spruce. These trees have been growing here since 1957. Note the absence of the lush plant understory usually found beneath deciduous trees. Conifers lay down a dense bed of acidic pine needles which prevents the seed of competing broad-leaf plants from taking hold. Only acid-tolerant ferns and grasses grow well in this gloomy blue shade.

Just before post #11 look for a river birch. This easily identified tree appears to have a fatal case of acne: its bark is broken into peeling salmon pink and reddish brown patches. Common in the mid-Atlantic states, the river birch, as its name implies, thrives on wet sites, making it useful in erosion control.

Rancocas Creek, the only major Pine Barrens river to flow to the Delaware.

Just beyond post #11 (0.3 mile into the walk), turn left and descend a woods road to the north branch of Rancocas Creek. The way down into the stream flood plain is lined by red maple, holly, sweet gum and umbrella magnolia. The magnolia, with its glossy two-foot-long leaves, is easy to spot. This is a southern tree, common in the Great Smoky Mountains of North Carolina. Its white flowers, blooming in spring, are as ostentatious as its leaves, forming a beautiful (but disagreeable smelling) six-to-ten-inch-wide cup.

A dense growth of sweet pepperbush, spicebush and winterberry hides the banks of the creek from view. At about 0.6 mile into your walk the woods road ends at Rancocas Creek on a muddy stream bank imprinted with the tracks of white-tailed deer, mice and shrews. Look for wading great blue herons standing on stiltlike legs amid the cattails, arrow arum and pickerelweed.

The Rancocas Creek forms the second largest watershed in the Pine Barrens and is the only major Pine Barrens stream to flow west into the Delaware River Basin. All other major South Jersey streams flow to the Atlantic.

The edge of the wide, amber-colored creek is lined with head-high aquatic sunflowers in autumn. The stream's wild rice marsh attracts migratory waterfowl, including wood ducks, northern pintails, and green-winged and blue-winged teals.

The green-winged teal is one of the fastest flying ducks, making it a favored and challenging target for duck hunters. While it's easy to condemn sportsmen as villains who diminish species, the survival of waterfowl and their habitat in the U.S. has been significantly enhanced by the advocacy of hunting organizations such as Ducks Unlimited.

Return the way you came from the shore of Rancocas Creek to the Nature Trail and turn left, picking up where you left off at post #12.

The trail now loops through a dark forest dominated by hard-to-miss sweet gum. This tree's distinctive five-pointed-star-shaped leaves and its green fruit resembling a spiked medieval mace make it a perfect candidate for Tree Identification 101. Sweet gum is a valuable southern timber tree used in furniture making and as plywood and pulpwood. The tree was named for a medicinal chewing gum early settlers produced from it.

The trail loops back toward the Nature Center through a mature forest of sweet gum, black oak, tulip tree, beech, and red maple. In April and May more than twenty species of migrant warblers pass through these woods. The yellow-billed cuckoo, Carolina wren, scarlet tanager, and barred owl nest here. The yellow-billed cuckoo's taste for hairy and spiny caterpillar species (which other birds avoid) makes it a valuable natural control for pests like the tent caterpillar and gypsy moth caterpillar. The cuckoo has evolved a mechanism for eliminating indigestible caterpillar parts. Spiny caterpillar hairs mat in the bird's stomach, then the stomach lining is shed and the cuckoo merely grows a new one.

The Nature Trail circles back to the forest-field edge at post #23, where frost grape vines hang like frayed ropes from black cherry and sassafras saplings. In a hundred feet the trail pops into the open back at the Nature Center parking lot (1.5 miles).

Hours, Fees and Facilities

The Rancocas Nature Center is open Tuesday through Sunday from 9:00 A.M. to 5:00 P.M., and closed Mondays and holidays. Admission free. Dogs and bicycles are not permitted on the trail.

Getting There

From I-295 use Exit 45A for Rancocas Road. In 1.7 miles turn right into the Rancocas Nature Center.

For More Information

Rancocas Nature Center, 794 Rancocas Road, Mount Holly, NJ 08060; 609-261-2495.

New Jersey Audubon Society, P.O. Box 126, Bernardsville, NJ 07924; 908-204-8998.

Apple Pie Hill Firetower

Wharton State Forest

- 8 miles
- 5.5 hours
- Challenging, due to length

A vista stretching from Philadelphia to the Atlantic Ocean

Walking in the Pine Barrens is like hiking along an ancient ocean bottom. The Outer Coastal Plain disappeared beneath ocean waves many times in the past 135 million years, and the sea laid down a gently sloping and nearly featureless terrain of permeable sand, silt, and clay more than a half-mile thick.

Hiking here is also like walking atop a great desert oasis. While the Pine Barrens receive more than forty inches of rain annually, that water drains quickly away, allowing only the hardiest of trees and heathlike shrubs to survive in bone-dry soils. But just below ground plentiful life-giving waters flow. A staggering 17 trillion gallons are cached in the Cohansey formation, New Jersey's largest aquifer. This crystal-pure water feeds 200,000 acres of Pine Barrens bog and swamp, plus its many sleepy miles of winding river.

The value of this aquifer was not lost on Pennsylvania financier Joseph Wharton, who began buying up the Pine Barrens in 1876. Wharton hoped to build canals and aqueducts with which to bring its sweet waters to the lips of millions of thirsty Philadelphians. The New Jersey legislature blocked Wharton's plan, and his 97,000 wooded acres became Wharton State Forest in 1955. Recognition of the value of the Pinelands aquifer has since thwarted other plans to cover the Outer Coastal Plain with model cities and a jetport.

There are no natural vistas from which to overlook the vast pine and oak wildlands overlaying the Cohansey formation aquifer. But 205-foot-high Apple Pie Hill with its firetower offers a stunning man-made view of this, the most extensive primitive tract remaining along the mid-Atlantic seaboard.

This 8.0-mile-out-and-back hike along the Batona Trail is one of the longest walks featured in this book, but, with an altitude gain of just a few hundred feet, is not overly challenging. Highlights include a cedar swamp, upland pine and oak forest, and the extraordinary view from Apple Pie Hill.

Apple Pie Hill Firetower

Apple Pie Hill
Firetower ■

Batona Trail (pink-blazed)

Skit Branch

Carranza Road

△

primitive
campground

START

P

■
Carranza
Memorial

TO
RT. 206

N

The walk begins in the parking area of the Carranza Memorial. This obelisk with its faded inscription marks the ill-fated end to a goodwill flight made by aviator Emilio Carranza. "Mexico's Lone Eagle" successfully flew a Ryan monoplane, of the type used by Charles Lindbergh, from Mexico City to Washington, D.C., and New York City in 1928. A Pine Barrens thunderstorm brought down the twenty-three-year-old pilot on his flight home.

Walk across the road from the Carranza Memorial and turn right. In a few hundred feet turn left and follow the pink blazes of the Batona Trail as they lead into the woods. The fifty-mile-long Batona Trail was built by the Batona Hiking Club of Philadelphia between 1961 and 1967. You'll be following the pink blazes for the entire hike.

Look closely. Beside the trail we found earthstars sprinkled in the sand. This tiny fungus is perfectly adapted to Pine Barrens desert-dry soil conditions. Only about two inches across, these tiny gray puffballs are surrounded by four to eight dark, star-like rays. The puffball (with a small hole in its top) is the fruiting body of the earthstar, and when sent skittering along by wind it spills forth its spores. Possessing no chlorophyll, the earthstar doesn't directly use the sun as a food source but derives its nutrients from organic matter found in the soil.

About 0.3 mile into your walk you arrive at Batona Primitive Camp (a camping permit is required from Wharton State Forest). The camp has tent sites, a water pump and outhouses. Follow the pink blazes through the campground.

The trail penetrates a forest of pitch pine, short-leaf pine, blackjack oak and post oak, the predominant trees seen on most of this walk. All four species thrive in nutrient-poor, acidic Pine Barrens soils. Pitch pines once were tapped for their thick, sticky sap called oleoresin, which was distilled into turpentine. Cut trees were also burned to boil off tar and pitch used to waterproof ship bottoms. Short-leaf pine is valued as lumber and pulpwood. In the 1800s, blackjack oak was primarily used as firewood and for charcoal. Post oak was more valuable, with its wood serving as mine timbers, posts and railroad ties.

Just beyond the campground the trail repeatedly intersects with a sand road (watch blazes closely). Beneath the pines and oaks, a scrubby understory of blueberries, sheep laurel, golden (Pine Barrens) heather, and reindeer lichen thrives.

The pink-blazed Batona Trail intersects the sand road one last time, turns left, and crosses the Skit Branch of the Batsto River on a major bridge at about 1.0 mile.

Like all Pine Barrens streams, this one is the color of steeped tea. This "cedar water" is rich in the tannin found in tree bark and leaves. Don't let its dark appearance fool you. Sailors once prized Pine Barrens cedar water because it stayed fresh and potable longer (never drink unfiltered water in the wild!).

While cedar waters are very acidic, with a 5.0 pH, they also support significant plant life. Along Skit Branch's peaty shores flourish insectivorous sundews and golden club, an aquatic herb with long-stalked leaves. Golden club blooms with a compact spike of yellow flowers in April and May. Fragrant waterlilies with pinkish white flowers blossom here from June to October.

The Carranza Memorial commemorates the ill-fated goodwill flight of "Mexico's Lone Eagle," who crashed his plane here in 1928.

After crossing the stream the trail immediately turns right, as it leaves the sand road for the last time. The path now straddles the boundary between upland and wetland. To your left, the drier pitch pine and oak forest continues unabated, with its mountain laurel, inkberry and sand myrtle understory. To your right, the dark reaches of a cedar swamp beckon. Bordering the still waters are highbush blueberry, dangleberry and leatherleaf shrubs. Farther in, stately Atlantic white cedars rise from sphagnum moss hummocks. The tree trunks glisten eerily with bluish green santee lichen. Woodpeckers have worked over the silver skeletons of dead cedars killed by a recent forest fire.

The trail crosses three small walking bridges before leaving the swamp behind at about 2.0 miles, and begins to climb into a dry pine and oak upland. Here we saw ants at work. They brought dark clay particles up from underground, building a chocolate brown mound atop white surface sand. Their excavations demonstrate the complex soil substrata displayed in the Pine Barrens. Thirteen major soil varieties top the Cohansey formation.

The trail crosses two small unnamed hills (rising to just 139 feet and 104 feet) before ascending to Apple Pie Hill (205 feet), the highest elevation in the Pine Barrens.

The view from the tower sweeps in an unbroken plain from horizon to horizon. It overlooks what John McPhee calls "a bewildering green country," 2,250 square miles, or 1.4 million acres, of flat, sandy, acidic and sterile soils blanketed by pitch pine and oak forests and cedar bogs. Here, within a major transportation corridor between New York City, Philadelphia and Atlantic City, there are few people and paved roads and no factories. On a clear day the skyscrapers of Philadelphia can be spotted, as can the silvery water towers marking New Jersey's many Atlantic Ocean barrier island towns. Mount Holly, a mere bump, climbs 183 feet above sea level to the west.

Apple Pie Hill is composed of Beacon Hill formation gravels and is slightly more erosion resistant than surrounding sands and clays. It may have been deposited by ancient rivers that once drained the Pine Barrens. The firetower surveys a vast country and in dry times offers a first defense against wildfire, which can burn through leaf litter, dry underbrush and resinous pines at the speed of a runaway freight train.

Amazingly, as we stared down from the tower top we saw a tree on the ground beneath us with huge, floppy tropical leaves. How this single invasive royal paulownia tree found its way here we could only guess. Perhaps it arrived as a seed carried in a bird's intestine, or maybe it was planted by a fire warden in need of its cheery, fragrant violet spring blooms. This native of China has become a New Jersey pest, popping up everywhere from the Palisades to the Piedmont and Pine Barrens. One botanist estimates that a single royal paulownia annually produces 21 million seeds. He also figured that if all those seeds grew, the offspring of that single tree would, by the third generation, produce enough royal paulownias to cover 20,442 worlds the size of our Earth!

When you've finished marveling at the sprawling Pine Barrens wilderness surrounding this lone firetower and royal paulownia tree, return the way you came to the Carranza Memorial parking area.

Hours, Fees and Facilities

The Batona Trail is open daily year-round and allows camping with a permit at designated sites.

Getting There

From U.S. 70, take U.S. 206 south and turn left (east) at the sign that directs you to the town of Tabernacle and the Carranza Monument. In 2.3 miles cross County 532 in Tabernacle. The Carranza Memorial parking area is 7.0 miles farther straight ahead on your right.

For More Information

Wharton State Forest, Batsto, R.D. 9, Hammonton, NJ 08037; 609-561-0024.
    To volunteer with the Batona Trail Club: 215-659-3921.

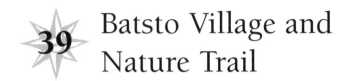

39 Batsto Village and Nature Trail

Wharton State Forest

- 2 miles
- 1.5 hours (not counting village walking tour)
- Easy

Explore the town that bog iron built

Bog iron breathed industrial life into the Pine Barrens. Starting in the 1700s, South Jersey ironmasters dredged streams and wetlands for iron ore, built iron furnaces and towns, clearcut forests and manufactured charcoal for fuel. They supplied pots, pans, and weapons to a booming colonial economy.

The bog iron business was also an ecological disaster. Dredging wrecked wetlands and disrupted streams. Each of thirty South Jersey furnaces consumed the charcoal equivalent of a thousand acres of woodland each year. When Pennsylvania became the new iron industry leader in the 1840s, Pine Barrens furnaces failed, leaving behind ghost towns and a scarred landscape.

Batsto is the iron town that wouldn't die. While many Pine Barrens communities are known today only for their legends and ruins, this one stayed alive. It began as a dirty little Pittsburgh with roaring blast furnace, pounding forge hammers, and acrid soot-filled air. Batsto's iron was thrown at British troops twice as cannonballs—first in the Revolution, then in the War of 1812. Batsto also forged peacetime products: iron water pipe, stoves, and fences.

When the bog iron business went bust in 1848, the town bounced back as a glass maker. It turned Pine Barrens sand into window panes and New York City lamplights. With the exhaustion of local forests by 1867, the glass industry also succumbed. South Jersey land baron and gentleman farmer Joseph Wharton stepped in and saved the community. He ruled his 97,000-acre Pine Barrens empire from Batsto until 1909. Today, the town has risen again as a historic village and headquarters to the 109,000-acre Wharton State Forest.

This 2.0-mile circuit hike invites walkers to explore Pine Barrens cultural and natural history. It utilizes part of the Batsto Pond Nature Trail, then loops back into town along unblazed but easy-to-follow sand roads. It ends with a tour of Batsto Village and its working gristmill and shingle-making sawmill. The town's odd name

Batsto Pond

Nature
Trail
Post K

Nature Trail

Nature Trail

sand road

sand road

sand road

sand road

N

0.25 mile

START

P

BATSTO
VILLAGE

542

**Batsto Village
& Nature Trail**

comes from the Swedish *batstu* for "steam bath," which was then borrowed and redefined by Native Americans to mean "bathing place."

Start at the visitor center by picking up a Nature Trail guide. Exit the back of the building and enter the village along the main road. To the left is an ore boat that was archaeologically exhumed from the bottom of Batsto Lake in 1957. Such boats hauled ore along South Jersey's little rivers to waiting iron furnaces.

Also to your left along the road is a heap of bog iron ore. This red mineral, called limonite or ironstone, was once mixed with bear grease by Lenape Native Americans and used as body paint.

The creation of bog iron is not so much a geological process as a botanical and biological one. Limonite forms when acidic vegetative "cedar water" in streams and ground water leaches iron salts out of greensands (marls or greensands are the fecal pellets of ancient marine filter-feeding organisms). The iron-rich cedar water forms a rust brown and oily blue slick on stream surfaces, where air and bacteria oxidize it. This slick then settles to the stream bottom and mixes with sand and muck to become thick beds of red ironstone.

The road next passes a charcoal kilning exhibit. Charcoal fueled iron and glass furnaces. It was made by slowly burning wood in an oxygen-starved charcoal pit to drive off tars, resins and impurities, leaving behind almost pure carbon. Charcoal burns at much higher temperatures than wood and produces the extreme heat needed to liquefy iron ore and glass.

The tulip tree–lined village road continues past the ironmasters' mansion and home to Joseph Wharton. While Wharton's nineteenth-century scheme to siphon off Pine Barrens water for thirsty Philadelphians was thwarted by the New Jersey legislature, he was able to retire to his vast Pine Barrens domain, which still bears his name.

Just before reaching the bridge and dam on Batsto Pond (0.1 mile into your walk), turn right onto the Nature Trail. Batsto Pond, like most Pine Barrens ponds, is artificial. It was dammed in 1766 to provide pollution-free water power to operate a sawmill, gristmill, and the huge bellows that forced air into the iron furnace, superheating and melting the ore.

At Nature Trail post A you are invited to compare two tree species. On the lake side of the path are native Atlantic white cedars which grow in Coastal Plain bogs from Maine southward. The Pine Barrens today supports some of the largest Atlantic white cedar groves. To the right are northern white cedars, an inland New England tree not native to New Jersey. Known as the arborvitae, or "tree of life," it is said that tea steeped from northern white cedar needles saved French explorer Jacques Cartier and his men from scurvy on their Canadian expedition of 1535. The needles are rich in vitamin C.

The trail passes along Batsto Pond through thick undergrowth of greenbrier and beneath a loose canopy formed by black oak, post oak, blackjack oak, shortleaf pine and pitch pine. Greenbrier (also called catbrier) is a thorn-covered vine that forms impenetrable Pinelands thickets and feeds gray catbirds, cardinals and

While Batsto Village is quiet today, it was once a sooty, noisy industrial town, maker of iron and glass.

hermit thrushes with its berries. Greenbrier harbors the hunted: rabbits, voles, and mice seek shelter from diving raptors in the barbed-wire-like tangles.

At Nature Trail post F you can survey Batsto Pond for turtles. Common in Pine Barrens waters are red-bellied turtles (feeding on aquatic vegetation, insect larvae and small fish), eastern mud turtles (a bottom feeder often coated with mud), and the stinkpot turtle (evocatively named for its musky secretions).

Yellow-rumped warblers abound in this forest, the northernmost extension of their winter range (we counted thirty in ten minutes one October afternoon). They are easily identified when they fly and flash their yellow rumps. This conspicuous bird is the only warbler to winter regularly in the Pine Barrens.

At Nature Trail post H look near your feet for golden heather (also called Pine Barrens heather). This little plant with bristly, needle-like leaves blooms with bright yellow flowers in mid-May. It colonizes open sand along trails and roads. Pine Barrens flora is unique for its mix of northern and southern species. Fourteen northern species like golden heather reach their southern limits here, while more than a hundred species, such as Pine Barrens gentian and bog asphodel, are at their northern limits. Most of these species appeared here since the start of a period of global warming at the end of the last Ice Age 15,000 years ago.

The path traverses a hardwood swamp at post J, where sweet bay magnolia mixes with red maples and black tupelos (black gums). The sweet bay, or swamp, magnolia has long-lasting, large, cup-shaped creamy white flowers appearing in late May and staying until July. It was named the beavertree by early settlers who baited beaver traps with its fleshy roots.

At post K the Nature Trail begins to loop to the right back toward the village. (If you would rather stick with the blazed path, follow the Nature Trail through post S back to where you began). For the slightly more adventurous, continue straight ahead. An easy-to-follow but unblazed trail edges the pond shore over some wet spots on bog bridging. It passes beneath pitch pine and post oak and amid sheep laurel, mountain laurel, bracken fern and sweet pepperbush.

In a short distance this unmarked trail intersects a sand road (1.0 mile). Follow this road right for about 0.25 mile until it intersects with another major sand road. Bear right again on this sand road.

These sand roads, pocked by white-tailed deer tracks, are typical of the hundreds, perhaps thousands, of signless miles of roads which weave aimlessly through the Pine Barrens. The loose sugar sand often hopelessly mires the tires of unwary four-wheelers.

At about 1.9 miles into your walk the sand road reaches a split-rail fence and chain-link fence. Make your way around both fences. A short stretch of sand road brings you back to the visitor center parking lot at 2.0 miles.

Tour Batsto village and its more than thirty buildings, including historic homes, barns, blacksmith shop, and working gristmill. Enjoy a shady picnic lunch and contemplate "idyllic" nineteenth-century life as it must have been within sight of the smoke-belching, ear-shattering blast furnace.

Hours, Fees and Facilities

Batsto village grounds are open dawn to dusk. The visitor center is open 9:00 A.M. to 4:30 P.M. daily. Buildings and facilities are closed New Year's, Thanksgiving and Christmas Days. A parking fee is charged from Memorial Day weekend through Labor Day weekend on weekends and holidays.

Getting There

Take the Garden State Parkway south to Exit 52 for New Gretna. Turn left onto Route 654 and in 1.0 mile turn right on US 9. In 1.5 miles turn right onto Route 542. Drive 13 miles and turn right into Batsto village.

For More Information

Wharton State Forest, Batsto, R.D. 9, Hammonton, NJ 08037; 609-561-0024.

40 Parvin State Park

- 4.6 miles
- 3.5 hours
- Moderate; sometimes wet

Immense biological diversity in a tiny state park

Where habitats collide, botanical and biological diversity rules. In Parvin State Park, northern and southern ecosystems meet in a preserve that lies just below the Mason-Dixon Line. Here oak-pine upland, swamp hardwood forest, stream flood plain, and Atlantic white cedar bog habitats weave together into a rich woodland tapestry.

Parvin State Park is known as a hidden gem of the New Jersey park system. This tiny preserve, at a mere 1,135 acres, explodes with life. It boasts 40 tree types, 61 woody shrubs, 17 ferns and club mosses, plus 200 herbaceous flowering plants. Migrant and nesting birds number at more than 135 species. White-tailed deer, river otter, raccoon, skunk, turtles, salamanders and nonpoisonous snakes thrive amid dense foliage.

The explanation for so much variety packed into such a tight space is a concept biologists call the ecotone. An ecotone marks the boundary between two or more ecosystems or habitats. In an ecotone the species of one habitat freely mix, interact, and compete with those of another for soil moisture and nutrients, light, space, and food. In these transition zones species variety tends to be rich.

This 4.6-mile loop walk uses the Parvin Lake Trail, Long Trail, and Thundergust Lake Trail to sample this wealth of life. One caution: trail blazing was poor on our hike here in 1997. However, this little park is surrounded by paved roads; it's difficult to stay lost for long. But, if a little perplexity isn't your style, avoid this hike. Mountain bikes are also common in Parvin, forcing hikers to step aside for their quick passage.

Begin by walking from the parking lot toward the park office and beach (you can buy an excellent detailed trail map at the park office). Turn sharply right just before reaching the building. The green-blazed Parvin Lake Trail leads immediately into the woods.

Forest diversity is instantly apparent. Parvin is a jumble of northern and southern, upland and wetland plant species, all jostling for dominance. In the first few hundred yards of this hike we identified six oak species (white, scarlet, chest-

Parvin State Park

nut, northern red, southern red, and post oak), three pines (white, short-leaf, and pitch pine), and two hickories (bitternut and shagbark), plus sassafras, sweet gum, black cherry, red maple, flowering dogwood, and holly trees.

The forest floor was equally luxuriant. A chaotic jungle of shrubs (arrowwood, mountain laurel, winterberry, greenbrier, and sweet pepperbush) and vines (wild grape, Virginia creeper, and poison ivy) compete for light and space. Waist-high cinnamon fern, partridgeberry and wintergreen spread out over the leaf litter.

Experienced birders spy assorted warblers, vireos, and scarlet tanagers in these wet woods during spring migration. Regular nesting birds at Parvin Park include Acadian flycatchers, yellow-billed cuckoos, barred owls, and Kentucky warblers. For best birding, walk here in late April and early May before lush leaf growth obscures the action. This is a hike where the tree, wildflower, and bird books are a must.

The first 0.9 mile of this walk feels like Christmas: festive American holly trees with prickly, glistening evergreen leaves and red berries in autumn flourish in damp soils. American holly's beauty was nearly its undoing in parts of the U.S. Overpruning for Yuletide decoration killed many of these slow-growing trees. Holly is spread primarily by berry-eating birds and mammals. Robins overwinter in South Jersey hardwood swamps and rely on the sugar-rich berries for survival.

Another common tree along this trail section is the southern red oak (or Spanish oak). This tree has distinctive leaves with a long, narrow central lobe, plus one to three shorter lobes on either side of a bell-shaped base. A large graceful tree, the Spanish oak is valued as an ornamental but not for its lumber, which is inferior to that of its relative, the northern red oak.

At 0.9 mile the green-blazed Parvin Lake Trail turns abruptly left. Continue straight ahead on the red-blazed Long Trail. There are picnic grounds and a toilet to the right. At 1.0 mile the white-blazed Nature Trail goes off to the right and reconnects with the Long Trail at 1.2 miles. Stay on the Long Trail.

Muddy Run, a branch of the Maurice River, now parallels the path on your left. The trail descends into an Atlantic white cedar swamp, passing among black tupelos, sweet bay magnolias, sensitive fern, royal fern, and, in drier spots, eastern burning bush (also known as the wahoo tree). In fall, burning bush is hard to miss, with bright red-orange fruit capsules and hot-pink leaves. The Native American term for the plant was *wahoo*. Could this perhaps have something to do with the purgative effect of its powdered bark?

Arrow arum, an aquatic relative of skunk cabbage, jack-in-the-pulpit and wild calla, is abundant in the stream flood plain. It has foot-long glossy arrow-shaped leaves. It flowers in June and wears green berries in autumn.

The Long Trail crosses Muddy Run on a bridge at 1.6 miles. Willows and red maples rise over the creek. Willow bark was long used by Native Americans as a pain reliever. Modern science caught up with aboriginal peoples in 1829 when glucoside salicin, a basic aspirin ingredient, was isolated and marketed.

Muddy Run rewards patient warbler watchers in spring. Prothonotary warblers have been sighted nesting in tree cavities near this bridge in past years. This

*Warbler watchers are rewarded at the bridge over
Muddy Run.*

golden bird, common to southern cypress swamps and bayous, is at the northern
extreme of its breeding range in South Jersey.

The name Muddy Run seems to be a misnomer. When we walked here the
stream ran crystal clear over a gravel bottom. Absent was the tannin-rich, tea-col-
ored "cedar water" found in the Pine Barrens.

Trail markings from this point on are almost nonexistent. Selecting the correct
path requires careful attention and map reading.

The Long Trail climbs slightly away from Muddy Run and at 1.7 miles intersects a short side trail to the left which meets Forest Road. Continue straight ahead
on the Long Trail, crossing an unnamed trail at 1.9 miles.

The path now curves slowly left, passing through much-drier terrain. An
upland forest of oak and pine takes over. White oak, red oak, hickories, and varied pines rise above sweet pepperbush, greenbrier, mountain laurel, scrub oak and
blueberry bushes.

At 2.7 miles the Long Trail reaches a T. Turn right on the Long Trail, which in a few hundred feet crosses a sand road and meets the Flat Trail (which turns to the left). Continue straight ahead, ignoring a right turn onto the Lost Trail. At 3.0 miles you arrive at a triangular trail junction. Stay to the right, following the Long Trail. At 3.1 miles the Long Trail intersects the Lost Trail again. Continue straight ahead. The Long Path intersects the Black Oak Trail at a paved dead end on the left. Continue straight ahead.

The Long Trail intersects with the yellow-blazed Thundergust Lake Trail at a stream bridge at 3.5 miles. Walk straight ahead, then curve to the left through the picnic area. Congratulations, you've completed the most confusing part of the walk and are back in civilization! The pretty shore of Thundergust Lake is on your left. The lake shore is overhung with black tupelo and holly and lined with sweet pepperbush and ferns. We saw great blue herons and green herons wading amid the duckweed, and red-bellied turtles sunning on snags in October.

At 4.0 miles you reach the far end of Thundergust Lake. Swerve left, cross a major park road, and follow the Parvin Lake Trail (the shore of Parvin Lake will be on your left). From here you can see the point at which you started, the park office and beach across the lake.

The trail passes over a horseshoe-shaped concrete spillway, a reminder that there are few natural lakes in South Jersey. Lamuel Parvin bought this land in 1796 with the intention of damming Muddy Run to turn a sawmill water wheel. The property became a state park in 1930 at the start of the Great Depression. While Hitler solved Germany's unemployment problems by arming his nation's youth with guns, Franklin Roosevelt armed America's financially strapped young men with shovels. The Civilian Conservation Corps built Parvin's roads, trails, cabins and beach.

Follow the trail as it curves left around Parvin Lake and returns you to the park office at 4.6 miles.

Hours, Fees and Facilities

The trails of Parvin State Park are open dawn to dusk year-round. From September 30 to May 1, office hours are 8:00 A.M. to 3:30 P.M. weekdays (closed on weekends). From May 1 through September 30 the office is open seven days a week.

Getting There

Take Route 55 south of Glassboro to Exit 45. Drive south on Route 553 for about 8 miles to Centerton. Turn left on Route 540 for about 2 miles. Parvin Park is on the right.

For More Information

Parvin State Park, R.D. 1, Box 374, Elmer, NJ 08318; 609-358-8616.

Atlantic Shore Region

41 Sandy Hook, Old Dune Trail

Gateway National Recreation Area

- 1.0 mile (plus optional additional 1.1-mile loop)
- 1 or 2 hours
- Easy

Witness the diversity of coastal life

Gateway National Recreation Area, including the 6.5-mile long sand spit known as Sandy Hook, is a study in diversity. Fresh water from the Hudson and Raritan River watersheds mingles with the saline waters of Long Island Sound. This creates an estuary ecosystem unlike that of open ocean or inland river, yet combining elements of both. Sandy Hook itself supports four types of plant communities (beach/dune, shrub thicket, mixed forest and holly forest) and stands as a buffer between open ocean to the east and sheltered salt marsh to the west.

Located on the edge of one of the most populated areas of this continent, Gateway has played diverse roles in the protection (and, ironically, possible self-destruction) of human inhabitants of the area. On Sandy Hook a lighthouse built in 1764 still operates today, the Coast Guard patrols the coast, and Fort Hancock—decommissioned by the military in 1972—serves as a museum and environmental research facility. Abandoned Nike missile sites attest to the Cold War bunker mentality. Fortunately, the better angels of our nature prevailed; in October of 1972, Congress proclaimed Gateway and San Francisco's Golden Gate Park the first urban National Recreation Areas.

Thus, Sandy Hook affords a rare sight indeed: a stretch of Jersey Shore virtually undeveloped. Endangered piping plovers nest here every summer. Holly trees, some more than 100 years old, canopy a variety of plants that would be considered unique anywhere.

Sandy Hook

Nike Pond

observation platform

dunes and fragile vegetation

North to optional additional loop walk

dirt road

shore

dunes and fragile vegetation

Atlantic Ocean

shore

Holly Forest

lots of seashells!

Area E Parking Lot

BEWARE! Poison Ivy

START

P

Visitor Center

N

A pre–Memorial Day or post–Labor Day visit to Sandy Hook offers a chance to explore the dunes—via trails only—without summer crowds of beach-goers. A winter walk may reward you with a glimpse of a snowy owl, a visitor from the far North. Even the off-season sun on these dunes can be unrelenting. No matter what time of year you walk here, don't let the short distance lull you into thinking you need not carry water or wear a hat.

Begin at the visitor center, itself a former lifesaving station of historic interest. Inside, displays alert you to some of the creatures you might see (kids of all ages will enjoy learning the names of shells they'll likely find on the beach). Pick up a brochure for the self-guided nature trail.

Leave the visitor center, heading back toward the main road. Almost immediately, turn right onto the Old Dune Trail.

Note at once that this is a natural laboratory for the close study of poison ivy, which attains the size of small shrubs here. You definitely do not want to stray off the trail or even casually brush against the foliage. Shiny green in spring, dull green in summer, and flaming red in autumn, think of poison ivy for what it is: a successful member of this ecosystem and a provider of food for the glorious avian life of this coastal habitat.

Wildflowers such as beach goldenrod and pokeweed, and grasses like switch grass, line the trail. Tolerance is the key to life on the dunes: shrubs like bayberry (with its pale blue fruit clusters in autumn, used to scent candles) and groundsel (with small white summer flowers and silky white autumn tufts) tolerate dry, nutrient-poor sand, salty breezes, and occasional inundation by salt surf during storm-driven high tides.

The prize for tolerance, however, must go to the prickly pear cactus, a reminder that life in dry sand, accumulated salt residue, and incessant wind resembles life in a desert. The prickly pear cactus stores fresh water in its padlike stalks, and its needles are actually modified leaves (less surface area means less water loss from transpiration).

Sandy Hook is a veritable paradise for birds. About 350 species either nest here or find temporary sustenance and shelter during spring and fall migrations. The native trees you see along the trail (red cedar, black cherry, holly) and the shrubs (winged sumac, beach plum, beach rose, and the garden escapee, multiflora rose) all provide succulent fruits and well-protected nesting sites for songbirds. The bark of some of the taller trees shows the work of woodpeckers. Small mammals such as mice, shrews and rabbits attract raptors.

The trail crosses a road and then immediately enters the dunelands again. Take a moment to look around at this remarkable density of plant life. Without the sand-stabilizing effects of this root network, the dunes would eventually be carried away by wind and wave, and Sandy Hook would cease to exist. Within 0.2 mile, you'll be amazed to find yourself in a forest. Years of vegetative recycling have laid down a layer of richer soil above the sand. Holly trees, which grow only an inch or so each year, tower overhead; their thick evergreen leaves retain moisture.

Keep going straight (paralleling the road to your left and the beach to your right) as the trail crosses an old dirt road. You are in the vicinity of an abandoned Nike missile site, an eerie reminder of the dark side of human nature.

Just as the path makes a right turn, an observation platform offers a vista out over a small freshwater pond. Take a moment to observe the abundant bird life or look for raccoon footprints around the base of the platform.

Smaller plants dominate the landscape again as you near the beach. Golden heather, seaside goldenrod, and tall wormwood line the way to the front dune.

Once out on the beach, you can see north to New York City. You'll want to head south (right) to complete this loop walk. (Option: explore the beach northward, entering the dunes again at parking area F; at the visitor center, a trail map is available for a 1.1-mile loop walk around the South Beach Dune Trail).

Sea shells abound, washed up on shore by the tides (see sidebar). Follow the beach south for about 0.3 mile; watch for power lines and the visitor center tower on your right. This is the end of the walk, if you can pull yourself away from the allure of sand and surf.

Beach grasses act as a skeleton for the dunes, withstanding the power of wind and wave.

🐚 *SEE SOME SEA SHELLS*

Translucent amber jingle shells. Ridged and furrowed oysters. Scallops in hues of blue and gray. Blue mussels like the sky at twilight. These are just a few of the bivalves (two-shelled mollusks) you'll find along the beach at Sandy Hook. Snail shells (univalves) also abound. The pleasing shapes and subtle colors of slipper shells, channeled whelks, knobbed whelks, and northern moon snails are a joy to observe.

Remember that the "dead" shells you find along the beach once housed living animals. The shell offered protection from predators and from periods of exposure to air (shell-less slugs produce slime instead). Calcium carbonate, concentrated in the animal's blood, is secreted by an organ called the mantle to form the shell. As the snail or clam grows, it adds more calcium carbonate to the edge of the existing shell. Pigmentation cells in the mantle produce colors and patterns.

A shell is not foolproof protection. Some snails bore through the shells of living bivalves to eat the soft animal within, while sea gulls regularly drop live mollusks (as well as crabs) from on high, smashing the shells on rocks. If you take a shell or two home as a souvenir of your walk at Sandy Hook, make sure the animal no longer resides within.

Mollusks first evolved about 600 million years ago, making them one of the oldest living forms of life on Earth. Today, the phylum Mollusca is the second largest group of animals, with more than 50,000 species (only the phylum Arthropoda—insects, spiders, crabs and their kin—has more species). Snails and clams also live in freshwater habitats, and snails live on land and even in trees in the tropics. Octopus, squid, nautaloids, nudibranchs (shell-less marine mollusks resembling ornate slugs), chitons (tiny armadillo-looking mollusks with eight-sectioned shells), and the slugs in your garden are all members of the phylum Mollusca.

Hours, Fees and Facilities

Visitor center open daily 10:00 A.M. to 5:00 P.M. Parking fees collected from Memorial Day through Labor Day.

Getting There

Take Exit 117 of the Garden State Parkway to Route 36 east. Follow signs for the Atlantic Highlands and Sandy Hook, Gateway National Recreation Area. After crossing the bridge onto Sandy Hook, follow signs to the park entrance. The visitor center is 2 miles ahead on the right.

For More Information

Sandy Hook Unit, Gateway National Recreation Area, P.O. Box 530, Fort Hancock, NJ 07732; 908-872-0115.

—chapter and sidebar by Jean LeBlanc

Cattus Island
42

Ocean County Park

- 3.2 miles
- 2 hours
- Easy; flat

Visit a salt marsh, home to osprey and diamondback terrapin

When the last glacial age subsided 15,000 years ago, meltwater from mile-thick layers of ice swelled the world's oceans, causing them to rise and drown lowland coasts. As the climate warmed, two salt-tolerant marsh grasses took hold in shallow sheltered bays and estuaries along the Atlantic seaboard.

Salt hay (*Spartina patens*), a fine, slender grass, colonized near the shore and above the high-tide level. Cordgrass (*Spartina alterniflora*), a taller, coarser, extremely salt tolerant plant, took hold farther from shore at midtide level.

These two grasses form the basis for an ecosystem that is among the most bountiful found on Earth. Salt marshes are the lifeblood of our oceans, adding nutrients and oxygen to coastal waters while removing pollutants. They provide vital nurseries to many commercially valuable fish. Tuna, clams, shrimp, oysters and other shellfish are dependent on tidal wetlands for survival. Thousands of migratory shorebirds and waterfowl also rely on salt marshes for food and resting and nesting places.

From colonial times down to the mid–twentieth century, most Americans failed to recognize the ecological value of these wetlands. Salt marshes were seen only as resources to be exploited. Salt hay was harvested to feed cattle. Tidal wetlands were diked, drained, and built upon. They were ditched and sprayed with DDT and other pesticides to kill mosquitoes. Oil spills, industrial pollution, urban sewage and garbage choked the marshes.

Today half of the 12,500 square miles of salt marsh that once lined the Atlantic coast is gone. New Jersey has lost more than a million acres, and what remains is not nearly as healthy as it once was. But in recent years the tide has begun to turn, as the public has come to understand the worth of these wetlands.

Cattus Island County Park and its Cooper Environmental Center naturalists have contributed to this public appreciation. This 500-acre Ocean County park protects a salt marsh at the heart of Barnegat Bay. Surrounded on all sides by beach

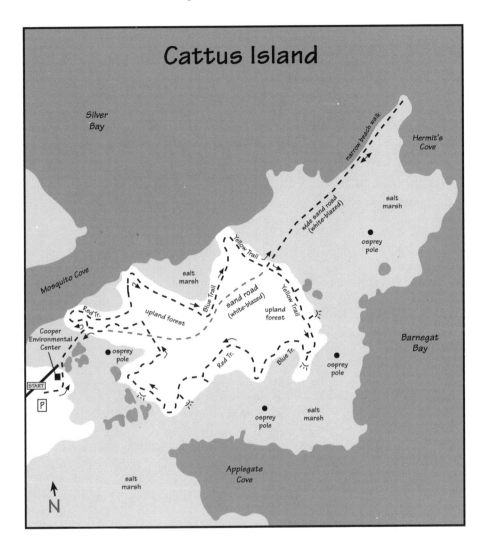

development and pleasure-boat docks, this fine preserve boasts breeding osprey, migrating warblers and diamondback terrapin.

Begin this 3.2-mile loop hike with a tour of the environmental center. Be sure to ask plenty of questions; the naturalists are particularly friendly and knowledgeable.

From the back of the building follow the White Trail leading out onto the marsh causeway raised above the bay. Cattus Island is not truly an island but rather a very wet peninsula. It consists of an upland completely encircled by an expansive salt marsh.

As you walk out onto the causeway, notice the salt hay (closest to shore) and the cordgrass (farther out in the marsh). Salt typically sucks water out of living cells, destroying them. But salt-marsh grasses have developed an ingenious adaptation that allows them to convert salt water into fresh: A root membrane filters out most of the salt. Any remaining brine is excreted by glands in the plant's leaves.

From the causeway the waters of Applegate Cove lie to your right, while those of Mosquito Cove lie to your left. The much-cursed mosquito (jokingly called New Jersey's state bird) is prolific in coastal salt marshes. While a pest to humans, this insect is a boon to hungry birds and fish.

A scattering of red cedar and groundsel trees and bayberry bushes dot the causeway. The bayberry is easily recognized when its waxy green berries darken to blue-gray by late summer. Often lasting through the winter, they offer meals to such songbirds as the yellow-rumped warbler, to shorebirds, and to red foxes. Bayberry takes the edict "be fruitful and multiply" seriously. Its tiny but numerous seeds (55,000 to a pound!), diffused in animal droppings, ensure that the plant is widespread.

At the end of the causeway (about 0.2 mile into the walk) leave the White Trail by turning left on the Red Trail. This path follows the edge between upland and marsh habitat. As you walk on dry land amid pitch pine, holly, southern red oak, blackjack oak, sweet bay magnolia, and greenbrier, you can repeatedly look left out into the open salt marsh.

The adjacency of marsh and upland enriches species diversity. The uplands, for example, provide shelter to nesting eastern phoebes and other songbirds, while the marsh provides insects as food.

The wooded upland through which you are walking was once the port of call for Revolutionary War privateer Timothy Page. Privateers were licensed pirates invited by the Continental Congress to raid British shipping. Later the island was the site for a sawmill, and by the 1890s it became a weekend retreat. Sold to developers in the 1960s, it narrowly escaped being built upon when New Jersey enacted tough wetland-protection laws. Cattus Island opened as an Ocean County park in 1976.

Continue following the marsh edge by leaving the Red Trail and turning left on the Blue Trail (roughly 0.7 mile into the walk). In a few hundred feet, leave the Blue Trail and turn left on the Yellow Trail. When the Yellow Trail intersects with the wide sand road of the White Trail at about 1.0 mile, turn left on the White Trail and follow it out onto a causeway which extends through the marsh into the bay. Look for the hoof prints of white-tailed deer in the soft sand at your feet.

As you walk the causeway, scout the marsh to the right for osprey towers. Such towers were placed by the park to encourage nesting raptors. One pair of ospreys has nested actively here for more than a decade. The pair arrives at Cattus Island to breed in late March and is gone by September, though migrating ospreys continue passing through until late in the fall. These large majestic birds, known as fish hawks, were nearly eliminated by eggshell-thinning DDT in the 1950s and 1960s but are enjoying a promising recovery. They fly and hover above the surface of the bay, then dive steeply and snatch fish with their talons.

Continue following the White Trail to where it dead-ends at a sandy point on the shore of Hermit's Cove (about 1.5 miles into the hike). A sweeping view of Barnegat Bay surrounds you. Backtrack along the White Trail over the causeway, and upon returning to the forested upland turn left on the Yellow Trail.

Cattus Island is a haven for birds in an otherwise suburbanized coastal area. In springtime thirty species of warbler, including common yellowthroats, black-throated blue, and cerulean warblers, may be spotted. In summer great blue herons and great and snowy egrets frequent the marsh. In spring and fall migrating raptors such as red-tailed hawks, northern harriers, merlins, and rare peregrine falcons stop to rest. Goldfinches, house finches, Carolina chickadees and tufted titmice overwinter in the thickets of the island uplands.

The fact that the diamondback terrapin makes its home in the Cattus Island salt marsh attests to the cleanness of Barnegat Bay. This little turtle can't tolerate polluted waters. Just five to eight inches long, the diamondback terrapin was considered such a gourmet delicacy in the early 1900s that it brought $7 per inch, which soon made it scarce. Less sought after as a soup ingredient these days, the little turtle has made something of a comeback. It lays its eggs in the sand at the edge of the Cattus Island marsh. Skunks and raccoons frequently prey on the eggs before they can hatch.

Continue following the edge between forest and marsh. When the Yellow Trail ends at the Blue Trail, turn left, following the Blue Trail briefly to where it ends at an intersection with the Red Trail. Turn left on the Red Trail and follow it as it circles back to intersect with the White Trail. Turn left on the White Trail and return over the causeway to the Cooper Environmental Center at 3.2 miles.

Hours, Fees and Facilities

Cattus Island trails are open daily from 8:00 A.M. to dusk. Cooper Environmental Center is open in winter from 10:00 A.M to 4:00 P.M. and in summer from 9:00 A.M. to 5:00 P.M. Admission is free.

Getting There

From the Garden State Parkway take Exit 82. Follow Route 37 east for about 4.4 miles, then use a right-hand jug handle to make a left turn onto Fischer Boulevard. (Spur Route 549). In about 2 miles turn right on Cattus Island Boulevard. The park entrance road is a hundred yards on the left and leads to the Cooper Environmental Center in about 1 mile.

For More Information

Cattus Island Park, Cooper Environmental Center, 1170 Cattus Island Boulevard, Toms River, NJ 08753; 732-270-6960.

43 Island Beach State Park

*Explore dynamic coastal habitats shaped by
a tumult of tide, wind and storm*

New Jersey's barrier islands, stretching from Sandy Hook to Cape May, are utterly ephemeral. Just 15,000 years ago they didn't exist. At that time much of the world's water lay locked within mile-thick glaciers. Earth's oceans were shallower and the Atlantic coast lay eighty miles east of its present location.

When a global warming trend melted away the continental ice sheet, torrential rivers flooded outward from the glaciers. In New Jersey, these streams hurled tons of sand and gravel—flecks of quartz, garnet and magnetite, the remains of ancient mountains—from the Highlands toward the sea.

Glacial melting also caused the world's oceans to rise, inundating the leading edge of the Coastal Plain. Violent tides swept sand up from the sea floor and heaped it in narrow islands lining the coast. These barrier islands, with their beaches, dunes, marshes, lagoons and back bays, were constantly reshaped by the flux of stream and tidal deposition and by rising ocean levels.

These radical alterations took place within the memory of the human race. New Jersey archaeologists surmise that the 12,000-year-old coastal campsites of Paleolithic hunter-gatherers are lost to us, submerged beneath the sea covering the continental shelf. Likewise, change continues: nineteenth-century farm fields are salt marsh today and will be brackish lagoons tomorrow.

Human-influenced global warming may be quickening the pace of change. The sea now rises one inch every six years, driving barrier beaches westward about two feet annually. Storms speed this movement. Hurricanes and nor'easters alter the face of the coast within hours, melting away beaches, closing or opening inlets, and extending or contracting islands.

Island Beach State Park (ten miles long but just a few hundred yards wide) protects one of the best unspoiled barrier island ecosystems on the North Atlantic. Unburdened by boardwalks and beach houses, life here continues to adapt to turbulent coastal conditions begun less than 15,000 years ago.

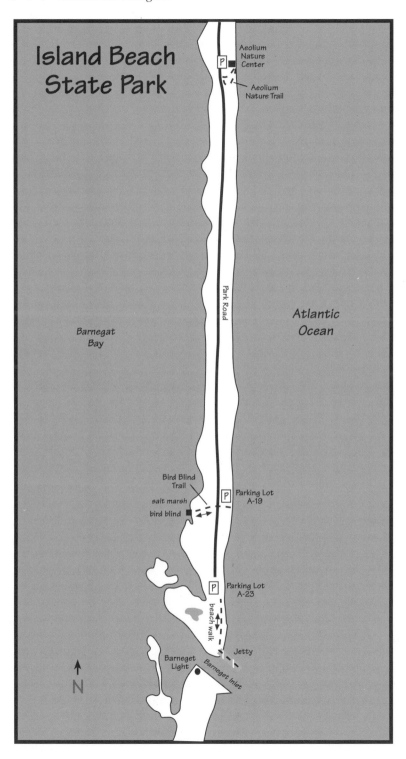

Island Beach
State Park

Aeolium
Nature
Center

Aeolium
Nature Trail

Park Road

Atlantic
Ocean

Barnegat
Bay

Bird Blind
Trail

salt marsh

bird blind

Parking Lot
A-19

Parking Lot
A-23

beach walk

Jetty

Barneget
Light

Barneget Inlet

N

This 4.1-mile walk explores three park locales. It begins with a tour of the Aeolium Nature Center and a stroll along its 0.1-mile self-guided trail. It continues with a 0.5-mile-out-and-back walk from beach to back bay, and ends with a 3.5-mile-out-and-back hike along ocean beach to the south tip of the park, where a jetty juts seaward, offering views of Barnegat Inlet and Barnegat Light.

Enjoy hands-on exhibits at the state park's Aeolium Nature Center (a Greek word for "wind"), a fun place for kids. We were perplexed by the difference between bottled samples of coarse-grained beach sand from Sandy Hook thirty-five miles to the north and fine-grained sand from Island Beach State Park. The explanation is simple. The heavily silted Raritan River deposits the weightiest, coarsest suspended particles at its Sandy Hook mouth. Lighter, finer sands are then carried steadily southward toward Cape May by waves striking barrier island beaches at an angle. This effect, called littoral drift, makes and unmakes inlets, sand spits, points and hooks, islands and peninsulas.

The 0.1-mile Aeolium Nature Trail loop offers an introduction to barrier island flora. Begin at the butterfly garden, where we saw autumn monarchs sipping nectar from wild bergamot and butterfly bushes before winging on to Mexico.

The trail penetrates an old dune area covered in a dense thicket community. The foliage and roots of red cedar, sassafras, black cherry, shining sumac, holly and pitch pine serve as windbreaks and anchors, reducing erosion and holding together tenuous sands. Without plant roots acting as internal skeletons, dunes would quickly blow away.

Low-lying plants provide dune-stabilizing anchorages, too. Sheep laurel, greenbrier, bayberry, Virginia creeper and blueberry form an impenetrable understory where cedar waxwings and other birds find cover and plentiful fruit. Beach plum is a showy dune species with masses of white spring flowers and plump autumn plums enjoyed by birds and red foxes.

The trail passes among other plants ideally suited to arid, sun-scorched dune life. Prickly pear, a native eastern cactus, blossoms with yellow flowers in July. Its thickened stems possess tremendous water-storage capacity, while its spines are modified leaves, minimized in size to reduce water loss. The plant can also withstand internal temperatures of up to 145°F. Woolly Hudsonia, or beach heather, spreads in a three-inch-tall yellow carpet around Memorial Day. Its tiny needlelike leaves minimize evaporation. Seaside goldenrod offers a fine flowering display after Labor Day. It, too, has succulent stems to store extra water, an adaptation not needed by inland goldenrods. These dune plants are very vulnerable to trampling, so always stay on trails.

Now that you've familiarized yourself with barrier island habitats, drive south along the park road to parking lot A-19. Take a short hundred-yard jaunt east, crossing from primary dunes to beach. Watch for plumes of seaside goldenrod, clumps of beach wormword (commonly known as dusty miller, a beneficial dune-building exotic plant from Asia), and tufts of beach grass.

Return to the parking lot and walk a short distance south along the road. Turn right on the 0.25-mile Bird Blind Trail. This secluded sand road offers a 0.5-mile

Barrier islands are dynamic, always in motion, as these lengths of snow fence drowned in sand attest.

round-trip walk to the back bay. It traverses red cedar woodland. Holly, cedar, black cherry and shadbush rise ever taller as you walk farther from the harsh habitat near the beach. Rugosa rose, bayberry, shining sumac, poison ivy and bearberry fill in a dense understory.

In 0.25 mile the trail passes among a few groundsel trees, then bursts into the open at the quiet bay. The enclosed Spizzle Creek Bird Blind overlooks an expansive salt marsh. New Jersey's sheltered bays provide refuge to migratory waterfowl and shorebirds.

Return to your car the way you came and drive south to where the road ends at parking lot A-23. This parking area once marked the southern tip of the park. But in the past ninety years littoral drift has piled up more than 1.5 miles of new dune extending farther southward.

From the parking lot walk out to the beach, where Atlantic surf rolls up on the shore. Turn right and head south toward Barnegat Light, built in 1858. Stay out of fragile dunes, which provide nesting spots for shorebirds and wintering grounds for an occasional snowy owl. This beach walk is not quite as solitary as one might hope. Four-wheel-drive vehicles and gleaming campers are parked like immense metal shells along the beach. Anglers, like hermit crabs, depend on their "hard shell" habitats for protection from the elements.

The beach is littered with tide-tossed debris. Look for moon jellies (three-inch-diameter translucent lenses), bay scallop shells (made familiar by the Shell Oil Company logo), and Atlantic surf clams and northern quahog shells (offered by countless beachcombing children to vacationing parents as ashtrays). Starfish also wash ashore. This invertebrate is no fish. Sea star is a more apt name for this five-armed fierce predator, which feeds on oysters by applying the powerful suction of its tubular feet to open shells. Anyone who has ever tried to pry open a live oyster by hand will appreciate the sea star's strength.

Oysters, a commonly found New Jersey shellfish, prove the "strength-in-numbers" law of the sea. This mollusk at various stages of its life cycle provides food to the sea star; flatworm; oyster drill; flounder and other fish; birds such as the scoter and oystercatcher; and, of course, humans. Each female oyster lays 50 million eggs per spawning season to assure species survival, also inadvertently aiding in the survival of its many predators.

At the south tip of Island Beach State Park, a stone jetty extends into the ocean and is intended to halt the littoral drift of sands into Barnegat Inlet. A steady flow of pleasure boats roars through the inlet. On the far shore the picturesque silhouette of Barnegat Light stands in profile against the sky. If weather is good and waves are low, a rock-hopping walk over the jetty is fun.

Return the way you came up the beach. At 3.5 miles keep eyes open for a first gap in the dune fence, marking the way back to parking lot A-23.

Hours, Fees and Facilities

Island Beach State Park is open 8:00 A.M. to 8:00 P.M. in summer, and 8:00 A.M. to dusk in winter. The Aeolium Nature Center is usually open 9:00 A.M. to 4:30 P.M. Park fees are $6 on weekdays, $7 on weekends, Memorial Day to Labor Day; and $4 the rest of the year.

Getting There

Take the Garden State Parkway to Exit 82. Follow Route 37 east over Barnegat Bay Bridge, turning right on Route 35 south (Central Avenue) and driving 2.5 miles. After paying at the park gate look for the Aeolium Nature Center 1.5 miles ahead on the left. Parking lot A-23 is about 6.5 miles farther south. Note: the park is crowded and parking hard to find on summer weekends.

For More Information

Island Beach State Park, Seaside Park, NJ 08752; 732-793-0506.

44 Holgate

Edwin B. Forsythe National Wildlife Refuge

- 5.5 miles
- 4 hours
- Moderate; flat, but walking in soft sand can be tiring
- Best in September, closed during nesting season
  (April 1 to August 31)

Investigate the domain of piping plovers,
least terns and black skimmers

Holgate at first glance appears to be a hike for minimalists who thrive only on overlapping plains of beige, brown, gray, and blue, where sandy shore and grassy dune merge with a horizon line of sea and sky.

But this initial minimalist image is all illusion. Holgate is an ecosystem in motion. It is one of the last New Jersey barrier islands unrestricted by jetty, sea wall, and condominium, or dredged for sand to perpetuate public swimming. It is a dynamic place, an unspoiled sand beach, low dune, mud flat, and salt marsh shaped and reshaped by the herculean powers of surf and storm. Any creature that thrives here must adapt to the relentless flux.

Naturally enough, birds with their gliding and soaring mobility are the most visible rulers of this shifting landscape. Least terns, piping plovers, and black skimmers—all on New Jersey's list of endangered species—nest, incubate their eggs, and raise their fledglings on Holgate's exposed beaches. Back from the shoreline amid the older dunes, egrets, herons and ibis breed among tangled stands of bayberry and marsh elder.

This 5.5-mile-out-and-back barrier island walk extends 2.75 miles into the ocean and bay, ending on a low, hook-shaped sand spit battered by whitecapped waves. The hike directions are the simplest of any in this book: Head south from the parking area along the hard-packed beach. Stay out of the fragile posted dunes. Continue walking until you run out of land.

Civilization—cottages and motels—abruptly vanishes just beyond the Holgate parking area. A few plants have taken tenuous hold in sheltered spots. Seaside goldenrod blooms in yellow spikes in autumn, and a few scattered bayberry bushes rise above snatches of dune grass. Within a few yards a sign announces your entrance into the wilderness area of the Holgate Unit of the Edwin B. Forsythe National Wildlife Refuge. Cats, dogs and kites, all harmful to wildlife, are prohibited.

Ahead, a sand spit sweeps away in a seemingly infinite brown arc. On the left, the ocean breaks and crashes onto a gently rising expanse of beach which stops abruptly at the low, grass-covered dunes. To the far right, Little Egg Harbor separates Holgate from the mainland.

This is a federal refuge for endangered birds. A refuge differs from a park in that wildlife needs come first. People are forbidden entry during the critical nesting season between April 1 and August 30. The birders' loss is the birds' gain. Skittish black skimmers, for example, which can find no safe haven at New Jersey's other beaches, flourish here (see sidebar).

From September 1 to March 31 you'll share this beach with other walkers and 4-wheel-drive vehicles. We were pleased to find on our visit that the drivers were well-mannered, slow-moving anglers. The same can't be said for two hot-dogging jet-skiers spewing noise and gas fumes, while disturbing birds and walkers. These leaf blowers and chain saws of the sea reminded us just how easily the serenity of this fragile ecosystem can be disrupted.

The beach at Holgate at first glance seems to be a wasteland, a desert landscape speckled by debris and dried grasses. A closer look reveals the intricate cycle of life.

The sea feeds the shore. Look for curving black swash marks made on the beach by the leading edge of waves. Each swash left by the flood is a litter of seaweed, algae, plankton, tiny crabs, and dead fish which is scavenged by beach creatures. The algae are consumed by sand worms and the plankton siphoned away by clams underground. Surf-edge feeders, like piping plovers, feast upon the crabs and clams. Nothing goes to waste: dung and feathers dropped by birds decompose to provide phosphates for nutrient-poor sand, nurturing plants like seaside goldenrod and sea-rocket.

A smorgasbord of edible tidbits isn't the only thing provided by the sea. Shifting tides deposit flotsam: driftwood, pebbles and broken shells which serve as camouflage for nesting terns. Black skimmers build their nests atop wracks of dried seaweed (called eelgrass) in summer.

A walk along the beach at Holgate in autumn reveals a continuous play of tide, sand and sun. Low sandbars are overwashed by each incoming wave. Little bays fill up with a rush of shallow water and tiny stranded minnows are scooped up by pouncing birds. Sanderlings skitter and race along the bars just ahead of your own shadow and feed on tiny mollusks and crustaceans.

Birds at Holgate ebb and flow with the seasons. Endangered plovers, terns and skimmers nest here in summer, a time when walkers aren't allowed. But you can still see these birds loafing and feeding through September. The fall migration season is also the time to observe black-bellied plovers, godwits, willets, sanderlings and sandpipers. Thousands of migrating barn swallows stop here in early September to feast on insects.

Winter rewards with more than beach solitude. Snowy owls, who migrate here from Canada, hunt over the bayside salt marsh. A few seals even show up at Holgate in March. The first Arctic seals appeared on New Jersey beaches in winter 1988. These migrating harp and hooded seals are usually young animals, probably unable to compete with adults in commercially overfished Arctic waters.

In autumn it's fun to stop and watch anglers surf-cast for striped bass and bluefish. Like the shorebirds, bluefish are migrators. They annually travel along the continental shelf from Nova Scotia to Uruguay in schools of like-sized individuals (preventing them from practicing their propensity for species cannibalism!). The Jersey coast serves as a spawning ground and its estuaries as important nurseries for young bluefish.

As you approach the end of the island at 2.75 miles, the landscape becomes nearly featureless, as the dunes diminish in size and the beach tapers away into a graveyard of shells and a few straggling stems of beach grass. The mile-wide Beach Haven

Inlet stretches before you into nothingness. Just offshore to the south is the last sandy vestige of Tucker Island. Fifty years ago the island boasted a village and life-guard station, but both fell victim to the tides. At this seemingly remote spot, the skyline of Atlantic City with its gambling tables is visible to the southwest. From the end of the sand spit, either return the way you came or explore a little farther along the bay side of the refuge, obeying posted signs. Holgate in autumn offers a deeply meditative walk, a place to contemplate the realm of surf, silence and shorebirds.

🪶 A LOOK AT BLACK SKIMMERS

The black skimmer is a beach nester, and that has nearly doomed it in New Jersey. Unlike the unflappable gull, the black skimmer flees its nest at the sight of a human being and stays away until the threat has passed. The bird is victim to habi-tat loss and to domestic animals like cats which eat its eggs.

The black skimmer is a distinctive-looking bird; black on top, snowy white beneath, with red legs. Its long lower bill protrudes well beyond its upper one, allowing it to eat on the wing. A precision night flyer, the skimmer usually feeds after dark, plowing along at water level, slicing the water's surface and scooping up small fish. Foraging by touch, the bill snaps closed when the bird feels a fish. The skimmer is easily identified when not feeding. It sometimes relaxes its lower bill and flies along with its mouth dangling open, appearing less than streamlined.

In summer black skimmers breed among the least terns on secluded New Jer-sey beaches. They make simple nests atop dried eelgrass wracks or by squatting and spinning their bodies into the soft sand.

While you won't see black skimmers nesting at Holgate, since the beach and dunes are off-limits during their breeding season, you may see young birds mak-ing practice flights and honing their skimming skills in September. By the end of the month the birds leave their New Jersey colonies for winter quarters as far away as the tropics.

Hours, Fees and Facilities

Holgate is open dawn to dusk from September 1 to March 31. It is closed during nesting season from April 1 to August 31.

Getting There

From the Garden State Parkway, take Exit 63 for Manahawkin. Follow Route 72 east for 7 miles onto Long Beach Island. At the third traffic light turn right onto Bay Avenue (Long Beach Boulevard). Continue straight for 9.0 miles to the park-ing area at the end of the road.

For More Information

Edwin B. Forsythe National Wildlife Refuge, Great Creek Road, P.O. Box 72, Oceanville, NJ 08231-0072; 609-652-1665.

45 Brigantine

Edwin B. Forsythe National Wildlife Refuge

- 3.1 to 8.0 miles
- 1 to 5 hours
- Easy to moderate

New Jersey's own "wild kingdom" and birders' high

As a crimson sun rose out of Great Bay we heard a distant host of barking birds. A graceful shimmer, a shifting curve of white shapes, eclipsed the sun and rose-colored clouds as the nasal *bowk!-bowk!* grew louder. Weeks later, as I write this, I'm amazed to hear the birds drowning out my own excited words on my pocket tape recorder. The pure-white snow geese swept before us in graceful formation, settling into the marsh by the hundreds, then by the thousands.

This stunning October event took place at "Brig," short for Brigantine, a refuge beloved by birders. Founded in 1939 to protect the migratory routes of the American black duck and Atlantic brant, this sprawling coastal refuge was combined with Barnegat and Holgate preserves and renamed the Edwin B. Forsythe National Wildlife Refuge in 1984. Today it provides a resting, feeding and/or breeding ground for more than 300 bird species.

The annual avian spectacle is rich beyond words. The refuge is at the heart of the Atlantic flyway, a sky corridor dotted by wetland stopping places and traveled by multitudes of migratory birds. Ecotones, biologically rich transition zones where habitats meet, make Brig an even more enticing place. Waders, waterfowl, seabirds, shorebirds, raptors and songbirds reign more than 40,000 acres of salt meadow and salt marsh, freshwater marsh, open bay, channels and sand islands edged by upland oak-pine forest, brush and field habitat.

Hikers will enjoy the Leeds Ecotrail (0.5-mile loop) and South Tower walk (2.4 miles out and back), which offer a sampling of life in the freshwater marsh. The James F. Akers Woodland Trail (0.25-mile loop) explores a dense woodland habitat. The Self-Guiding Wildlife Drive can also be driven by car, bicycled or walked in its 8.0-mile loop entirety. While the road is designed for easy auto access, pedestrians benefit from continuous intimate contact with the sweeping grandeur of the marsh. This chapter discusses all of these hike options.

Remember that there is no shade in the marsh. Avoid walking in severe weather, wear appropriate clothing, and bring foul-weather gear, plus a hat, food, water

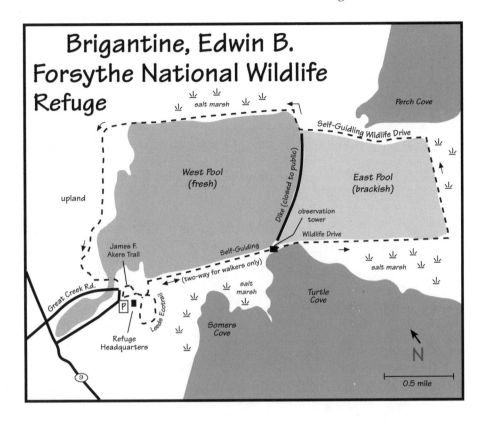

Brigantine, Edwin B. Forsythe National Wildlife Refuge

salt marsh

Perch Cove

Self-Guiding Wildlife Drive

West Pool
(fresh)

East Pool
(brackish)

upland

Dike (closed to public)

observation
tower

Wildlife Drive

James F.
Akers Trail

Self-Guiding

(two-way for walkers only)

salt
marsh

salt marsh

Great Creek Rd.

Leeds Ecotrail

P

Turtle
Cove

Somers
Cove

Refuge
Headquarters

N

9

0.5 mile

and insect repellent. Biting flies (a meal for birds) will make a meal of you when summer winds aren't blowing. The ideal time to walk Brig is on cool spring or autumn days at dawn when migrations are at their peak. Don't forget your binoculars and bird book.

Start your tour with a visit to the refuge headquarters at the parking area. Pick up maps and a bird list, and check out the register of recent sightings with its handy grid for pinpointing bird locations (this book has been playfully nicknamed "the book of lies" by those unable to spot the species noted on those pages). Be sure to write in your own discoveries when you complete your tour.

Just a short walk beyond the headquarters on the right is the 0.5-mile loop of the Leeds Ecotrail. A boardwalk threads through a wetland blanketed by marsh cordgrass. This undistinguished-looking grass, regularly inundated by the tides, is the staff of life to marsh birds. Snow geese (see sidebar) feed on its roots in winter, while its seeds are eaten by black ducks. The grass also indirectly nurtures many other species. Bacteria attack tiny floating fragments of the plant. Then fiddler crabs, mullet and clams ingest the plant fragments and digest the bacteria. The mullet, crabs, and clams in turn provide food for foraging shorebirds. Rarely seen diamondback terrapin, secretive rails, and muskrat also find shelter among the grasses.

The Leeds Ecotrail moves onto higher ground where cordgrass and phragmites give way to bushy groundsel trees, which in turn give way to black cherry, sassafras, and cedar. The path enters a secluded woods where arrowwood, Virginia creeper, and shining sumac fill in a brushy understory. Insect-eating bluebirds and phoebes supplement their fall diets with sassafras fruit. White oak, southern red oak and pitch pine join the forest mix. Mockingbirds, robins and thrushes, rabbits, foxes, and the elusive long-tailed weasel frequent this upland. The trail exits the woods abruptly, passing through an edge of marsh elders, a salt-tolerant shrub that offers nesting habitat to marsh wrens, seaside sparrows and red-winged blackbirds.

Upon completing the Leeds Ecotrail loop, retrace your steps past the headquarters building to the 0.25-mile James F. Akers Woodland Trail. This self-guided nature trail circles among upland cedars (whose stringy bark is used by squirrels and birds as nesting material), oaks (whose acorns feed birds and mammals), and pitch pines (offering cover and food to white-tailed deer).

After finishing the Akers Woodland Trail, return to the headquarters building and travel by foot, bicycle or car along the Self-Guiding Wildlife Drive. At about 0.2 mile, turn sharply right into the open marsh. The 900-acre West Pool, an artificial freshwater impoundment, lies to your left. Migratory waterfowl rest, drink, and feed in this pool. In spring and fall, wood ducks are prominent, while magnificent flocks of Atlantic brant stop here daily to wash salt residue from feathers and to savor fresh water.

About 1.0 mile out into the marsh is the South Tower, a must-do-climb where you can observe the meeting of three wetland habitats. A dike on the left side of the road forms a border between the freshwater West Pool and brackish 700-acre East Pool, while tidal Turtle Cove lies to your right. From the observation tower we watched thousands of snow geese resting on an October morning. Among them were crowds of cormorants, snowy egrets, great egrets and great blue herons. We were also thrilled to spot a single peregrine falcon perched atop an abandoned osprey nest.

If you are walking, you have the choice of returning to the headquarters parking lot by backtracking the way you came (1.2 additional miles) or by completing the 8.0-mile loop of the Self-Guiding Wildlife Drive (6.8 additional miles). Cars must complete the 8.0-mile loop, since the road is one-way.

If you choose to complete the loop, follow the road as it passes all the way around the East Pool, turning left at 2.7 miles with views right to 16,000 acres of protected marsh and bay. The road turns left again at 3.4 miles and returns to forested upland at 5.9 miles. The road climbs gently uphill through field and forest and returns to the refuge headquarters at 8.0 miles.

After enjoying the wonders of the marsh, don't disregard forest birding possibilities. The treeline at water's edge offers especially productive winter golden and bald eagle watching. A friendly birder shared his spotting scope with us, allowing us to observe a bald eagle perched atop a treeline oak.

Brig provides an ever changing palette of birds. In August, shorebirds and warblers head south. In September ducks gather, while the first snow geese arrive in

October. In November and December more than 100,000 geese and ducks congregate before flying south. Midwinter is a quieter time, with the best viewing during thaws. At mid-March, waterfowl come north, with wading birds and shorebirds arriving in April and May. Warblers are back in May.

When not watching birds, give the birders a look. Whether standing absolutely still with binoculars pressed to eyes (like egrets poised to snatch up a fish) or exchanging excited hand gestures (like a flock of ducks taking flight), they offer a lovable human side to Forsythe.

🦃 TOO MANY SNOW GEESE...

The spiritually moving spectacle of flocking snow geese settling into a marsh makes one feel that all is well with the world. Sadly, in June 1997 *Audubon* magazine writer Kevin Krajick reported that the bird's stellar success is not a sign of ecological health but of well-meaning wildlife-management policies run amok.

The birds, fattened upon plentiful U.S. farm grains and protected within a string of national refuges like Forsythe, have multiplied alarmingly. Numbers of lesser snow geese in the midwestern U.S. have jumped from 2 million in 1970 toward 5 million. Along the Atlantic flyway, greater snow geese estimates have shot from 50,000 in the mid-1960s to more than 600,000.

The birds' population boom has devastated its Arctic summer breeding grounds. Grubbing snow geese rip up every last tuft of tundra grass, turning that fragile ecosystem into overgrazed wasteland. Slow-recovering flora take decades to regenerate, starving out other migratory bird species. The ravenous animals are also putting severe pressure on U.S. farm crops and refuge habitat. Biologists have come to an unsettling conclusion: Snow geese numbers must be cut by up to 50 percent in the next five years to reestablish a natural balance and save the tundra.

Hours, Fees and Facilities

Open dawn to dusk, $4 per car. Annual pass, $15.

Getting There

From northern New Jersey, take the Garden State Parkway south to Exit 48. Follow US 9 south for 6.0 miles and turn left on Great Creek Road into the refuge. Park in the main lot next to the headquarters.

For More Information

Edwin B. Forsythe National Wildlife Refuge, Great Creek Road, P.O. Box 72, Oceanville, NJ 08231-0072; 609-652-1665.

46

Cape May
Point State Park

- 2 miles
- 1 hour
- Easy

Experience the wonder of the Atlantic flyway in autumn

A late-summer cold front blasts out of the northwest, and in the dark of night all across the northern U.S. and Canada, birds take flight. By September up to 12 million per evening appear on airport radar screens. They pour south on powerful tail winds in an ancient migration that still intrigues ornithologists. One great focus for the continent's southward migration is Cape May, New Jersey.

Cape May peninsula is to migrating raptors, songbirds, and butterflies what a rest stop is to tired motorists on the Garden State Parkway: a place to reconnoiter, refuel, and restore. It is the last land a southward flyer encounters before making the challenging thirteen-mile open water crossing of Delaware Bay. Cape May Point is a wedge-shaped attracter, a narrowing funnel of land that concentrates birds and butterflies within its revitalizing marshes and the plenty of its forests and fields.

The migration opens in August when a few ospreys and bald eagles appear over the point. It peaks in autumn when trees virtually drip with birds. More than 80,000 raptors—sharp-shinned and broad-winged hawks, harriers, kestrels, merlins and peregrines—glide through in a single season. More than 200 species of songbird also make the passage. Flycatchers, thrushes, vireos, and warblers wing toward the tropics. Migrating waterfowl and shorebirds add raucous cries and calls to the Cape May cacophony. Amid this tumult, the monarch butterfly passes voicelessly. Fluttering south on orange wings, this feather-light flyer follows an instinctual map on a 2,000-mile journey to an ancestral wintering ground to which it has never traveled before.

Cape May Point State Park, once a military base that protected Delaware Bay with gun emplacements and concrete bunkers, is now a boon to birders. In the fall its 300 acres and five miles of trail can be as thick with binocular-wielding naturalists as with the bird species they come to observe.

This 2.0-mile loop walk samples the Red, Yellow and Blue Trails and explores woods, thicket, pond, marsh, dune and beach habitat. While a fall hike rewards with the migratory spectacle, the preserve is worth a visit anytime.

Check out the visitor center exhibits, then cross the parking lot to the trail-head. All three trails (Red, Yellow and Blue) begin on a boardwalk at the same spot. Just to the right of the trailhead is the Hawk Watch Platform. Crowded in autumn, this is a prime place to gaze at the migration. Cape May holds seasonal migration records for many of the fifteen species of raptors, including sharp-shinned hawk (61,800 sightings), kestrel (30,268), broad-winged hawk (14,000), osprey (5,400), and peregrine (702). Ornithologists still marvel at the means for the migration, studying how birds find their way (see sidebar).

In a short distance turn sharply left, following the Red Trail (also called the Nature Trail). Phragmites (reed grass) immediately surrounds you. This wetland plant thrives where humans have disturbed marshlands. It chokes out other species like cattail, valuable food to wildlife. While phragmites has little nutritional worth, it does have some worth: least bitterns and marsh wrens roost and nest within its protecting cover.

On a spring walk the sunny face of yellow thistle stared up at us from beside the boardwalk. Edging salt marshes, this plant blossoms with a rounded yellow flower hung amid radiating rays of spiny leaves. While celebrated for its birds, Cape May Point boasts more than 240 wildflower species. Showiest along the trail are multiflora rose (blooming white from May to June), trumpet creeper (reddish orange flowers from July to September), and seaside goldenrod (blossoming on dunes from August to November).

More than 385 bird species and 104 butterfly species have been spotted in Cape May County. The area's vital location along the Atlantic flyway promotes this diversity, but so does the richness of edible flora. The county is an ecotone, a transition zone where the plants of North and South merge. Nature Trail marker #2 is bayberry, a northern species, while #4 is wax myrtle, its southern counterpart. Both shrubs thrive in the Cape May transition zone.

Walking along the boardwalk, note that phragmites has colonized wet ground to the left and that red cedars have taken hold in drier, higher ground to the right. The blue-gray berries produced by the red cedar are not really berries but modified cones, a food for robins and cedar waxwings.

At Nature Trail marker #7, a side trail branches left to a dead end at a nature photography blind overlooking Lighthouse Pond West. Stop for impressive views of Cape May Light, built in 1859. Marsh birds, painted turtles, bullfrogs, muskrat, and red fox rely on freshwater ponds like this one.

The Red Trail passes through woody thickets of cedar, pitch pine and poison ivy, a valuable plant with white berries that feeds thirty-five bird and mammal species. Some deciduous trees are dying out here due to the intrusion of saltwater. The Atlantic Ocean is rising along this coast by one inch every six years, a trend starting at the end of the last Ice Age that may be accelerating due to global warming. The Cape May Lighthouse is the third light station at this location; the other two became victims of the encroaching sea.

At marker #12, the Red Trail reaches Lighthouse Pond East, where we watched mute swans, egrets, pied-billed grebes and coots sharing open water in May. The sociable coot, a dark gray ducklike bird with a white bill, would rather dive when frightened than fly away. It is an adept swimmer, making brief forays underwater to eat vegetation. We also spotted swooping barn swallows. From late August to early October massed numbers of tree swallows, in the tens of thousands, descend on Cape May, lining its telephone wires.

After passing marker #15 leave the Red Trail, turning left onto the combined Yellow and Blue Trails. This path alternates between boardwalk and dry ground, passing among sassafras and dying cedars that support climbing tangles of multiflora rose. Sun-dappled patches of wild geranium pepper the forest floor. The sweet scent of red cedar and the roar of nearby surf fill the air.

When the Blue Trail proceeds straight ahead, turn right on the Yellow Trail, passing among dense vegetation. More than 200 species of migrating songbirds forage for seeds, fruits and insects within this shore-side jungle. Countless common migrants like the catbird, with its squeaky-gate call; yellow warbler and red-eyed vireo may be joined occasionally by regionally rare birds like the western tanager.

In a short distance the Yellow Trail edges Shallow Pond East. Such saltwater ponds harbor New Jersey endangered birds like the black skimmer, least tern and piping plover. In summer, they breed on beaches and dunes. Easily disturbed by walkers, they abandon their nests until the threat passes.

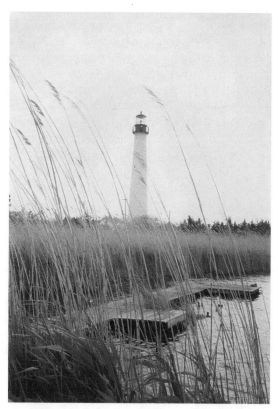

Cape May Lighthouse, built in 1859, overlooks the spectacular fall migration of raptors, songbirds and monarch butterflies.

Just beyond the dunes, the Yellow Trail turns right, offering a short walk along the Atlantic shore before returning to the parking lot.

🦴 MYSTERIOUS MIGRATIONS

Linnaeus, the eighteenth-century Swede who gave us our modern system of plant and animal classification, dismissed the then new-fangled theory that small song-birds flew thousands of miles to escape northern winters. He, like the ancients, theorized that swallows dove deep beneath the surface of lake and river, buried themselves in mud and hibernated away the cold months.

The truth is far more fantastic. The mass migration of birds is on a scale that stirs the imagination. It seems unfathomable that birds like the Arctic tern, the champion long-distance flyer, can repeatedly make its 22,000-mile round trip from Arctic to Antarctica and back with pinpoint accuracy.

Why migrate? The seasonal commute offers the best of both worlds: bountiful food supply and avoidance of stressful winter conditions. Many migrating birds breed in summer within the plenty of northern deciduous forests or the insect-rich Arctic, while waiting out winter months in tropical climes.

The "how" of migration has proven harder to decipher. Ongoing investigation reveals that birds utilize visual cues and internal clocks. They know the position of sun, moon and stars at particular times of day and follow coastlines and mountain ranges. They even seem to recognize particular groves of trees. They may have an innate directional sense, possibly using Earth's magnetic field, sound, faint smells, or even gravity to find their way.

Hours, Fees and Facilities

The park is open dawn to dusk year-round. The environmental center is open seven days a week April to October (8:00 A.M. to 6:00 P.M.), and Wednesday to Sunday (9:00 A.M. to 4:00 P.M.) in winter. Admission free.

Getting There

Take the Garden State Parkway south to its end, where it joins Lafayette Street (Route 633) into the city of Cape May. Bear right onto West Perry Street, which will turn into Sunset Boulevard. Go west on Sunset Boulevard (Route 606) and turn left on Lighthouse Avenue. The park entrance is on the left in 0.7 mile. Park in the main lot.

For More Information

Cape May Point State Park, P.O. Box 107, Cape May Point, NJ 08212; 609-884-2159.

Birding information: New Jersey Audubon Society Cape May Bird Observatory, Northwood Center; 609-884-2736.

Appendix A

Useful Names and Addresses

General

American Hiking Society
P.O. Box 20160
Washington, DC 20041–2160
Amhiker@aol.com
301-565-6704

Appalachian Mountain Club
5 Joy Street
Boston, MA 02108
outdoors.org
617-523-0655

Appalachian Mountain Club
New York–New Jersey Chapter
5 Tudor City Place
New York, NY
212-986-1430

Appalachian Trail Conference
P.O. Box 807
Harpers Ferry, WV 25425
info@atconf.org
304-535-6331

The Canal Society of New Jersey
P.O. Box 737
Morristown NJ 07963
908-722-9556

Garden State EnviroNet
(Conservation and parks info on-line)
e-mail: mailbox@gsenet.org
voice mail: (Phil Reynolds): 973-586-4128

New Jersey Audubon Society
P.O. Box 693
Bernardsville, NJ 07924
908-766-5787

New Jersey Conservation Foundation
Bamboo Brook
170 Longview Road
Far Hills, NJ 07931
908-234-1225.

New Jersey RailTrails
P.O. Box 23
Pluckemin, NJ 07978

New York-New Jersey Trail Conference
232 Madison Ave., Suite 802
New York, NY 10016
212-685-9699; e-mail:nynjtc@aol.com

The Nature Conservancy
Kay Environmental Center
200 Pottersville Road, Chester, NJ
908-879-7262

Pine Barrens Preservation Alliance
114 Hanover Street
Pemberton, NJ 08068

Sierra Club
57 Mountain Avenue
Princeton, NJ 08540
609-924-3141

State Government

New Jersey Department of
Environmental Protection
401 E. State Street
CN 402
Trenton, NJ 08625-0402
609-777-DEP3

New Jersey Division of Fish, Game and
Wildlife
501 East State Street
CN 400
Trenton, NJ 08625
609-292-2965

New Jersey Division of Parks and
Forestry
CN 404
Trenton, NJ 08625
609-984-0370

New Jersey Natural Lands Trust
501 East State Street
CN 404
Trenton, NJ 08625
609-984-1339

New Jersey Pinelands Commission
PO Box 7
New Lisbon, NJ 08064
County Government

Essex County Park Commission
115 Clifton Avenue
Newark, NJ 07104
973-621-7199.

Monmouth County Park System
Thompson Park
Newman Springs Road
Lincroft, NJ 07738
732-842-4000.

Morris County Park Commission
53 East Hanover Avenue
PO Box 1295
Morristown, NJ 07962
973-326-7600

Ocean County Parks and Recreation
1198 Bandon Rd.
Toms River 08753
732-506-9090

Somerset County Park Commission
P.O. Box 5327
North Branch 08876
908-722-1200

Appendix B

Recommended Reading

Abbott, R. Tucker. *Seashells of North America.* New York: Golden Press, 1968. 280 pp.

Boyd, Howard P. *A Field Guide to the Pine Barrens of New Jersey: Its Flora, Fauna, Ecology and Historic Sites.* Medford, NJ: Plexus Publishing, 1991. 423 pp.

Boyle, William J. *A Guide to Bird Finding in New Jersey.* New Brunswick, NJ: Rutgers University Press, 1986. 512 pp.

Brockman, C. Frank. *Golden Guide to Trees of North America.* Racine, WI: Golden Books Publishing Company, 1986. 280 pp.

Bull, John, and John Farrand Jr. *National Audubon Society Field Guide to North American Birds: Eastern Region.* New York: Alfred A. Knopf, 1996. 797 pp.

Burger, Joanna. *A Naturalist along the Jersey Shore.* New Brunswick, NJ: Rutgers University Press, 1996. 304 pp.

Cobb, Boughton. *Peterson Field Guides: Ferns.* Boston: Houghton Mifflin, 1984. 281 pp.

Collins, Beryl Robichaud, and Karl H. Anderson. *Plant Communities of New Jersey: A Study in Landscape Diversity.* New Brunswick, NJ: Rutgers University Press, 1994. 287 pp.

Dann, Kevin, and Gordon Miller. *30 Walks in New Jersey.* New Brunswick, NJ: Rutgers University Press, 1983. 243 pp.

Dupont, Ronald J., Jr. *Vernon 200: A Bicentennial History of the Township of Vernon, New Jersey, 1792-1992.* McAfee, NJ: Friends of the Dorothy E. Henry Library, 1992. 226 pp.

Dupont, Ronald J., Jr., and Kevin Wright. *High Point of the Blue Mountains.* New Jersey: Sussex County Historical Society, 1990. 104 pp.

Eastman, John. *Birds of Forest, Yard & Thicket.* Mechanicsburg, PA: Stackpole Books, 1997. 328 pp.

Eastman, John. *The Book of Forest and Thicket.* Mechanicsburg, PA: Stackpole Books, 1992. 212 pp.

Eastman, John. *The Book of Swamp and Bog.* Mechanicsburg, PA: Stackpole Books, 1995. 237 pp.

Gosner, Kenneth L. *Peterson Field Guides: Atlantic Seashore.* Boston: Houghton Mifflin, 1978. 329 pp.

Grimm, William Carey. *The Illustrated Book of Trees.* Mechanicsburg, PA: Stackpole Books, 1983. 493 pp.

Harlow, William M. *Trees of the Eastern and Central United States and Canada.* New York: Dover Publications, 1957. 288 pp.

Jorgensen, Neil. *A Sierra Club Naturalist's Guide: Southern New England.* San Francisco: Sierra Club Books, 1978. 417 pp.

Kraft, Herbert C. *The Lenape: Archaeology, History, and Ethnography.* Newark: New Jersey Historical Society, 1986. 303 pp.

Lenik, Edward J. *Iron Mine Trails.* New York: New York–New Jersey Trail Conference, 1996. 160 pp.

Little, Elbert L. *National Audubon Society Field Guide to North American Trees: Eastern Region.* New York: Alfred A. Knopf, 1980. 714 pp.

Lyons, Janet, and Sandra Jordan. *Walking the Wetlands: A Hiker's Guide to Common Plants and Animals of Marshes, Bogs, and Swamps.* New York: John Wiley & Sons, 1989. 222 pp.

McPhee, John. *The Pine Barrens.* New York: Farrar, Straus and Giroux, 1968. 157 pp.

Neiring, William A., and Nancy C. Olmstead. *National Audubon Society Field Guide to North American Wildflowers: Eastern Region.* New York: Alfred A. Knopf, 1979. 887 pp.

Newcomb, Lawrence. *Wildflower Guide.* Boston: Little, Brown, 1977. 490 pp.

New York–New Jersey Trail Conference, *New York Walk Book.* New York: Doubleday. 1984. 393 pp.

Perry, Bill. *A Sierra Club Naturalist's Guide: The Middle Atlantic Coast, Cape Hatteras to Cape Cod.* San Francisco: Sierra Club Books, 1985. 470 pp.

Peterson, Roger Tory. *Peterson Field Guide: Eastern Birds.* Boston: Houghton Mifflin, 1980. 384 pp.

Reynolds, Phil. *Garden State EnviroNet:* mailbox@gsenet.org.

Rezendes, Paul. *Tracking & the Art of Seeing: How to Read Animal Tracks & Sign.* Charlotte, VT: Camden House Publishing, 1992. 320 pp.

Roberts, David C. *Peterson Field Guide: Geology of Eastern North America.* Boston: Houghton Mifflin, 1996. 402 pp.

Rue, Leonard Lee, III. *New Jersey Out-of-Doors: A History of Its Flora and Fauna.* Washington, NJ: Hicks Printing Co., 1964. 96 pp.

Scherer, Glenn, and Don Hopey. *Exploring the Appalachian Trail: Hikes in the Mid-Atlantic States.* Mechanicsburg, PA: Stackpole Books, 1998. 371 pp.

Scofield, Bruce, Stella Green, and H. Neil Zimmerman. *50 Hikes in New Jersey.* Woodstock, VT: Backcountry Publications, 1997. 238 pp.

Searfoss, Glenn. *Skulls and Bones: A Guide to the Skeletal Structures and Behavior of North American Mammals.* Mechanicsburg, PA: Stackpole Books, 1995. 277 pp.

Serrao, John. *Nature's Events: A Notebook of the Unfolding Seasons.* Mechanicsburg, PA: Stackpole Books, 1992. 292 pp.

Stutz, Bruce. *Natural Lives, Modern Times: People and Places of the Delaware River.* New York: Crown Publishers, 1992. 390 pp.

Teal, John, and Mildred Teal. *Life and Death of the Salt Marsh.* New York: Ballantine Books, 1969.

Whitaker, John O., Jr. *National Audubon Society Field Guide to North American Mammals.* New York: Alfred A. Knopf, 1996. 937 pp.

Widmer, Kemble. *The Geology and Geography of New Jersey.* New Jersey Historical Series. Princeton, NJ: D. Van Nostrand, 1964. 189 pp.

Zatz, Arline, and Joel Zatz. *Best Hikes with Children in New Jersey.* Seattle: Mountaineers, 1992. 254 pp.

About the Author

G lenn Scherer is a New Jersey outdoor and environmental writer and coauthor of *Exploring the Appalachian Trail (Mid-Atlantic States)* and *Exploring the Appalachian Trail (Northern New England)*. He is contributing editor for *Appalachian Trailway News* and publishes his work in *Backpacker* magazine, *Outside, AMC Outdoors, American Hiker,* and *New Jersey Country Roads.*

C ontributor Jean LeBlanc grew up in Massachusetts and inherited her love of the outdoors from her parents. She is a nationally published essayist, poet and reviewer. Her column on the flora of the Appalachian Trail entitled "Growing Wild" appears regularly in *Appalachian Trailway News.*

Alphabetical Listing of Walks

About the AMC

B egin a new adventure!

Join the Appalachian Mountain Club, the oldest and largest outdoor recreation club in the United States. Since 1876, the Appalachian Mountain Club has helped people experience the majesty and solitude of the Northeast outdoors. Our mission is to promote the protection, enjoyment, and wise use of the mountains, rivers, and trails of the Northeast.

Members enjoy discounts on all AMC programs, facilities, and books:

Outdoor Adventure Programs
We offer more than 100 workshops on hiking, canoeing, cross-country skiing, biking, and rock climbing as well as guided trips for hikers, canoers, and skiers.

Facilities: Mountain Huts and Visitor Centers
The AMC maintains backcountry huts in the White Mountains of New Hampshire and visitor centers throughout the Northeast, from Maine to New Jersey.

Books & Maps
Guides and maps to the mountains, streams and forests of the Northeast — from Maine to North Carolina — and outdoor skill books from backcountry experts on topics from winter camping to fly fishing.

The Appalachian Mountain Club
5 Joy Street
Boston, MA 02108
617-523-0636

Find us on the web at www.outdoors.org

Other Titles of Interest from AMC Books

Visit the AMC Bookstore at **www.outdoors.org**

Nature Walks in Northern Vermont

Nature Hikes in the White Mountains

Nature Walks in the Berkshire Hills

Nature Walks in and around New York City

Nature Walks in Southern New Hampshire

Nature Walks in the New Hampshire Lakes Region

Nature Walks in Southern Maine

Nature Walks in Central Massachusetts

Nature Walks near Philadelphia

Quiet Water Canoe Guide: New York

Quiet Water Canoe Guide: New Hampshire/Vermont

Quiet Water Canoe Guide: Maine

Quiet Water Canoe Guide: Massachusetts/Connecticut/Rhode Island

AMC Guide to Freshwater Fishing in New England:
   How and Where to Fish in all six New England States

Watercolor Painting on the Trail:
   A Hiking Artist's Handbook

Seashells in My Pocket:
   A Child's Guide to Exploring the Atlantic Coast

Into the Mountains:
   Stories of New England's Most Celebrated Peaks

The Complete Guide to Trail Building and Maintenance